SHARIA SHUBRA

SHARIA RAMSES

SHARIA BUR SAID

Ramses
Station

S.H. EL-SAHARA

KHAN
EL-KHALILI

AL-AZHAR
MOSQUE

SH. QASR
EL-NIL

MOHAMMED MAHMOUD

AL-AZHAR
BUS STATION

FARID

Old City Walls

RIA SALAH SALEM

SHEIK RIHAN

D0958441

SHARIA BUR SAID

ARABIC

AT A GLANCE

PHRASE BOOK & DICTIONARY FOR TRAVELERS

BY HILARY WISE, Ph.D.
Senior Research Fellow
Queen Mary and Westfield College
University of London

Second Edition

BARRON'S

All inquiries should be addressed to:
Barron's Educational Series, Inc.
250 Wireless Boulevard
Hauppauge, New York 11788
http://www.barronseduc.com

International Standard Book No. 0-7641-1248-1

Library of Congress Catalog Card No. 00-131724

Illustrations: Juan Suarez

PRINTED IN HONG KONG
9 8 7 6 5 4 3

NOV 1 2 2002

4

CONTENTS

PREFACE

So you're taking a trip to a fascinating part of the world. That's exciting! In more ways than one, this new phrase book will prove an invaluable companion that will make your stay far more interesting and truly unforgettable.

This phrase book is part of a comprehensive series from Barron's Educational Series, Inc. In these books we present the phrases and words that a traveler most often needs for a brief visit to a foreign country, where the customs and language are often different. Each of the phrase books highlights the terms particular to that country, in situations that the tourist is most likely to encounter. With a specially developed key to pronunciation, this book will enable you to communicate quickly and confidently in colloquial terms. It is intended not only for beginners with no knowledge of the language, but also for those who have already studied it and have some familiarity with it.

Some of the unique features and highlights of the Barron's series are:

- Easy-to-follow *phonetic pronunciations* for all words and phrases in the book.
- Compact *dictionary* of commonly used words and phrases — built right into this phrase book so there's no need to carry a separate dictionary.
- Useful phrases for the *tourist*, grouped together by subject matter in a logical way so that the appropriate phrase is easy to locate when you need it.
- Special phrases for the *business traveler*, including banking terms, trade and contract negotiations, and secretarial services.
- Thorough section on *food and drink*, with comprehensive food terms you will find on menus; these terms are often difficult or impossible to locate in dictionaries, but our section gives you a description of the preparation as well as a definition of what it is.

■ *Emergency phrases* and terms you hope you won't need: legal complications, medical problems, theft or loss of valuables, replacement or repair of watches, cameras, and the like.

■ *Sightseeing itineraries*, shopping tips, practical travel tips, and regional food specialties to help you get off the beaten path and into the countryside, to the small towns and cities, and to the neighboring areas.

■ A *reference section* providing: expressions of time, days of the week, weather, countries and nationalities, directions, and information on Islamic festivals.

■ A brief *grammar section*, with the basic elements of the language quickly explained.

Enjoy your vacation and travel with confidence. You have a friend by your side.

ACKNOWLEDGMENTS

We would like to thank the following individuals for their assistance on this project: Hala N. Barakat, Hany M. El-Hosseiny, Ashraf Hossein, Ibrahim Gendy, Afaf El-Menoufy, and Eyad Amer; also Dr. Valerie Becker, Anthony Rutgen and Barney Allan of Anthony Rudkin Associates.

INTRODUCTION

There can be few parts of the world where a foreigner's efforts to speak the language are more appreciated than in the Middle East. Even the ability to exchange greetings and express thanks will arouse interest and establish an immediate bond. The wider your knowledge, the warmer your welcome in countries renowned for their hospitality to strangers.

Who Speaks Arabic?

Arabic is spoken by over 200 million people in more than 20 different countries, from Morocco in the west to Iraq in the east, and as far south as Somalia and the Sudan. As the language of the Koran, the holy book of Islam, it is taught as a second language in Muslim states throughout the world. Arabic originated in Saudi Arabia in pre-Islamic times, and spread rapidly in the wake of the Arab conquests from the seventh century. The languages of northern India, Turkey, Iran, Portugal, and Spain are full of words of Arabic origin.

Modern spoken Arabic varies a good deal from country to country, differing as much as, say, Spanish and Italian. The classical, written language has, however, changed little over the centuries, and is the accepted literary language throughout the Arab world.

What Kind of Arabic?

As a visitor to the Middle East you have to decide which kind of Arabic is going to be most useful to you. Although Classical Arabic has a standard form, and carries high prestige, it is primarily a written language, used for all literary purposes; it is only spoken on very formal occasions; for example, when someone is making an official speech. Grammatically it is far more complex than spoken Arabic.

Local dialects are used for all everyday communication, at work and in the home, and will clearly be of more practical use to the average tourist or businessperson. But which of the many dialects should you choose?

Egyptian Arabic

Egypt is at the heart of the Arab world, geographically, historically, and politically. With over 60 million inhabitants, it has by far the highest population of any Arab country, and more than 2 million teachers, doctors, businesspersons, and workers of all kinds are to be found in the wealthier Arab countries. Because Egypt also produces films, songs, and TV series that are immensely popular throughout the Arab world, Egyptian Arabic has acquired a special prestige, and even in remote areas people are familiar with the dialect.

Other Dialects

Egyptian is similar to the dialects of the eastern Mediterranean — Lebanese, Syrian, Palestinian, and Jordanian — and to Sudanese. The dialects of North Africa, from Morocco to Libya, have features in common, as do the dialects of Saudi Arabia and the Gulf. The main differences in pronunciation, and in some key everyday expressions, are outlined on page 208, so that you will have some idea what to expect if you are traveling in the Middle East outside Egypt.

But if you use Egyptian Arabic you will have no problem being understood, and many people will be able to adapt their own accent to help you.

Using the Book

Most of the expressions in the book are given in Egyptian Arabic, using the Western alphabet.

Occasionally an alternative is provided, when a different expression is widely used elsewhere. For instance, the Egyptian word for *room* is *'oh-Da*, but **ghur**-*fa* is the usual word in many other Arab countries; both are given, the Egyptian word being listed first: *'oh-Da*/**ghur**-*fa*. If two words are given separated by a comma, they are both equally common in Egyptian.

In addition, a translation is given in literary Arabic, using the Arabic script. This is so you can point to a word or phrase, or circle it in pencil, if you want to make sure you've been understood. Or an Arabic speaker may point to the appropriate phrase if *he* or *she* wants to communicate with *you*. The literary version given here in the Arabic script is not the "high" Classical Arabic of the Koran. It is a simplified variety that should be accessible to speakers who may not have had many years of formal education.

If you are going to point to phrases in the book, it's a good idea to make it clear that you are in fact using Egyptian Arabic (*c*a-ra-bee **maS**-ree); otherwise it may be assumed that you are learning literary Arabic and people may struggle to use Classical forms in their own speech for your benefit!

You can manage perfectly well *without* learning the Arabic script, though a guide is provided on page 204 for the really ambitious. With a little effort you will be able to decipher simple notices, street names, and the names of shops. The kind of signs you'll encounter most often are given on pages 162–163.

QUICK PRONUNCIATION GUIDE

Most of the sounds of Arabic are similar to sounds used in English; there are just a few that are unfamiliar to English ears. As with any language, a positive approach is much more important than getting the sounds exactly right.

THE VOWELS

SHORT VOWELS		EXAMPLES
a	as in *bat*	**ba**-lad (town, country)
e	as in *met*	**ka**-me-ra (camera)
i	as in *bit*	*bint* (girl, daughter)
u	as in *book*	**buk**-ra (tomorrow)
o	as in *dog*	do-**laar** (dollar)

LONG VOWELS		EXAMPLES
aa	as in *father*	**Daa**-nee (lamb)
eh	as in *met*, but lengthened	*heht!* (bring!)
ee	as in *feed*	*meen?* (who?)
ey	as in *they*, but lengthened	*feyn?* (where?)
oo	as in *mood*	*shoof!* (look!)
oh	as in *phone*	*yohm* (day)

All these long vowels should be pronounced "pure," with the lips held in the same position throughout (as in Spanish or French).

COMPLEX VOWELS (i.e., where the lips *do* change position)		EXAMPLES
ay	as in *try*	*kub-**bay**-ya* (glass)
aw	as in *out*	***daw**-sha* (noise)

THE CONSONANTS

The following consonants are pronounced as in English: **p, b, t, d, f, v, k, g, h, j, l, m, n, s, z, w, y**.

Notice that **s** is always as in *see*, never as in *his*, and the **g** is always "hard" as in *good*, never "soft" as in *age*. Also:

- **l** is the "clear" British English type, rather than the "dark" American sound.
- **r** is a brief tap of the tongue-tip against the teeth, as in Spanish.
- **h** may be used in positions in which it doesn't occur in English, such as before consonants. Make it nice and breathy: *ah-lan!* (Hi!). (Exceptions are the sequences *oh* as in *yohm* and *eh* as in *heht!*, which always represent long, pure vowels, not a vowel plus aspirate *h*.)

	CONSONANT	EXAMPLES
sh	as in *sheet*	*sheek* (check)
kh	a "soft" **k** sound, as in Scottish *loch*	*kham-sa* (five)
gh	a guttural **g** sound, rather like the French *r*	*gha-nee* (rich)
H	a rough, heavily aspirated **h** (as if you've swallowed something hot!)	*Hubb* (love)
q	like **k**, but made further back, so that it has a "darker" quality	*il-quds* (Jerusalem)
' or "	a glottal stop, or catch, found in Cockney and Scottish English, replacing a *t*, as in *bi'er* for "bitter," and *Sco'ish* for "Scottish."*	*ma-"ehs* (size)

* Two symbols are used for this sound because they represent two different sounds in some other dialects; *'a-lam* (pain) and *"a-lam* (pen) sound the same in Egyptian Arabic, but are different in many other varieties. See page 208.

	CONSONANT	EXAMPLES
c	made by contracting the muscles at the back of the throat. If you use a glottal stop instead ('), you'll still be understood!	^cehl! (great!)

Double Consonants

When the same consonant is written twice, it should be pronounced long. So you should hang on to the *t* in *sit-ta* (six) and the *l* in "*ul-lee* (tell me).

"Heavy" Consonants

There are four "heavy" consonants in Egyptian Arabic, represented in this book by **T**, **D**, **S**, and **Z**. They are like **t**, **d**, **s**, and **z**, except that they are pronounced with loose, lax lip and tongue muscles:

LETTER	EXAMPLES
T	**Tay**-yib (good, fine)
D	**D**eyf (guest)
S	**Saa**-la (hall)
Z	a-**Zunn** (I think)

These consonants affect the surrounding sounds; as you'll hear from listening to the tape, the whole word will often have a laxer, "heavier" articulation.

Stressed Syllables

The stressed syllables, which are printed in bold type, should be pronounced more loudly and emphatically than the others (think of the difference stress makes in English **bill**ow versus be**low**).

It's important to pronounce a long vowel really long (and "pure") in a stressed syllable; for example, *ee* will be longer in *ta-la-teen* (thirty) than in *bin-tee* (my daughter).

There is a tendency to drop some unstressed vowels. For example, the first vowel in *khu-**Saa**-ra* (pity) is likely to be dropped in a phrase like *ya kh-**Saa**-ra!* (What a pity!). When one word ends in a vowel and the next begins with one, the second vowel is usually dropped; so **ma**-ᶜa *is-sa-**leh**-ma* (lit., with peace; good-bye) becomes **ma**-ᶜa *s-sa-**leh**-ma*.

A "helping" vowel — usually **i** — is often introduced between two words if one word ends in two consonants and the next begins with one:

shuft (I saw) + *mu-**Ham**-mad* (Mohammed) is often pronounced **shuf**-ti *mu-**Ham**-mad*.

Stress usually falls on the penultimate syllable of the word (see *mu-**Ham**-mad* and *is-sa-**leh**-ma*, above). But if the final syllable ends in two consonants, as in *ka-**tabt*** (I wrote), or in a long vowel plus one consonant, as in *ba-**neht*** (girls), or *ta-la-**teen*** (thirty), then this syllable carries the stress.

THE BASICS FOR
GETTING BY

The expressions listed below will help you make contact with people, obtain essential information, and express your needs and views. They are the basic building blocks of everyday conversation, which are needed in most situations. Try to learn as many as you can before you leave; you can then combine them freely with words appropriate to each situation as it arises.

Masculine and Feminine

A distinction is often made between the masculine and feminine in Arabic. For instance, to say "How are you?" you'd say *iz-zay-yak?* to a man, but *iz-zay-yik?* to a woman. And if you are a man you'd say *ᶜa-wiz* for "I want," but you'd say *ᶜaw-za* if you're a woman. In this book the feminine forms are given in square brackets.

GREETINGS

Hello!		***ah*-lan!**	أهلاً
	or	***ah*-lan wa *sah*-lan!**	أهلاً وسهلاً
How are you?		*iz-**zay**-yak? [iz-**zay**-yik?]*	ازيك ؟
	or	*keyf **Heh**-lak?*	
		*[keyf **Heh**-lik?]*	كيف حالك؟
Fine.		***kway**-yis [kway-**yi**-sa]*,	كويس
		*il-**Ham**-du lil-leh*	[كويسة]، الحمد لله
	or	*bi kheyr,*	بخير،
		*il-**Ham**-du lil-leh*	الحمد لله

Pleased to meet you.	*it-shar-**raf**-na*	تشرفنا
Good-bye.	***ma**-ᶜa s-sa-**leh**-ma*	مع السلامة

PLEASE AND THANK YOU

Please.	*min **faD**-lak [min **faD**-lik]*	من فضلك
Thank you.	***shuk**-ran*	شكراً
Thank you very much.	*'al-fi shukr*	شكراً جزيلاً
You're welcome.	*ᶜaf-wan*	عفواً

COMMON EXPRESSIONS

yes	*'**ay**-wa*	نعم
no	*la'*	لا
fine, O.K.	***Tay**-yib, oh-**key***	طيب
There is/are, is/are there?	*fee (?)*	(هل) يوجد / توجد
There isn't/ aren't (any)	*ma **feesh***	لا يوجد / توجد
Here you are/ do join us/go ahead	*it-**faD**-Dal [it-faD-**Da**-lee]*	تفضل / تفضلي
Maybe.	***yim**-kin*	يمكن، ربما
Never mind.	*ma-ᶜa-**lish***	لا بأس، حصل خير

What a pity!	*ya kh-**Saa**-ra!*	يا خسارة!
Honest to God! (protestation)	*wal-**laa**-hee!, wal-**laah** il ^ca-**Zeem!***	والله العظيم !
Please … (excuse me)	*law sa-**maHt***	من فضلك
Sorry.	*'**eh**-sif ['**as**-fa]*	آسف [آسفة]
Let's go!	*__yal__-la!*	هيا!
Just a minute.	*__laH__-Za*	لحظة
Wait.	*is-**tan**-na*	إنتظر
That's enough.	*ki-**feh**-ya **ki**-da*	كفاية
Great! Wonderful!	*^c**ehl**! mum-**tehz!***	عال! ممتاز!
Wow! (amazement)	*ya sa-**lehm!***	شيء عجيب
Look!	*shoof! [**shoo**-fee]*	انظر [انظري] !
I don't mind, I've no objection.	*ma-^can-**deesh meh**-ni^c*	ليس عندي مانع
I think (so).	*a-**Zunn***	أظن
I don't think (so).	*ma-**Zun**-nish*	لا أظن
I (let's) hope so (God willing).	*'in **shaa**' al-**laah***	إن شاء الله
and	*wi*	و
but	*__leh__-kin*	لكن
or	*'aw*	أو

PRONOUNS

I (am) — .	***a**-na* — .	أنا —
You (are) — .	***in**-ta [**in**-tee]* — .	أنت —
He (is) — .	***huw**-wa* — .	هو —
She (is) — .	***hee**-ya* — .	هى —
We (are) — .	***iH**-na* — .	نحن —
You (pl.) are — .	*in-**tum**-ma* — .	أنتم —
They (are) — .	***hum**-ma* — .	هم —

REQUESTS

Bring me — .	***gib**-lee* — .	احضر لي —
Give me — .	*id-**dee**-nee* — .	اعطني —
▦ this/that one	▦ *da*	هذا
I want — .	*ᶜ**a**-wiz [ᶜ**aw**-za]* — .	أريد —
I want to go — .	*ᶜ**a**-wiz [ᶜ**aw**-za] a-**rooH**** — .	
		أريد أن أذهب —
▦ to see — .	▦ *a-**shoof*** —	أرى —
▦ to buy — .	▦ *ash-**ti**-ree* —	أشتري —
▦ to eat — .	▦ *'**eh**-kul* — .	آكل —
▦ to drink — .	▦ *ash-rab* — .	أشرب —

I don't want — .	*mish ᶜa-wiz [ᶜaw-za]* — .	لا أريد — .
a lot	*ki-teer*	كثير
a little	*shway-ya, "a-leel*	قليل
more	*'ak-tar*	أكثر
Is it possible — ? Can you — ?	*mum-kin* — ?	هل من الممكن — ؟
It is possible.	*mum-kin.*	ممكن
It isn't possible.	*mish mum-kin.*	مستحيل
Do you know — ?	*tiᶜ-raf* — ? [*tiᶜ-ra-fee* — ?]	هل تعرف —؟
I don't know.	*maᶜ-rafsh.*	لا أعرف

QUESTIONS

Where is/are —?	*feyn* —?	أين —؟
Where is <u>the bathroom?</u>	*feyn it-twa-litt?*	أين التواليت؟
bus	*il-'u-tu-bees*	الأوتوبيس
telephone	*it-ti-li-fohn*	التليفون
What is/are — ?	*'eyh* — ?	ما — ؟
What's this/that?	*'eyh da?*	ما هذا ؟
What's the matter?	*fee 'eyh?*	ماذا جرى ؟
When?	*'im-ta?*	متى؟

Why?	*leyh?*	لماذا؟
Why not?	*leyh **la'**?*	لماذا لا ؟
Who?	*meen?*	من ؟
How?	*iz-**zayy**?, keyf?*	ازي ؟ كيف ؟
Which — ?	*'**an**-hee — ?*	أي — ؟
How much?	*kam? bi kam?*	كم، بكم؟
How many?	*kam?*	كم ؟

TIME AND PLACE

here	***hi**-na*	هنا
there	*hi-**nehk***	هناك
up(stairs)	*foh"*	فوق
down(stairs)	*taHt*	تحت
in(side)	***go**-wa*	في الداخل
out(side)	***bar**-ra*	في الخارج
near	*"u-**ray**-yib*	قريب
far	*bi-^{c}**eed***	بعيد
now	*dil-**wa**"-tee*	الآن
later	*ba^c-**deyn***	بعد ذلك
soon	*"u-**ray**-yib*	قريباً
today	*'in-na-**har**-da/il-**yohm***	اليوم

tomorrow	**buk**-ra	غداً
yesterday	'im-**beh**-riH/'ams	أمس
usually	c a-**da**-tan	عادةً
never	'a-ba-dan	أبداً

COMMUNICATING

Do you speak English?	bi-tit-**kal**-lim [bi-tit-kal-**li**-mee] in-gi-**lee**-zee?	هل تتكلم الانجليزية ؟
Does anyone here speak English?	fee-Hadd **hi**-na bi-yit-**kal**-lim in-gi-**lee**-zee?	هل يوجد شخص يتكلم الانجليزية ؟
Do you understand?	fi-**himt** [fi-**him**-tee] ?	هل فهمت ؟
I don't understand.	mish **feh**-him [**fah**-ma] .	لم أفهم
Please speak slowly.	kal-**lim**-nee bir-**raa**-Ha min **faD**-lak.	أرجو ان تتكلم على مهلك
I speak a little Arabic.	bat-**kal**-lim a-ra-bee **shway**-ya.	أتكلم العربية قليلا
▨ Egyptian Arabic	▨ a-ra-bee **maS**-ree	اللهجة المصرية
What's — in Arabic?	**tib**-"a 'eyh — bil-**a**-ra-bee?	ماهو — بالعربية؟
Please could you help me?	min-**faD**-lak, **mum**-kin ti-sa-**id**-nee?	من فضلك، هل يمكن أن تساعدني ؟

Please show me the phrase in the book.	min *faD*-lak, war-*ree*-nee il-*gum*-la fil-ki-*tehb*.	من فضلك أشر إلى الجملة في الكتاب
Please write it down.	ik-tib-*hoo*-lee, min *faD*-lak.	اكتبه لي، من فضلك

PROBLEMS

Go away!	*im*-shee!	امش!
Leave me alone.	*sib*-nee fi *Heh*-lee.	اتركني
Behave yourself.	ᶜeyb, iH-*ti*-rim *naf*-sak.	احترم نفسك
Please help me.	min *faD*-lak, sa-ᶜid-nee.	أرجو أن تساعدني
I'm lost.	*a*-na tuht.	ضللت الطريق، تهت
Nonsense.	ka-*lehm feh*-righ!	كلام فارغ!
I'll get the police.	ha-*gib*-lak il-bu-*leeS*.	سأطلب لك البوليس

SOME USEFUL ADJECTIVES

good, nice	*kway*-yis, *Tay*-yib	جيد، طيب
beautiful	Hilw, ga-*meel*	حلو، جميل
bad, ugly	*wi*-Hish	سيء

awful	*fa-Zee^c*	فظيع
expensive	**gheh**-*lee*	غالي
cheap	*ri-**kheeS***	رخيص
old (people)	*ki-**beer***	كبير
(things)	*"a-**deem***	قديم
new	*gi-**deed***	جديد
young, small	*Su-**ghay**-yar*	صغير
big	*ki-**beer***	كبير
noisy	*daw-**sha**-gee*	صخاب
quiet	**heh**-*dee*	هادىء
full	*mal-**yehn***	ملىء
empty	*faa-Dee*, *feh-righ*	فارغ
long, tall	*Ta-**weel***	طويل
short	*"u-**Say**-yar*	قصير
thirsty	*^caT-**shaan***	عطشان
hungry	*ga-^c**ehn***	جوعان، جائع
tired	*ta^c-**behn***	متعب
ill	*^cay-**yehn***, *ma-**reeD***	مريض
angry, upset	*za^c-**lehn***	غاضب
happy, pleased	*mab-**SooT***	مبسوط
kind	**Tay**-*yib*, *la-**Teef***	طيب، لطيف

generous	*ka-**reem***	كريم
mean	*ba-**kheel***	بخيل
easy	*sahl*	سهل
difficult	*Sa^cb*	صعب
correct	*maZ-**booT***	تمام ، مضبوط
incorrect	*mish maZ-**booT***	غير مضبوط
early	***bad**-ree*	باكر
late	***wakh**-ree, mu-ta-'**akh**-khir*	متأخر

NUMBERS

0	*Sifr*	٠
1	***weh**-Hid*	١
2	*it-**neyn***	٢
3	*ta-**leh**-ta*	٣
4	*ar-**ba**-^ca*	٤
5	***kham**-sa*	٥
6	***sit**-ta*	٦
7	***sab**-^ca*	٧
8	*ta-**man**-ya*	٨
9	***tis**-^ca*	٩
10	*^c**a**-sha-ra*	١٠

11	Hi-**daa**-shar	١١
12	it-**naa**-shar	١٢
13	ta-lat-**taa**-shar	١٣
14	ar-ba^c-**taa**-shar	١٤
15	kha-mas-**taa**-shar	١٥
16	sit-**taa**-shar	١٦
17	sa-ba^c-**taa**-shar	١٧
18	ta-man-**taa**-shar	١٨
19	ti-sa^c-**taa**-shar	١٩
20	^{c}ish-**reen**	٢٠
21	**weh**-Hid wi ^{c}ish-**reen**	٢١
22	it-**neyn** wi ^{c}ish-**reen**	٢٢
30	ta-la-**teen**	٣٠
40	ar-bi-^{c}**een**	٤٠
50	kham-**seen**	٥٠
60	sit-**teen**	٦٠
70	sab-^{c}**een**	٧٠
80	ta-man-**yeen**	٨٠
90	tis-^{c}**een**	٩٠
100	**mee**-ya	١٠٠
200	mee-**teyn**	٢٠٠

300	*tul-tu-**mee**-ya*	٣٠٠
400	*rub-ᶜu-**mee**-ya*	٤٠٠
500	*khum-su-**mee**-ya*	٥٠٠
600	*sut-tu-**mee**-ya*	٦٠٠
700	*sub-ᶜu-**mee**-ya*	٧٠٠
800	*tum-nu-**mee**-ya*	٨٠٠
900	*tus-ᶜu-**mee**-ya*	٩٠٠
1000	*'alf*	١٠٠٠
2000	*'al-**feyn***	٢٠٠٠
3000	***ta**-lat a-**lehf***	٣٠٠٠
4000	***ar**-baᶜ ta-**lehf***	٤٠٠٠
5000	***kha**-mas ta-**lehf***	٥٠٠٠
6000	*sitt a-**lehf***	٦٠٠٠
7000	***sa**-baᶜ ta-**lehf***	٧٠٠٠
8000	***ta**-man ta-**lehf***	٨٠٠٠
9000	***ti**-saᶜ ta-**lehf***	٩٠٠٠
10,000	*ᶜa-shar ta-**lehf***	١٠٠٠٠
100,000	*meet 'alf*	١٠٠٠٠٠
1,000,000	*mil-**yohn***	١٠٠٠٠٠٠

WHEN YOU ARRIVE

Visitors will need a visa for most Arab countries; these are sometimes obtainable at the point of entry; but it is usually simpler to get them before you leave. If you are touring the Middle East, and expect to come back to the same country, check on the possibility of getting a multiple-entry visa, and also whether you will need an exit visa.

PASSPORT CONTROL

My name is——.	*'is*-mee ——.	—— اسمي
I'm <u>American</u>	*a-na am-ree-**keh**-nee* [am-ree-keh-**nee**-ya] .	أنا امريكي [امريكية]
▪ British	▪ bri-**Taa**-nee [bri-Taa-**nee**-ya]	بريطاني [بريطانية]
▪ Canadian	▪ **ka**-na-dee [ka-na-**dee**-ya]	كندي [كندية]
▪ Australian	▪ os-**traa**-lee [os-tra-**lee**-ya]	استرالي [استرالية]
My address is ——.	ᶜ*in-**weh**-nee* ——.	—— عنواني
I'm staying at ——.	*a-na **neh**-zil [**naz**-la] fi* ——.	أنا أقيم ب ——
Here are (is) ——.	it-**faD**-Dal ——.	—— تفضل
▪ my documents	▪ il-'aw-**reh**″	أوراقي
▪ my passport	▪ il-bas-**boor**/ ga-**wehz** is-**sa**-far	جواز سفري

■ my identification card	■ *bi-**Ta**″-ti ish-shakh-**See**-ya* بطاقتي الشخصية
■ my embarkation card	■ *il-**bor**-ding kard* بطاقة الصعود
■ my disembarka-tion card	■ *kart il-wu-**Sool*** بطاقة الوصول

I have (I don't have) a visa.	*^can-dee (ma-^can-deesh) vee-za.* معي (لا يوجد معي) تأشيرة

I'm (traveling) —.	*da **sa**-far —.* أنا مسافر [مسافرة]
■ on business	■ *shughl* في عمل
■ on vacation	■ *'a-**geh**-za* في عطلة، اجازة

I'll be staying —.	***ha**″-^cud —.* سابقى —
■ a few days	■ ***ka**-za yohm* عدة أيام
■ a week	■ *'is-**boo**^c* أسبوع
■ a month	■ *shahr* شهر

I'm traveling <u>alone</u>.	*a-na mi-**seh**-fir [mi-**saf**-ra] li **waH**-dee.* أنا اسافر وحدي
■ with my family	■ *ma-^ca ^c**eyl**-tee/ '**us**-ri-tee* مع اسرتي
■ with my wife	■ *ma-^ca m-**raa**-tee/ **zohg**-tee* مع زوجتي
■ with my husband	■ *ma-^ca **goh**-zee* مع زوجي

BAGGAGE AND PORTERS

Where is the baggage claim?	*il-ᶜafsh feyn?*	أين مكان إستلام الأمتعة؟
This bag (these bags) are mine.	*ish-shan-Ta dee (ish-shu-naT dee) bi-taᶜ-tee.*	هذه حقيبتي (حقائبي)
This is mine.	*dee bi-taᶜ-tee.*	هذه لي
Is there a baggage cart?	*fee trol-lee?*	هل توجد عربة أمتعة؟
Is there a porter?	*fee shay-yehl?*	هل هناك شيال؟
Be careful!	**Heh-sib!**	احذر !
I'll carry that.	***a-na** ha-**sheel** da.*	سأحمل هذه الحقيبة
I'm missing one bag.	*fee **shan-Ta na″-Sa.***	فقدت حقيبة
I've lost my luggage.	*Daaᶜ **min-nee** il ᶜafsh.*	فقدت أمتعتي
How much do I owe you?	*ᶜa-wiz **kam?***	كم تريد؟
Thank you.	**shuk-ran.**	شكراً
That's for you.	*da ᶜa-la-**sheh**-nak.*	تفضل، هذا لك

CUSTOMS

I have nothing to declare.	***a-na** fi Hu-**dood** il-mas-**mooH.***	أنا في حدود المسموح

I have <u>one carton</u> of cigarettes.	*ma-^ceh-ya khar-**Too**-shit sa-geh-yir.*	معي خرطوشة سجائر
▪ two cartons	▪ *khar-Toosh-**teyn***	خرطوشتين
I have one bottle <u>of whiskey</u>.	*ma-^ceh-ya "i-zeh-zit **wis**-kee.*	معي زجاجة ويسكي
▪ of wine	▪ *ni-**beet***	نبيذ
▪ of perfume	▪ *^ciTr*	عطر
I have nothing else.	*ma ma-^ceesh Ha-ga **tan**-ya.*	لا يوجد معي شيء آخر
These are gifts.	*dee ha-**deh**-ya.*	هذه هدايا
They are for my personal use.	*dee li-'is-ti^c-**meh**-lee ish-**shakh**-See.*	إنها لاستعمالي الشخصي
It isn't new.	*dee mish gi-**dee**-da.*	إنها ليست جديدة
Do I have to pay duty?	*leh-zim ad-fa^c ga-**meh**-rik?*	هل يجب أن أدفع ضريبة؟
Where do I pay?	*ad-fa^c feyn?*	أين أدفع؟
Can I pay with dollars?	***mum**-kin ad-fa^c bid-do-**laar**?*	هل يمكن أن أدفع بالدولار؟

Bureaucracy

Dealings with government officials over visas, customs clearance, residence permits, and so on may be slow and frustrating. Showing impatience and irritation usually has an adverse effect, however. Try to get the official(s) on your side by a warm and friendly but courteous approach.

Make use of any contact you have in the office or Ministry, however tenuous. Ideally, go with someone who is familiar with the procedures involved. If a particular bureaucratic process is known to take forever, take along a stack of post-cards to write or a book to read.

OTHER AIRPORT INFORMATION

Can I book a hotel room from here?	*mum*-kin *aH*-giz '*oh*-Da/ *ghur*-fa min *hi*-na?	هل استطيع حجز غرفة بفندق من هنا؟
Is there a post office in the airport?	fee *mak*-tab ba-*reed* fil-ma-*Taar*?	هل يوجد مكتب بريد في المطار؟
Is there a bank open?	fee bank *feh*-tiH?	هل يوجد بنك مفتوح؟
Can I make a phone call from here?	*mum*-kin *a^c*-mil ti-li-*fohn* min *hi*-na?	هل استطيع إجراء مكالمة من هنا؟
Where can I rent a car?	mi-*neyn* a-'*ag*-gar ^c a-ra-*bee*-ya/ say-*yaa*-ra?	من أين أستطيع إستئجار سيارة؟

GETTING INTO TOWN

| Where can I get a taxi? | a-*leh*-"ee *tak*-see feyn? | أين أجد تاكسي؟ |
| Is there a meter? | fee ^c ad-*dehd*? | هل يوجد عداد؟ |

Is there a bus into town?	*fee 'u-tu-**bees** li wiST il-**ba**-lad?*	هل يوجد أوتوبيس لوسط المدينة؟
Where is the stop?	*il-ma-**HaT**-Ta feyn?*	أين المحطة؟
When does it leave?	*bi-**yiT**-la^c '**im**-ta?*	متى يرحل؟
How much will it cost?	*ha-**yeh**-khud kam?*	كم الأجرة؟
How long does it take?	*ir-**riH**-la bi-**teh**-khud "**ad**-di 'eyh?*	ما مدة الرحلة؟
I want to go to the — Hotel.	*^ca-wiz [^caw-za] a-**rooH** 'u-**teel** —.*	أريد الذهاب إلى فندق —
I want to go to this address.	*^ca-wiz [^caw-za] a-**rooH** il-^cin-**wehn** da.*	أريد الذهاب إلى هذا العنوان
I am with a group.	*a-na ma-^ca mag-**moo**-^ca.*	أنا مع مجموعة

BANKING AND MONEY MATTERS

The basic currencies in the major Arab countries are as follows:

dinar (*dee-naar*): Iraq, Algeria, Tunisia, Jordan, Libya, Bahrain, and Kuwait.

riyal (*ree-yehl*): Saudi Arabia, Yemen, Oman, Qatar.

gineh (*gi-ney*): Egypt and the Sudan.

lira (*lee-ra*): Syria and Lebanon.

dirham (*dir-ham*): Morocco and the United Arab Emirates.

These are, of course, all independent currencies. They are all further divided into a hundred units. In Egypt a **gineh** is made up of 100 **piastres** ("*irsh*), which is also the smaller unit of currency in Lebanon. Sometimes the smaller unit is further divided; in Egypt one piastre is worth 10 **millimes** (*mil-leem*). In Jordan there are 1,000 **fils** (*fils*) to the dinar.

Sometimes paper money is used for very small denominations, being worth as little as a few cents.

Check on currency regulations before you leave; often there are restrictions on taking local currency out of the country. It may be necessary to prove you have spent a certain amount during your stay, so keep receipts of all exchange transactions.

bank	*bank*	بنك
branch	*far ͨ*	فرع
exchange	*taH-weel, Sarf*	تحويل، صرف
When do you <u>open</u>?	*bi-tif-ta-Hoo 'im-ta?*	متى تفتحون؟

English	Transliteration	Arabic
close?	*bi-ti"-fi-loo?*	تغلقون ؟
bank clerk	*mu-waZ-Zaf Hi-sa-beht*	موظف حسابات
cashier	*Sar-raaf*	صراف
window, counter	*shib-behk*	شباك
check (checks)	*sheek (shee-keht)*	شيك (شيكات)
checkbook	*daf-tar shee-keht*	دفتر شيكات
amount	*mab-lagh*	مبلغ
Please give me a receipt.	*id-dee-nee waSl min faD-lak [min faD-lik]*	اعطني إيصالا من فضلك
I'd like to open —.	*ᶜa-wiz af-taH —.*	أريد أن أفتح — .
▪ a current account	▪ *Hi-sehb geh-ree*	حساب جاري
▪ a deposit account	▪ *Hi-sehb wa-dee-ᶜa*	حساب وديعة
What is the interest rate?	*siᶜr il-fay-da kam?*	كم سعر الفائدة؟
(About) five percent	*(Ha-weh-lee) kham-sa fil-mee-ya*	(تقريبا) خمسة بالمئة
▪ ten	▪ *ᶜa-sha-ra*	عشرة
I want to rent a safe.	*ᶜa-wiz [ᶜaw-za] a-'ag-gar khaz-na.*	أريد استئجار خزنة

I'd like to see the manager, please.	*a-wiz [*aw-za] a-shoof il-mu-deer, min faD-lak.	أريد أن أرى المدير، من فضلك

(For more banking and commercial terms see the mini business dictionary, page 186)

EXCHANGING MONEY

Is there a bank near here?	fee bank "u-ray-yib min hi-na?	هل يوجد بنك قريب؟
■ a money exchange	■ mak-tab Sarf	مكتب صرافة
■ a cash dispenser (ATM)	■ ma-ka-na li saHb il-fi-loos	آلة تعطي نقود
Where is the American Express office?	feyn mak-tab il-a-me-ri-kan eks-pres?	أين مكتب اميريكان إكسبريس؟
Can I change —?	mum-kin a-ghay-yar —?	هل يمكن أن أغير —
■ cash	■ fi-loos na"d	نقد
■ dollars	■ do-laa-raat	دولارات
■ traveler's checks	■ shee-keht si-yeh-Hee-ya	شيكات سياحية
Can I cash a personal check?	mum-kin aS-raf sheek khaaS?	هل يمكنني صرف شيك خاص؟
I have a credit card.	*an-dee kri-dit kard.	عندي بطاقة إعتماد، كريدت كارد

What's the <u>dollar</u> exchange rate?	*kam si^cr id-do-**laar**?*	كم سعر الدولار؟
▨ sterling	▨ *il-'is-tir-**lee**-nee*	الاسترليني
Is that the official rate?	*da is-si^cr ir-**ras**-mee?*	هل هذا السعر رسمي؟
Is there a black market rate?	*fee si^cr soo" **soo**-da?*	هل يوجد سعر سوق سوداء؟
Do I fill out a form?	*leh-zim am-la 'is-ti-**maa**-ra?*	هل يجب أن أملأ استمارة؟
Where do I sign?	*am-Dee feyn?*	أين أمضي؟
Here's my passport.	*it-**faD**-Dal il-bas-**boor**/ga-**wehz** is-**sa**-far.*	تفضل ها هو جواز السفر
I'd like to change <u>100</u> dollars.	*^ca-wiz a-**ghay**-yar <u>meet</u> do-**laar**.*	أريد تحويل ١٠٠ دولار
▨ 200	▨ *mee-**teyn***	٢٠٠
▨ 300	▨ *tul-tu-**meet***	٣٠٠
▨ 400	▨ *rub-^cu-**meet***	٤٠٠
▨ 500	▨ *khum-su-**meet***	٥٠٠
▨ 600	▨ *sut-tu-**meet***	٦٠٠
▨ 700	▨ *sub-^cu-**meet***	٧٠٠
▨ 800	▨ *tum-nu-**meet***	٨٠٠
▨ 900	▨ *tus-^cu-**meet***	٩٠٠
▨ 1000	▨ *'alf*	١٠٠٠

■ into local currency	*lil-ᶜ**um**-la l-ma-Hal-**lee**-ya*	للعملة المحلية

Can you give me <u>small bills</u>?	***mum**-kin tid-**dee**-nee 'aw-**reh**" Su-ghay-**ya**-ra?*	هل تستطيع أن تعطني أوراق صغيرة ؟
■ large bills?	■ *'aw-**reh**" ki-**bee**-ra?*	أوراق كبيرة
■ some small change?	■ ***fak**-ka?*	فكة

(See page 17 for numbers.)

AT THE HOTEL

The usual international hotels are to be found in the major cities, at international prices. More interesting places to stay are the few remaining grand hotels of a more leisurely era, such as the Cecil in Alexandria and the Old Cataract in Aswan. But with the help of the local tourist office you can find a room in any price range; generally speaking, you will get what you pay for.

CHECKING IN

Do you have a room?	*ᶜan-**du**-kum 'oh-Da/**ghur**-fa?*	هل عندكم غرفة؟
I have a reservation.	*ᶜan-dee Hagz.*	حجزت
I have no reservation.	*ma-ᶜan-**deesh** Hagz.*	لم أحجز
I'd like a single room.	*ᶜa-wiz [ᶜaw-za] 'oh-Da/**ghur**-fa bi si-**reer** weh-Hid.*	أريد غرفة مفردة
I'd like a double room.	*ᶜa-wiz [ᶜaw-za] 'oh-Da/**ghur**-fa lit-**neyn**.*	أريد غرفة مزدوجة
I'd like a room <u>with twin beds.</u>	*ᶜa-wiz [ᶜaw-za] 'oh-Da <u>bi si-ree-**reyn**</u>.*	أريد غرفة بسريرين
▤ with a shower	▤ *fee-ha dush*	بها دش
▤ with a bathroom	▤ *bi Ham-**mehm****	بحمام
▤ with a TV	▤ *fee-ha ti-li-viz-**yohn***	بها تليفزيون
▤ with a refrigerator	▤ *fee-ha tal-**leh**-ga*	بها برادة/ ثلاجة
▤ with a balcony	▤ *fee bal-**koh**-na*	لها بلكون/ شرفة

with air conditioning	*fee*-ha tak-*yeef* *ha*-wa	بها مكيف هواء
with hot water	*fee*-ha **may**-ya **sukh**-na	بها ماء ساخن
with a good view	**min**-ha **man**-Zar ga-**meel**	مطلة على منظر جميل
(not) facing the street	(mish) ᶜa-la-sh-**sheh**-riᶜ	(غير) مطلة على الشارع
facing the garden	ᶜa-la g-gi-**ney**-na	مطلة على الحديقة
on the sea	ᶜa-la l-**baHr**	على البحر
Can you try another hotel for me?	**mum**-kin ti-**shuf**-lee 'u-**teel** teh-**nee**?	هل تستطيع أن تجد لي فندقا آخرا؟
May I see the room?	**mum**-kin a-**shoof** il-'**oh**-Da/il-**ghur**-fa?	أريد أن أرى الغرفة
I like it.	ᶜa-ga-**bit**-nee.	تعجبني
I don't like it.	ma ᶜa-ga-bit-**neesh**.	لا تعجبني
Can I see another?	**mum**-kin a-**shoof** 'oh-Da **tan**-ya?	هل أستطيع أن أرى غرفة اخرى؟
larger	'**aw**-saᶜ	أوسع
smaller	'**aS**-ghar	أصغر
quieter	'**ah**-da	أهدا

■ cheaper	■ *'ar-khaS*	أرخص
■ better	■ *'aH-san*	أفضل
This is nice.	*dee kway-yi-sa.*	هذه جيدة
I'll take it.	*ha-khud-ha.*	سآخذها
What floor is it on?	*dee fee an-hee dohr?*	في أي طابق هي؟
Is there an elevator?	*fee 'a-san-Seer?*	
		هل يوجد مصعد / أسنسير؟
What's the rate?	*il-'oh-Da bi kam?*	كم السعر؟
Does it include <u>service</u>?	*da bil-khid-ma?*	
		هل يشمل الخدمة؟
■ taxes	■ *biD-Da-raa-yib*	الضرائب
■ breakfast	■ *bil-fi-Taar*	الافطار
How much is <u>bed and breakfast</u>?	*bi kam il-'oh-Da bil-fi-Taar?*	كم السعر بالافطار؟
■ full board (3 meals)	■ *bil-'akl*	للاقامة الكاملة
Is there a reduction for children?	*fee takh-feeD lil-'aT-faal?*	هل يوجد تخفيض للاطفال؟
Can you put another bed in the room?	*mum-kin ti-HuTT si-reer teh-nee fil-'oh-Da?*	هل تستطيع وضع سرير آخر في الغرفة؟
I will stay <u>one night</u>.	*ha"-cud ley-la waH-da.*	سأبقى ليلة واحدة

▦ two nights	▦ *leyl-teyn*	ليلتين
▦ a few days	▦ *ka-za yohm*	عدة أيام
▦ a week	▦ *'is-boo*ᶜ	أسبوع
▦ two weeks	▦ *'is-boo-*ᶜ*eyn*	أسبوعين

I don't know exactly how long.	*ma*ᶜ*-rafsh "ad-di 'eyh biZ-ZabT*
	لا أعرف المدة بالضبط

BREAKFAST

I'd like breakfast in the room.	ᶜ*a-wiz [*ᶜ*aw-za] il-fi-Taar fil-'oh-Da.*
	أريد الافطار بالغرفة
▦ for one	▦ *li weh-Hid* لشخص واحد
▦ for two	▦ *li 'it-neyn* لشخصين

Please send up —.	*min faD-lak gib-lee —.*
	أرجو أن ترسل —.

▦ coffee	▦ *"ah-wa*	قهوة
▦ tea	▦ *shayy*	شاي
▦ toast	▦ *tust*	خبز محمص، توست
▦ (with jam/honey)	▦ *(bil-mi-rab-ba/bil-*ᶜ*a-sal)*	
		(بالمربى / بالعسل)
▦ fruit juice	▦ ᶜ*a-Seer*	عصير فاكهة
▦ eggs	▦ *beyD*	بيض
▦ (scrambled/fried/ boiled)	▦ *(maD-roob/ma"-lee/mas-loo")*	
		(مضروب / مقلي / مسلوق)

■ an English
language newspaper

■ *ga-ree-da in-gi-lee-zee*

جريدة باللغة الانجليزية

HOTEL SERVICES

Where is
the elevator?

feyn il-'a-san-Seer?

أين المصعد/الاسنسير؟

■ the bathroom	■ *it-twa-litt*	التواليت
■ the restaurant	■ *il-maT-ᶜam*	المطعم
■ the phone	■ *it-ti-li-fohn*	التليفون
■ the bar	■ *il-baar*	البار
■ the swimming pool	■ *Ham-mehm is-si-beh-Ha*	حمام السباحة

I need
a chambermaid.

*ᶜa-wiz [ᶜaw-za]
shagh-gheh-la.*

احتاج لخادمة الغرفة

■ a bellboy	■ *far-raash*	لفراش
■ a hair dryer	■ *sish-waar*	لمجفف شعر
■ a reading lamp	■ *a-ba joo-ra*	لمصباح للقراءة

The room is
dirty.

il-'oh-Da wis-kha.

الغرفة قذرة

There are
mosquitoes.

fee na-moos.

يوجد ناموس

Please spray
the room.

rush-shi-lee l-'oh-Da min faD-lak.

أرجو أن ترش الغرفة

Please bring me <u>towels</u>.	*min* **faD**-*lak* **gib**-*lee* **fo**-*waT*.	أرجو ان تحضر لي مناشف، فوط
■ soap	■ *Sa*-**boon**	صابون
■ a pillow	■ *mi*-**khad**-*da*	مخدة
■ a blanket	■ *baT*-*Ta*-**nee**-*ya*	بطانية
■ ice	■ *talg*	ثلج
■ mineral water	■ **may**-*ya ma*ᶜ-*da*-**nee**-*ya*	مياه معدنية
■ hangers	■ *sham-ma-*ᶜ*eht*	شماعات
■ toilet paper	■ **wa**-*ra*" *twa*-**litt**	ورق تواليت
■ an adaptor	■ *mu*-**Haw**-*wil*	محول
■ a light bulb	■ **lam**-*ba*	لمبة
■ (bath) plug	■ *sad*-**deh**-*da*	سدادة
■ (electric) plug	■ **fee**-*sha*	فيشة
Just a minute!	**laH**-*Za* **waH**-*da!*	لحظة واحدة!
Come in!	*ud*-**khul!**	ادخل!
Thank you. Put it here.	**shuk**-*ran.* **HuT**-*Too* **hi**-*na.*	شكراً. ضعها هنا.
Please put a board under the mattress.	*min faD*-*lak HuTT* **lohH** *taHt il-mar-*ta-ba.	احتاج للوح تحت المرتبة.
There is no <u>(hot) water</u>.	*ma*-**feesh** <u>**may**-*ya*</u> (<u>**sukh**-*na*</u>).	لا يوجد ماء ساخن
■ electricity	■ *kah*-**ra**-*ba*	كهرباء

The <u>air conditioning</u> isn't working.	*it-tak-**yeef**^caT-**laan**.*	لا يعمل التكيف

▓ toilet	▓ *it-twa-**litt***	التواليت
▓ faucet	▓ *il-Ha-na-**fee**-ya*	الصنبور/الحنفية
▓ light	▓ *in-**noor***	النور
▓ radio	▓ *ir-**ra**-dyo*	الراديو
▓ TV	▓ *it-ti-li-viz-**yohn***	التليفزيون

Can you fix it <u>soon</u>?	***mum**-kin ti-Sal-**la**-Hoo bi-**sur**-^ca?*	هل تستطيع إصلاحه سريعاً؟

Is there <u>satellite TV</u>?	*fee ti-li-viz-**yohn** <u>sa-ti-**layt**?</u>*	هل يوجد تليفزيون بالقمر الصناعي؟

| ▓ cable TV? | ▓ <u>***key**-bil?*</u> | كابل؟ |

Are there English-language channels?	*fee qa-na-**weht** bil-'in-gi-**lee**-zee?*	هل هناك قنوات بالإنجليزية؟

Can you open this?	***mum**-kin tif-**taH**-lee da?*	هل تستطيع فتح هذا لي؟

I have lost my key.	*il-muf-**tehH** Daa^c **min**-nee.*	ضاع المفتاح مني

This is to be <u>laundered</u>.	*da <u>lil-gha-**seel**</u>.*	هذا للغسيل

| ▓ pressed | ▓ *lil-**mak**-wa* | للكي |

When will it be ready?	*hay-**koon** geh-hiz 'im-ta?*	متى سيكون جاهزاً؟

Are there any <u>messages</u> for me?	*fee <u>ri-**seh**-la</u> ^ca-**sheh**-nee?*	هل هناك رسائل لي؟
▨ letters	▨ *ga-wa-**beht***	خطابات
▨ packages	▨ *Tu-**rood***	طرود
Can you make a phone call for me?	***mum**-kin tuT-**lub**-lee ti-li-**fohn**?*	هل تستطيع ان تطلب مكالمة لي؟
I want to speak to Mr. —.	*^ca-**wiz** [^c**aw**-za-] a-**kal**-lim is-**say**-yid—.*	أريد ان اتكلم مع السيد —
▨ to Mrs. —.	▨ *ma-**dehm** —.*	السيدة —
Please give me an outside line.	*id-**dee**-nee il-**khaTT** min **faD**-lak.*	أرجو أن تعطني خطاً خارجياً
Do you have a a fax machine?	*^can-**du**-kum **ma**-ka-nit **faks**?*	هل عندكم جهاز فاكس؟
I want to send a fax.	*^ca-**wiz** [^c**aw**-za] ab-^cat **faks**.*	أريد أن أرسل فاكس.
This isn't legible.	*da mish **waa**-DiH.*	هذا ليس واضح.
I'd like to put this in your safe.	*^ca-**wiz** [^c**aw**-za] a-**HuTT** dee fil-**khaz**-na.*	أريد أن أضع هذا في الخزنة
I'd like my things from your safe.	*^ca-**wiz** [^c**aw**-za] 'eh-khud il-ha-**geht** bit-ta^c-tee min il-**khaz**-na*	أريد أشيائي من الخزنة من فضلك

CHECKING OUT

I'm leaving <u>today</u>.	*a-na mi-seh-fir mi-saf-ra in-na-haar-da/il-yohm.*	سأرحل اليوم
▪ tomorrow (morning)	▪ *buk-ra (iS-SubH)*	غداً (صباحاً)
I'd like the bill, please.	*id-dee-nee il-Hi-sehb min faD-lak.*	أريد الحساب، من فضلك
My room number is —.	*il-'oh-Da nim-ra —.*	رقم غرفتي —
There seems to be a mistake.	*fee gha-laT.*	يبدو هناك خطأ
What is this amount for?	*il-mab-lagh da ᶜa-shehn 'eyh?*	لماذا هذا المبلغ؟
Please check it again.	*law sa-maHt reh-giᶜ ᶜa-leyh teh-nee.*	أرجوك راجعها ثانية
Can I leave my luggage here till <u>noon</u>?	*mum-kin a-seeb ish-shu-naT hi-na li Hadd iD-Duhr?*	هل أستطيع ترك أمتعتي هنا حتى الظهر؟
▪ evening	▪ *il-mi-seh'*	المساء
Please have my luggage brought down.	*min faD-lak naz-zil ish-shu-naT.*	أرجوك انزل أمتعتي
I'm in a hurry.	*a-na mis-taᶜ-gil [mis-taᶜ-gi-la].*	أنا مستعجل [مستعجلة]

Please call a cab.	*min **faD**-lak uT-**lub**-lee **tak**-see.*
	أرجوك اطلب تاكسي
I'm going to the airport.	*a-na **reh**-yiH [**ray**-Ha] il-ma-**Taar**.*
	أنا ذاهب الى المطار

OTHER ACCOMMODATIONS

I want to rent a house.	*^c**a**-wiz [^c**aw**-za] a-'**ag**-gar **beyt**.*	أريد استئجار بيت
▓ an apartment	▓ *sha"-"a*	شقة
▓ an (un)furnished apartment	▓ *sha"-"a (mish) maf-**roo**-sha*	شقة (غير) مفروشة
▓ a furnished room	▓ *'oh-Da/**ghur**-fa maf-**roo**-sha*	غرفة مفروشة
▓ a houseboat	▓ *^caw-**weh**-ma*	عوامة
Do you know a good boarding house?	*ti^c-raf pin-si-**yohn** kway-yis?*	هل تعرف بنسيوناً جيداً ؟
Do you know a good real estate agent?	*ti^c-raf sim-**saar** kway-**yis**?*	هل تعرف سمساراً جيداً ؟
I need one (two) bedroom(s).	*^c**a**-wiz [^c**aw**-za] 'oh-Dit ('ohT-**teyn**) nohm.*	أريد غرفة نوم (غرفتين نوم)
▓ a living room	▓ *'oh-Dit gu-**loos***	غرفة الجلوس
▓ a good bathroom	▓ *Ham-**mehm**-**kway**-yis*	حمام جيد

How much is it <u>per week?</u>	*kam* *fil-'is-**boo**^c?*	كم إيجارها في الأسبوع؟
▨ per month	▨ *fish-**shahr***	في الشهر
▨ per year	▨ *fis-**sa**-na*	في السنة
I'll be staying <u>two weeks.</u>	*ha''-^c-ud* *'is-boo-^ceyn*	سأبقى أسبوعين
▨ one month	▨ *shahr*	شهر
▨ two months	▨ *shah-**reyn***	شهرين
▨ (about) three months	▨ *(Ha-weh-lee) ta-lat-**tush**-hur*	(حوالي) ثلاثة أشهر
Do you need a deposit?	*^ca-wiz ^car-boon?*	هل تحتاج لمقدم؟
Shall I pay in dollars?	*ad-fa^c bid-do-**laar**?*	هل أدفع بالدولار؟
Do you take key money?	*bi-**teh**-khud khu-**luww**?*	هل تريد وديعة/خلو؟
Can I use the kitchen?	*mum-kin as-ta^c-mil il-**maT**-bakh?*	هل أستطيع إستعمال المطبخ؟
Is there hot water?	*fee **may**-ya **sukh**-na?*	هل هناك ماء ساخن؟
Is there <u>a refrigerator?</u>	*fee tal-**leh**-ga?*	هل هناك ثلاجة؟
▨ a freezer	▨ *free-zar*	فريزر
Is there a youth hostel in town?	*fee beyt sha-**behb** fil-**ba**-lad?*	هل هناك بيت شباب في المدينة؟

| Can I park the car here? | **mum**-kin **ar**-kin il-ᶜa-ra-**bee**-ya **hi**-na? هل أستطيع ترك السيارة هنا؟ |
| Can I leave it here overnight? | **mum**-kin a-bay-**yit**-ha **hi**-na? هل استطيع ترك السيارة هنا ليلا ؟ |

THE BAWWAB

If you stay in an apartment building for any length of time you will discover the live-in doorkeeper (the *baw-wehb*) who is in charge of the overall security and daily maintenance of the building. It is important to establish good relations with this key individual; if willing, he can prove invaluable by taking and passing on messages, running small errands, acting as a go-between with local tradespeople and repairmen, and so forth.

You will contribute to his official monthly salary, but he should be tipped modestly for any extra services he performs. Find out from the neighbors what sums are appropriate. (Note: Foreigners are usually expected to be more generous than locals!) If you are on good terms, he can also be a fascinating source of gossip about the building and the area in general.

TIPPING

The usual rules for tipping apply in Arab hotels and restaurants as well. It is not customary in most Arab countries to tip taxi drivers, although it is increasingly expected of foreigners, and is certainly appreciated!

In the poorer Arab countries you sometimes find people anxious to perform small services for you: find a cab, carry your bag, clean your windshield. It is often less hassle to accept this with a good grace than to fend people off continually. Keep a supply of small change for the purpose.

In the major tourist centers — in countries like Morocco and Egypt — you will be approached by people wanting to act as a guide. If you decide the person has enough English — and useful local information — to be helpful, agree on a fee for his services in advance. Small boys can often be helpful in showing you out-of-the-way sites or guiding you back to civilization when you get lost. Again, it's often simpler to adopt one young "guide" at the outset; he will then repel rivals, and you will be left in relative peace.

If you are determined to go it alone, reply to overtures with a firm "No thank you," indicating that you have a guidebook and know where you are going. Above all, don't shout or get upset. Everyone has to earn a living. Judging when to tip can be a delicate matter, since people will often show great kindness and hospitality with no thought of reward. Then a small gift is much more acceptable than money, though you might persuade someone to accept the latter by insisting it's "for the children" (*ᶜa-shehn il-'aw-lehd*). Do it quietly and discreetly if possible.

GETTING AROUND TOWN

Taxis tend to be inexpensive (once you get to know the rates!), whereas buses are crowded and slow. Minibuses are faster because they fill up early on the route and don't stop to take on new passengers. In some of the larger cities streetcars still run. Cairo has a modest subway (underground) train service (**mit-roo**).

Within some cities, and between most, there is a system of shared taxis. The intercity ones will leave from a specific part of town — often near the railway or bus station. The taxi will leave once it's full (if you're in a hurry, you can pay for the remaining seats).

Shared taxis in town either operate along fixed routes like buses, or, hopefully, you hail a passing cab with the name of the place you want to get to. If it's going in that general direction, you'll be taken on board. The big hotels often have their own limousine service, which is comfortable and efficient but naturally a good deal more expensive.

In some of the countries in the Gulf it's best to use a taxi agency, since the freelance taxi drivers may not have much idea of local geography. Ask the advice of someone who has lived in the town for some time.

Do you have a map of the city?	*ᶜan*-dak kha-*ree*-Ta lil-*ba*-lad?	هل عندكم خريطة للمدينة؟
Where is — ?	— *feyn?*	أين —؟
How far is — ?	— *ᶜa*-la **buᶜd** "ad-di '*eyh*?	كم تبعد —؟
▪ the bus station	▪ *maw*-"af il-'u-tu-bee-**seht**	محطة الاوتوبيس
▪ the railway station	▪ ma-**HaT**-Tit is-**sik**-ka l-Ha-**deed**	محطة القطار

▨	the airport bus terminal	*maw-"af'u-tu-bees* il-ma-**Taar** موقف أوتوبيس المطار
▨	the museum	*il-mat-Haf* المتحف
▨	Qasr ElNil Street	*sheh-ri*ᶜ *"aSr in-neel* شارع قصر النيل
▨	Tahrir Square	*mi-dehn it-taH-reer*ميدان التحرير

I want to take
a cab to —.

ᶜ*a-wiz [*ᶜ*aw-za]* '*eh-khud*
tak-*see li* —.   — أريد أن آخذ تاكسي إلى

I want to go to —.

ᶜ*a-wiz [*ᶜ*aw-za] a-rooH* —.

— أريد الذهاب إلى

Can I take a
bus from here?

mum-*kin* '*eh-khud* '*u-tu-bees*
min **hi**-na?

هل أستطيع أن آخذ الاوتوبيس من هنا؟

Which number
is the bus?

'*u-tu-bees nim-ra* **kam**?

ما هو رقم الاوتوبيس؟

Can I go on foot?

mum-*kin am-shee-ha?*

هل أستطيع الذهاب سيراً؟

Is there a subway
station near here?

fee ma-HaT-Tit **mit**-*roo*
"*u-ray-yib min* **hi**-na?

هل توجد محطة مترو قريب؟

Is it far from here?

*da bi-*ᶜ*eed* ᶜ*an* **hi**-na?   هل هو بعيد؟

How much
will it cost?

*hay-***kal**-*lif* **kam**?   كم ستكلف؟

Do you have a meter?	*ᶜan-dak ᶜad-dehd?*	هل عندك عداد؟
How much do you charge per day?	*bi-teh-khud **kam** fil-yohm?*	كم الاجرة اليومية؟
I want to go and come back.	*ᶜa-wiz [ᶜaw-za] a-rooH war-gaᶜ.*	أريد الذهاب والعودة
Will you wait for me there?	***mum**-kin tis-tan-**neh**-nee hi-**nehk**?*	هل ستنتظرني هناك؟
Slow down!	*ᶜa-la **mah**-lak!*	قلل السرعة!
Please wait here a moment.	*is-**tan**-na **hi**-na shway-ya.*	من فضلك انتظر هنا لحظة
I'll be right back.	***har**-gaᶜ **Heh**-lan.*	سأعود حالاً
Turn <u>left</u> here.	***Haw**-wid shi-**mehl** **hi**-na*	الى اليسار هنا
■ right	■ yi-**meen**	الى اليمين
Straight on.	***dugh**-ree.*	الى الامام
Stop here.	*'u-"af **hi**-na.*	قف هنا
I'll get out here.	***han**-zil **hi**-na.*	سأنزل هنا.
How much do I owe you?	*ᶜa-wiz **kam**?*	كم تريد؟
Thanks. That's for you.	***shuk**-ran. da ᶜa-la-**sheh**-nak.*	شكراً. هذا لك
Please tell me where to get off.	*min **faD**-lak "**ul**-lee **an**-zil feyn.*	أرجوك قل لي أين انزل

SIGHTSEEING

Because the Arabic-speaking countries span such a vast area, each offers different attractions to the traveler. In North Africa, Morocco and Tunisia have the most developed tourist industries. A holiday there can combine relaxing on superb beaches with visits to medieval walled cities and to ancient Greek and Roman sites, or trips into the dramatic Atlas Mountains.

At the eastern end of the Mediterranean, in Syria, Jordan, and Lebanon, you will find some of the most spectacular monuments of the ancient world and of Islamic civilization, as well as marvelous swimming off the Mediterranean and Red Sea coasts. Though political turmoil in the area has discouraged foreign visitors, the intrepid traveler will be well rewarded. Not only will people be delighted to see you and want to show you the best of their country, you will be blissfully free of the hype and hassle that popular tourist centers tend to attract.

Egypt is understandably the Arab country best known to the foreign tourist. It has literally hundreds of miles of unspoiled beaches on its Mediterranean and Red Sea coasts; the coral reefs of the Red Sea and Sinai Peninsula offer some of the best snorkeling and scuba diving in the world.

Most visitors with limited time to spend will want to concentrate on the great temples, pyramids, and tombs of the Nile Valley. The daily flights from Cairo to Luxor and Aswan, as well as comfortable trains, make it easy to stop off at lesser-known sites en route. Or you can travel one way by Nile steamer, the best of which retain an old-world elegance and charm.

Travel facilities in Egypt are being improved all the time, so that it is now possible to combine visits to the major Pharaonic monuments with trips to the chain of oases in the Western Desert and to Sinai in the east, where the famous Greek Orthodox monastery of St. Catherine stands at the foot of Mount Sinai. This *can* all be done in a couple of weeks, but it is much more rewarding to take a little longer, to rest up in a quiet corner, absorb your impressions of the country, and get to know the people.

The main tourist centers offer accommodations ranging from the absolutely basic to international five-star standard. In the oases and smaller coastal resorts accommodations will be inexpensive and simple, if not Spartan.

Where is the Tourist Office?	**mak**-tab is-si-**yeh**-Ha feyn?	أين مكتب السياحة ؟
Do you have tourist information?	^can-**du**-kum is-ti^c-la-**meht** si-yeh-**Hee**-ya?	هل عندكم معلومات سياحية؟
Do you have a guidebook?	^can-**du**-kum da-**leel** si-yeh-**Hee**?	هل عندكم دليل سياحي؟
Are there tours of the city?	fee riH-**leht** si-ya-**Hee**-ya fil-**ba**-lad?	هل هناك جولات في المدينة؟
When does the bus leave?	bi-**yiT**-la ^c 'im-ta il-'u-tu-**bees**?	متى سيرحل الاوتوبيس؟
Where does it leave from?	il-ma-**HaT**-Ta feyn?	من أين سيرحل الاوتوبيس؟
How much does it cost?	bee-**kal**-lif kam?	كم تكلف؟
How long does it take?	ha-**yeh**-khud kam seh-^ca?	ما مدة الجولة؟
What are the main attractions?	'eyh 'a-**hamm** il-'a-**meh**-kin is-si-yeh-**Hee**-ya?	ما هي أهم الأماكن السياحية؟

I have only <u>one day.</u>	*^can-dee <u>yohm</u> bass*	لم يبق لي إلا يوماً واحداً
▧ two days	▧ *yoh-meyn*	يومين
▧ three days	▧ *ta-lat tee-yehm*	ثلاثة أيام
▧ one week	▧ *'is-boo^c*	أسبوع
I need a guide with good English.	*^ca-wiz [^caw-za] da-leel bi-yit-kal-lim in-gi-lee-zee kway-yis.*	احتاج لمرشد يتكلم الانجليزية بطلاقة
How much does he charge <u>per hour</u>?	*bi-yeh-khud kam <u>fis-seh-^ca</u>?*	كم يطلب في الساعة؟
▧ per day	▧ *fil-yohm*	في اليوم
I want to go to the <u>Islamic Museum.</u>	*^ca-wiz [^caw-za] a-rooH il-mat-Haf il-is-leh-mee.*	أريد أن أذهب الى المتحف الاسلامي
▧ The Egyptian Museum	▧ *il-mat-Haf il-maS-ree*	المتحف المصري
▧ Khan ElKhalili bazaar	▧ *khan il-kha-lee-lee*	خان الخليلي
▧ the Azhar mosque	▧ *geh-mi^c il-'az-har*	جامع الأزهر
▧ the Sultan Hasan mosque	▧ *geh-mi^c is-sul-Taan Ha-san*	جامع السلطان حسن
▧ the Citadel	▧ *il-"al-^ca*	القلعة
▧ the pyramids	▧ *il-ha-ram*	الهرم

■ the zoo	■ gi-**ney**-nit il-Ha-ya-wa-**neht**	حديقة الحيوان
■ the market, bazaar	■ is-**soo**"	السوق
■ the old city	■ il-ma-**dee**-na	المدينة القديمة
■ Sakkara	■ saq-**qaa**-ra	سقارة
■ Fayyoum	■ il-fay-**yoom**	الفيوم
■ the Valley of the Kings	■ **weh**-di l-mu-**look**	وادي الملوك
■ the Temple of Luxor	■ **ma**ᶜ-bad **lu**"-Sur	معبد الأقصر
■ the Temple of Hatshepsut	■ **ma**ᶜ-bad Hat-ship-**soot**	معبد الملكة حتشبسوت
■ Abu Simbel	■ 'a-boo **sim**-bil	ابو سمبل
mosque	**geh**-miᶜ	جامع
monuments, antiquities	il-'a-**saar**	الآثار
temple	**ma**ᶜ-bad	معبد
tomb	maq-**ba**-ra	مقبرة
Can I enter?	**mum**-kin **ad**-khul?	هل يمكن ان ادخل؟
At what time does it open?	bi-**yif**-taH is-**seh**-ᶜa kam?	متى يفتح؟
When does it close?	bi-**yi**"-fil is-**seh**-ᶜa kam?	متى يغلق؟

Is it open every day?	*bi-**yif**-taH **kul**-li yohm?*	هل يفتح كل يوم؟
What is the admission price?	*'eyh siᶜr id-du-**khool**?*	كم رسم الدخول؟
How much for children?	*bi kam lil-'aT-**faal**?*	كم رسم الدخول للاطفال؟
Do you know a good restaurant near here?	*tiᶜ-raf **maT**-ᶜam **kway**-yis "u-**ray**-yib min **hi**-na?*	هل تعرف مطعما جيدا قريبا من هنا؟
Is photography allowed?	*it-taS-**weer** mas-**mooH**?*	هل التصوير مسموح ؟
Do I need a permit?	*leh-zim taS-**reeH**?*	هل احتاج لتصريح؟
I have a permit from the Ministry.	*ma-ᶜ**eh**-ya taS-**reeH** min il-wi-**zaa**-ra*	معي تصريح من الوزارة
Let's rest and have a drink.	*nis-ta-**ray**-yaH wi **nish**-rab Ha-ga.*	فلنستريح ونشرب شيئا
Can you pick us up here in <u>one hour</u> exactly?	*<ins>**mum**</ins>-kin tir-gaᶜ-**li**-na baᶜd <u>**seh**-ᶜa</u> biZ-ZabT?*	هل تستطيع أن ترجع لنا هنا بعد ساعة بالضبط ؟
▇ two hours	▇ *saᶜ-**teyn***	بعد ساعتين

MOSQUES

Some of the most beautiful and historic buildings to be found in the Middle East are mosques; you will certainly want to visit a number on your trip.

Attitudes toward non-Muslim visitors vary a good deal. Many famous mosques, such as Ibn Tulun and AlAzhar in Cairo, are recognized as national monuments as well as places of worship, and it is easy to visit them as long as you are suitably dressed. Often, however, visitors are not admitted to some parts of the mosque while prayers are in progress. Check whether photography is permitted (you may have to leave your camera at the door).

The mosque is the social as well as the religious center of the community; in the early days of Islam especially all important public announcements were made from the pulpit (**min**-*bar*). Schools (*mad*-**ra**-*sas*) have always been associated with mosques, primarily to teach the Koran but also reading, writing, and arithmetic. A feature of the **geh**-*mi*ᶜ, or congregational mosque, is the large inner courtyard, where prayer or teaching may take place; this is usually absent from the smaller **mas**-*gids*, less monumental but often gems of Islamic architecture.

At the entrance to most mosques is a place to leave your shoes. Ask there whether it is all right to go in. Apart from removing your shoes, be sure you are properly dressed: shorts and halter tops are not acceptable. A skirt should cover the knee, and arms should be covered to the elbow. It is appreciated if women wear a headscarf.

Don't disturb anyone who is praying, and avoid walking between them and the **mih**-*rab* (niche) indicating the direction of Mecca. On leaving, you may want to put a contribution in the offerings box, which will go toward the upkeep of the mosque.

PLANNING A TRIP

TRAVEL BY AIR

When is there a flight to Aswan?	*Tay-**yaa**-rit 'aS-**waan** 'im-ta?*	متى تكون الرحلة إلى اسوان؟
▪ to Luxor	▪ *lu"-Sur*	إلى الاقصر
▪ to Sinai	▪ *see-na*	إلى سيناء
I'd like a single (one-way) ticket.	*ᶜa-wiz [ᶜaw-za] taz-**ka**-ra **reh**-yiH bass.*	أريد تذكرة ذهاب
▪ a return ticket	▪ *taz-**ka**-ra **reh**-yiH gayy*	تذكرة ذهاب وعودة
I want to cancel my reservation.	*ᶜa-wiz [ᶜaw-za] al-ghee il-**Hagz***	أريد إلغاء الحجز
▪ confirm	▪ *a-'**ak**-kid*	تأكيد الحجز
When should I be at the airport?	*leh-zim a-**koon** fil-ma-**Taar** 'im-ta?*	متى يجب أن أكون بالمطار؟
I'd like a seat — .	*ᶜa-wiz [ᶜaw-za] **kur**-see — .*	أريد مقعدا —
▪ by the window	▪ *gamb ish-shib-**behk***	بجانب الشباك
▪ on the aisle	▪ *ᶜal-ma-**marr***	على الممر
▪ in the smoking (nonsmoking) section	▪ *fi man-**Ti**-"it il-mu-dakh-khi-**neen** (**gheyr** il-mu-dakh-khi-**neen**)*	في الجزء المخصص للمدخنين (لغير المدخنين)

Tourist class	*da-ra-ga si-yeh-**Hee**-ya*	درجة سياحية
First class	*da-ra-ga 'oo-la*	درجة اولى
Business class	*da-ra-git il-'a^c-mehl*	درجة الأعمال
What is the fare?	*bi **kam** it-taz-**ka**-ra?*	بكم التذكرة؟
Can I pay by credit card?	*mum-kin ad-fa^c bi **kri**-dit kard?*	هل استطيع الدفع ببطاقة إعتماد؟
Is there an <u>earlier</u> flight?	*fee ma-^cehd **bad**-ree shway-ya?*	هل هناك رحلة قبل هذا الموعد؟
▦ later	▦ *mit-'**akh**-khar*	بعد هذا الموعد
Is there a daily flight?	*fee Tay-**yaa**-ra **kul**-li yohm?*	هل هناك رحلة يومية؟
When does it arrive?	*bi-**tiw**-Sal '**im**-ta?*	متى تصل؟
Where do I check my bags?	*a-**sag**-gil ish-**shu**-naT feyn?*	اين أسجل حقائبي؟
I have only hand luggage.	*ma-^c**eh**-ya **shu**-naT yad bass.*	ليس معي سوى حقائب يد
What gate do we leave from?	*bi-**nu**-khrug min '**an**-hee behb?*	من أي بوابة سنرحل؟

TRAVEL BY TRAIN AND BUS

Where is the ticket office?	*shib-**behk** it-ta-**zeh**-kir feyn?*	اين مكتب بيع التذاكر؟
May I see a schedule?	*mum-kin a-**shoof** gad-wal il-ma-wa-^ceed?*	هل استطيع أن ارى جدول المواعيد؟

When does the bus to Alexandria leave?	*il-'u-tu-bees lis-kin-di-ree-ya bi-yiT-la^c 'im-ta?*	متى يرحل الاوتوبيس إلى الاسكندرية؟

▪ the train	▪ *il-"aTr*	القطار

Is there a student rate?	*fee takh-feeD liT-Ta-la-ba?*	هل يوجد تخفيض للطلبة؟

I'd like a seat at the front.

I have a student card.	*ma-^ceh-ya kar-ney Taa-lib.*	معي بطاقة طالب

Does it take the desert road?	*bi-yeh-khud iT-Ta-ree" iS-SaH-reh-wee?*	هل ياخذ الطريق الصحراوي؟

Does it stop en route?	*bi-yu-"af fis-sik-ka?*	هل يقف على الطريق؟

I'd like a seat at the front.	*^ca-wiz [^caw-za] kur-see "ud-dehm.*	أريد مقعدا في المقدمة

Are the seats numbered?	*ik-ka-reh-see ^ca-ley-ha ni-mar?*	هل المقاعد مرقمة؟

A first class ticket, please.	*taz-ka-ra da-ra-ga-'oo-la, min faD-lak.*	أريد تذكرة درجة اولى من فضلك

▪ second class	▪ *da-ra-ga tan-ya*	درجة ثانية

Two tickets please.	*taz-kar-teyn, min faD-lak.*	تذكرتين من فضلك

Which platform?	*ra-Seef nim-ra kam?*	ما هو رقم الرصيف؟

I'd like a berth (couchette) to Luxor.	*^ca-wiz [^caw-za] ma-kehn fi ^ca-ra-bee-yit in-nohm li lu"-Sur.*	أريد مكانا بعربة النوم إلى الاقصر

■ two berths (couchettes)	■ *ma-ka-neyn*	مكانين
Is it air-conditioned?	*fee tak-yeef?*	هل هو مكيف الهواء؟
Where is the checked luggage office?	*feyn mak-tab il-'a-ma-neht?*	أين مكتب الامانات؟
Is this <u>the train</u> for Asyut?	*da"aTr 'as-yooT?*	هل هذا قطار اسيوط؟
■ the bus	■ *'u-tu-bees*	أوتوبيس
Is there a dining car on the train?	*fee ᶜa-ra-bee-yit 'akl fil-"aTr?*	هل هناك عربة طعام في القطار؟
■ a buffet car	■ *bu-feyh*	بفيه
What do you have <u>to eat?</u>	*ᶜan-dak 'ak-li 'eyh?*	ما هى انواع الأكل عندكم؟
■ to drink	■ *mash-roo-beht*	المشروبات
Is this seat taken?	*fee Hadd hi-na?*	هل هذا المقعد محجوز؟
Can I change to first class?	*mum-kin a-ghay-yar-ha li da-ra-ga 'oo-la?*	هل استطيع أن اغير للدرجة الاولى؟
Where are we now?	*iH-na feyn dil-wa"-tee?*	أين نحن الآن؟
What's the next stop?	*'eyh il-ma-HaT-Ta g-gay-ya?*	ما هي المحطة القادمة؟

TRAVEL BY BOAT

I'd like to
take a boat —.

^c*a-wiz [^caw-za]*
*'eh-khud **mar**-kib —.*

أريد أن آخذ سفينة

- from Cairo
  to Luxor

- *min maSr li **lu**"-Sur*

من القاهرة للاقصر

- from Luxor
  to Aswan

- *min **lu**"-Sur*
  *li-'aS-**waan***

من الاقصر لأسوان

I want to return
by air.

^c*a-wiz [^caw-za]*
*ar-ga^c biT-Tay-**yaa**-ra.*

أريد العودة بالطائرة

How long does
the cruise take?

*ir-**riH**-la bi-**teh**-khud kam yohm?*

ما مدة الرحلة؟

I'd like a cabin
<u>for one.</u>

^c*a-wiz [^caw-za] ka-**bee**-na*
*li **waH**-dee.*

أريد
حجرة/كابينة لشخص واحد

- for two people

- *lit-**neyn***

لشخصين

English	Transliteration	Arabic
Does it have a private bathroom?	*fee*-ha Ham-**mehm** khaSS?	هل لها حمام خاص؟
Where does it stop?	bi-**tu**-"af feyn?	أين تتوقف؟
Is there a <u>ferry</u>?	fee <u>mi-ʿad-**dee**-ya</u>?	هل هناك عبارة/معدية ؟
■ hydrofoil	■ hay-dro-**feel**	هيدروفيل
What time do we have to be back on board?	**leh**-zim nir-gaʿ lil-**mar**-kib is-**seh**-ʿa kam?	متى يجب أن نعود إلى السفينة؟
I'd like to take a sailboat ride —.	ʿ**a**-wiz [ʿaw-za]ʿ**a**-la] ' **eh**-khud fa-**loo**-ka — .	أريد أن اذهب في نزهة على مركب شراعي
■ around the island	■ Ha-wa-**leyn** ig-gi-**zee**-ra	حول الجزيرة
■ across the river	■ lin-**naH**-ya t-**tan**-ya	عبر النهر
■ for a couple of hours	■ li **mud**-dit saʿ-**teyn**	لمدة ساعتين
When will we get back?	ha-**nir**-gaʿ ' **im**-ta?	متى سنعود؟
Is the wind right?	ir-**reeH** mu-**nas**-ba?	هل الرياح مناسبة؟

OTHER MODES OF TRANSPORT

English	Transliteration	Arabic
Where does the river bus leave from?	feyn ma-**HaT**-Tit il-'u-tu-**bees** in-**nah**-ree?	أين محطة الاوتوبيس النهري؟

Can I take a streetcar/tram?	*mum-kin 'eh-khud tur-maay?*	هل أستطيع أن آخذ الترام ؟
Can I take a microbus?	*mum-kin 'eh-khud mee-kro-bus?*	هل أستطيع أن آخذ ميكروبس ؟
Can I hitchhike from here?	*mum-kin ar-kab oh-toh-stop min hi-na?*	هل أستطيع ركوب سيارة مارة من على الطريق ؟
Could you give me a lift to —?	*mum-kin ti-waS-Sal-nee li —?*	هل تستطيع توصيلي إلى —؟
Where can I get a shared taxi to —?	*mi-neyn 'eh-khud tak-see mush-ta-rak li — ?*	أين آخذ تاكسي مشترك (تاكسي بالنفر) إلى — ؟
I'd like to hire —.	*ᶜa-wiz [ᶜaw-za] a-'ag-gar —.*	أريد إستئجار —
▦ a motorbike/ scooter	▦ *mo-to-sikl*	دراجة بخارية
▦ a bicycle	▦ *ᶜa-ga-la*	دراجة
▦ a horsedrawn carriage	▦ *Han-Toor*	حنطور
▦ a donkey	▦ *Hu-maar*	حمار
▦ a camel	▦ *ga-mal*	جمل

ENTERTAINMENT AND DIVERSIONS

BEACH AND POOL

English	Transliteration	Arabic
I love swimming.	*ba-**Hibb** il-ᶜohm.*	أحب السباحة
It's very hot.	*id-**dun**-ya Harr **gid**-dan.*	الجو حار جداً
Is there a swimming pool?	*fee Ham-**mehm** si-**beh**-Ha?*	هل يوجد حمام سباحة ؟
Is there a sandy beach?	*fee plehj raml?*	هل يوجد شاطىء رملي؟
The water's beautiful.	*il-**may**-ya **Hil**-wa **gid**-dan.*	المياه جميلة
Is it safe to swim?	*il-ᶜohm hi-na 'a-**mehn**?*	هل السباحة مأمونة هنا؟
Is it deep?	*il-**baHr** hi-na ᶜa-**mee"**?*	هل المياه عميقة هنا ؟
Are there sharks?	*fee "u-**roosh**?*	هل توجد اسماك القرش؟
I'd like to go scuba diving.	*ᶜa-wiz [ᶜaw-za] **agh**-Tas.*	أريد الغطس
Do they give diving lessons?	*fee du-**roos** ghaTs?*	هل هناك دروس غطس؟
I want to buy a mask.	*ᶜa-wiz [ᶜaw-za] ash-ti-ree naD-**Daa**-rit baHr.*	أريد شراء قناع

a snorkel	*payp*	انبوبة للتنفس تحت الماء
flippers	*za-ᶜeh-nif*	زعانف
suntan lotion	*kreym li Hi-meh-yit il-bash-ra*	كريم لحماية البشرة
sunglasses	*naD-Daa-rit shams*	نظارات شمس
a sunhat	*bur-ney-Tit shams*	قبعة شمس
a swimsuit	*ma-yoh*	لباس بحر/ مايوه
a beach towel	*foo-Tit baHr*	منشفة شاطيء
an inflatable mattress	*mar-ta-bit baHr*	مرتبة بحر

I want to go <u>waterskiing.</u>	*ᶜa-wiz [ᶜaw-za] at-zaH-la^nᶜal-may-ya.*

أريد التزحلق على الماء

windsurfing	*aᶜ-mil wind-surf*	ركوب الأمواج

How much is it an hour?	*bi kam fis-seh-ᶜa?* كم في الساعة؟

I'd like to hire <u>an umbrella.</u>	*ᶜa-wiz [ᶜaw-za] a-'ag-gar sham-see-ya.* أريد إستئجار شمسية

a deck chair	*kur-see baHr*	كرسي شاطيء
a surfboard	*lohH ru-koob il-'am-wehg*	لوح ركوب الأمواج
skin diving equipment	*'a-da-weht ghaTs*	أدوات الغوص

Is there a diving club?	fee **neh**-dee ghaTs?	هل يوجد نادي غوص ؟
shells	**Sa**-daf	أصداف
coral	mur-**gehn**	مرجان
coral reefs	**shu**-ʿab mur-ga-**nee**-ya	شعب مرجانية
crabs	a-boo ga-**lam**-boo, ka-**boor**-ya	أبو جلمبو، سرطان البحر
sponges	sa-**fing**	إسفنج
Is swimming forbidden?	is-si-**beh**-Ha mam-**noo**-ʿa?	هل السباحة ممنوعة؟
Will you keep an eye on my things?	**mum**-kin ti-**khal**-li **beh**-lak min il-Ha-**geht dee**?	هل ترعى أشيائي؟
Is there a lifeguard?	fee ghaT-**Taas**?	هل هناك عامل إنقاذ / غطاس؟

SAILING AND FISHING

I'd like to hire a sailboat.	ʿa-wiz [ʿaw-za] a-'ag-gar **mar**-kib shi-**raa**-ʿee.	أريد إستئجار مركب شراعي
▦ a motorboat	▦ lansh	قارب بخاري
▦ a yacht	▦ yakht	يخت
I want to spend the whole day on the water.	ʿa-wiz [ʿaw-za] a-"aD-Dee yohm keh-mil fil-baHr	أريد قضاء يوماً كاملاً في البحر

Let's take a picnic.	*neh-khud il-'akl ma-ʿeh-na.*	
		دعنا نقوم بنزهة
the Mediterranean	*il-baHr il-'ab-yaD*	
		البحر الأبيض المتوسط
the Red Sea	*il-baHr il-'aH-mar*	البحر الأحمر
the Atlantic	*il-'aT-lan-Tee*	المحيط الاطلنطي
the sea is very <u>rough</u>.	*il-baHr <u>heh</u>-yig gid-dan.*	البحر هائج جداً
■ calm	■ *heh-dee*	هادىء
I don't feel very well.	*a-na Heh-sis [Has-sa] in-nee taʿ-behn [taʿ-beh-na]*	أنا متعب
Let's head back to shore.	*nir-gaʿ lil-barr.*	فلنرجع الى الشاطىء
Is there a boat race?	*fee si-beh" ma-reh-kib?*	هل هناك سباق مراكب؟
I'd like to go fishing — .	*ʿa-wiz [ʿaw-za] aS-Taad — .*	أريد الذهاب لصيد الأسماك — .
■ with rod and line	■ *biS-Sin-naa-ra*	بصنارة صيد
■ with nets	■ *bish-sha-ba-ka*	بالشبك
Can I come with you?	*mum-kin a-rooH ma-ʿeh-kum?*	هل أستطيع الذهاب معكم ؟
What bait should I use?	*as-taʿ-mil Taʿm 'eyh?*	ما الطعم الذي سأستعمله؟

Did you have a good catch?	iS-**Tad**-too **kway**-yis?	هل وفقت في الصيد؟
What's the name of this fish?	is-**sa**-mak da 'is-moo 'eyh?	ما اسم هذه السمكة؟

HUNTING

What do you hunt in this area?	bi-tiS-**Taa**-doo 'eyh fil-man-**Ti**-"a dee?	ماذا تصطادون في هذه المنطقة؟
I'd like to go hunting in the desert.	ᶜa-wiz [ᶜaw-za] aS-**Taad** fiS-**SaH**-ra.	أريد ان أصطاد في الصحراء
Can I rent <u>a shotgun</u>.	**mum**-kin a-'**ag**-gar bun-du-"**ee**-yit rashsh?	هل استطيع إستئجار بندقية رش؟
▧ a rifle	▧ bun-du-"**ee**-yit Seed	بندقية صيد
Do I need a permit?	**leh**-zim taS-**reeH**?	هل احتاج لتصريح؟
Are there <u>rabbits</u>?	fee 'a-**reh**-nib?	هل هناك أرانب ؟
▧ partridges	▧ **Ha**-gal	حجل
▧ pigeons	▧ Ha-**mehm**	حمام
▧ deer	▧ gha-**zehl**	غزال
▧ foxes	▧ ta-ᶜ**eh**-lib	ثعالب
Do you go hunting with hawks?	bi-tiS-**Taa**-doo biS-Su-"**oor**?	هل تصطاد بالصقور؟

Can you give me some cartridges?	*mum*-kin tid-***dee***-nee kha-ra-***Teesh***?	هل يمكنك أن تعطيني بعض الخراطيش؟

RIDING AND RACING

I'd like to hire a horse.	ᶜ***a***-wiz [ᶜ***aw***-za] a-'***ag***-gar <u>Hu-**Saan**</u>.	أريد إستئجار حصاناً
▓ a camel	▓ ***ga***-mal	جمل
Let's go riding in the desert.	***yal***-la ***nir***-kab kheyl fiS-**SaH**-ra.	فلنركب الخيل في الصحراء
I need some riding lessons.	ᶜ***a***-wiz [ᶜ***aw***-za] du-***roos*** ru-***koob*** il-***kheyl***.	احتاج لبعض الدروس في الفروسية
How much is <u>a lesson</u>?	id-***dars*** bi kam?	بكم الدرس؟
▓ a series of lessons	▓ mag-***moo***-ᶜit du-***roos***	مجموعة دروس
This horse is <u>lazy</u>.	il-Hu-**Saan** da kas-***lehn***.	هذا الحصان كسول
▓ bad-tempered	▓ ***shi***-ris	شرس
I want a <u>quiet</u> horse.	ᶜ***a***-wiz [ᶜ***aw***-za] Hu-**Saan** ***heh***-dee.	أريد حصانا هادئا
▓ lively	▓ na-***sheeT***	نشيط
Is there a racecourse near Cairo?	fee ***mal***-ᶜab si-**beh**" gamb il-qaa-**hi**-ra?	هل هناك ميدان سباق قريب من القاهرة؟

When are the races?	*fee si-beh" 'im-ta?*	متى تجرى السباقات؟
Are there camel races?	*fee si-beh" lig-gi-mehl?*	هل هناك سباق للجمال؟
Is betting allowed?	*ir-ri-hehn mas-mooH?*	هل الرهان مسموح؟

TENNIS, SQUASH, AND GOLF

Is there <u>a tennis court</u> here?	*fee **mal**-cab **ti**-nis **hi**-na?*	هل يوجد ملعب تنس هنا؟
■ a squash court	■ *mal-cab **skwash***	ملعب إسكواش
Is it a private club?	*da **neh**-dee khaaS?*	هل هذا نادي خاص؟
Do I have to be a member?	***leh**-zim a-koon cuDw?*	هل يجب أن أكون عضواً؟
Can I rent a racquet and balls?	***mum**-kin a-'ag-gar **maD**-rab wi **ko**-war?*	هل يمكن أن أستأجر مضرب وكور؟
Would you like a game?	*ca-wiz [caw-za] til-cab [til-ca-bee]?*	هل تريد أن تلعب معي؟
Is there a golf course nearby?	*fee **mal**-cab golf "u-ray-yib?*	هل يوجد ملعب جولف قريب؟
Can I become a temporary member?	***mum**-kin ab-"a cuDw mu-wa"-"at?*	هل يمكن أن أصبح عضو موقت؟
Can I rent golf clubs?	***mum**-kin a-'ag-gar ma-**Daa**-rib golf*	هل يمكن أن استأجر مضارب جولف؟

CAMPING

Is there a camp site near here?	*fee mu-**khay**-yam si-**yeh**-Hee "u-**ray**-yib?*	هل يوجد مخيم سياحي قريباً ؟
Can we spend the night here?	***mum**-kin ni-**beht** hi-na?*	هل يمكن أن نبيت هنا ؟
Is there <u>drinking water</u>?	*fee **may**-yit shurb?*	هل توجد مياه للشرب ؟
▪ a grocery store	▪ *ba"-"**ehl***	محل بقالة
Are there <u>showers</u>?	*fee du-**sheht**?*	هل توجد دشات ؟
▪ toilets	▪ *twa-**litt***	تواليت
Can we do some washing here?	***mum**-kin **nigh**-sil hi-na?*	هل يمكن أن نغسل هنا ؟

SOCCER

I'd like to see a soccer match.	*ᶜa-**wiz** [ᶜ**aw**-za] a-**shoof** matsh **koh**-ra.*	أريد أن أرى مباراة كرة القدم
Where is the match?	*il-**matsh** feyn?*	أين ستجري المباراة ؟
When does it begin?	*bi-yib-**ti**-dee 'im-ta?*	متى تبدأ ؟
Can you get tickets?	***mum**-kin ti-**gib**-lee ta-**zeh**-kir?*	هل تستطيع أن تشتري تذاكر لي ؟
Is it an international match?	*da matsh **daw**-lee?*	هل هي مباراة دولية ؟
Who is playing?	***meen** il-lee bi-**yil**-ᶜab?*	من يلعب ؟

When is the Cup Final?	*ni-**heh**-'ee il-**kehs** '**im**-ta?*	متى يكون نهائي الكأس ؟
Who won (the Cup)?	***meen keh**-sib (il-**kehs**)?*	من كسب (الكأس) ؟
Who do you support?	*bit-**shag**-ga^c [bit-shag-ga-^cee] meen?*	أي فريق تشجع ؟
What is the score?	*in-na-**tee**-ga kam?*	ما هي النتيجة؟
It was a draw.	*kehn ta-^c**eh**-dul.*	كانت تعادل
Foul!	*fawl!*	خطأ !
Goal!	*gohn!*	هدف!
Will it be shown on television?	*hay-**gee**-boo fit-til-li-viz-**yohn**?*	هل ستذاع في التليفزيون؟
Are they a famous team?	*dee **fir**-"a mash-**hoo**-ra?*	هل هذا الفريق مشهور؟

INDOOR ENTERTAINMENT

Do you play <u>chess</u>?	***til**-^cab [til-^c**a**-bee] sha-Ta-**rang**?*	هل تلعب الشطرنج؟
■ backgammon	■ ***Taw**-la*	الطاولة
■ roulette	■ *ru-**litt***	الروليت
■ poker	■ ***poh**-kar*	البوكر

| blackjack | **blak**-jak | البلاك جاك |
| pool | bil-**yar**-du | البلياردو |

Is gambling allowed? — il-"u-**maar** mas-**mooH**?

هل القمار مسموح؟

Do you have <u>videos</u>? — ⁶an-dak vi-dyo-**heht**?

هل عندك أفلام فيديو؟

| video games | 'al-⁶ehb vid-yo | ألعاب فيديو |
| a home computer | kom-**byoo**-tar man-zi-lee | كمبيوتر منزلي |

How many TV channels are there? — fee kam qa-**naat** ti-li-viz-**yohn**?

كم قناة تليفزيونية عندكم؟

Is this an <u>Egyptian</u> serial? — da mu-**sal**-sal **maS**-ree?

هل هذا مسلسل مصري؟

| American/English | am-ri-**keh**-nee/in-gi-**lee**-zee | أمريكي/انجليزي |

What's on at the movies? — fee 'af-**lehm** 'eyh fis-**si**-ni-ma?

ماذا يعرض في السينما؟

Is there an <u>open air</u> cinema? — fee **si**-ni-ma **Sey**-fee?

هل توجد دار عرض صيفية؟

| air-conditioned | mu-**kay**-ya-fa | مكيفة |

Is it an <u>Egyptian</u> film? — da film **maS**-ree?

هل هذا فلم مصري؟

■ American/English	*am-ri-**keh**-nee/in-gi-**lee**-zee*	امريكي / انجليزي
Is it dubbed <u>in English</u>?	*da mu-**da**-blaj <u>bi-lin-gi-**lee**-zee</u>?*	هل هو مترجم إلى الانجليزية؟
■ in Arabic	■ *bil-ʿa-ra-bee*	الى العربية
Is it subtitled in English?	*da mu-**tar**-gam bi-lin-gi-**lee**-zee?*	هل عليه ترجمة انجليزية؟
What time does the show <u>begin</u>?	*il-ʿ**arD** <u>bi-yib-**ti**-dee</u> 'im-ta?*	متى يبدأ العرض؟
■ end	■ *bi-yin-**ti**-hee*	ينتهي
Can I book seats (now)?	***mum**-kin a**H**-giz ka-**reh**-see (dil-**wa**"-tee)?*	هل أستطيع حجز الاماكن (الآن) ؟
We would like to go to <u>the theater</u>.	*ʿaw-**zeen** ni-**rooH** <u>il-**mas**-raH</u>.*	نريد الذهاب للمسرح
■ the opera	■ *il-'**o**-bi-ra*	للاوبرا
■ the ballet	■ *il-ba-**ley***	للباليه
■ folk dancing	■ *ir-**ra**"S ish-**sha**ʿ-bee*	لرقص شعبي
■ a concert	■ ***Haf**-la mu-si-**qee**-ya*	لحفل موسيقي
Is it Western or Oriental music?	*il-mu-si-**qee**-ya ghar-**bee**-ya **wal**-la shar-"**ee**-ya?*	هل هي موسيقى غربية أم شرقية؟

That singer is very famous isn't he (she)?	*il-mu-**ghan**-nee da [il-mu-ghan-**nee**-ya dee] mash-**hoor** [mash-**hoo**-ra] **gid**-dan, mish **ki**-da?*	هذا المغني (المغنية) مشهور(ة) جداً، اليس كذلك؟
What's his (her) name?	*'**is**-moo ['is-**ma**-ha] 'eyh?*	ما اسمه (اسمها)؟
I'd like to go to a nightclub.	*ᶜ**a**-wiz [ᶜ**aw**-za] a-**rooH** mal-ha **lay**-lee.*	أريد الذهاب الى ملهى ليلى
Which <u>club</u> has good belly dancing?	*an-hee **mal**-ha fee ra″S ba-la-dee **kway**-yis?*	في أي ملهى يوجد رقص شرقي جيد؟
▪ restaurant	▪ *maT-ᶜam*	مطعم

Is there an <u>Oriental</u> cabaret?	*fee ka-ba-rey shar-"ee?*	هل هناك كباريه شرقي؟
▪ Western-style	▪ *ghar-bee*	غربي
Can you get us a table near the dance floor?	*mum-kin ti-leh-"ee-lee Ta-ra-bey-za gamb il-beest?*	هل تستطيع أن تجد لنا طاولة قريبة من حلبة الرقص؟
When does the floor show start?	*il-ᶜarD bi-yib-ti-dee 'im-ta?*	متى يبدأ العرض؟
Is there a discotheque in the hotel?	*fee dis-ko fil-'u-teel?*	هل يوجد ديسكو في الفندق؟
It's very crowded.	*da zaH-ma gid-dan.*	إنه مزدحم جداً
I'd like to go home.	*ᶜa-wiz [ᶜaw-za] a-raw-waH.*	أريد العودة الى المنزل
I'd like to go back to the hotel.	*ᶜa-wiz [ᶜaw-za] a-raw-waH lil-'u-teel.*	أريد العودة الى الفندق

EATING OUT

Part of the fun of your trip will be experimenting with Middle Eastern cuisine — one of the most subtle and varied in the world. The dishes mentioned here are to be found in most Arab countries, though each has its own regional specialties.

In North Africa, couscous (**kus**-ku-see), fine grains of semolina, steamed, forms the basis for many dishes, whereas further east rice and beans are the staple food. Meat is served either charcoal-grilled or braised slowly in the oven. Because most Arab countries border an ocean, seafood is abundant.

Lunchtime is from about one o'clock till three, dinner from eight till eleven. This means you can — in theory! — sleep off your lunch in the hottest part of the day, and make the most of the cool of the evening.

lunch	il-**gha**-da
dinner	il-^c**a**-sha

Big hotels serve Western as well as local dishes, and French and Italian restaurants are to be found in most major cities. Cairo offers an incredible range, from Hungarian to Japanese, whereas in the Gulf you will have the chance to try excellent Indian food. American-style chicken and hamburger restaurants and take-outs are becoming increasingly popular throughout the region.

Good guidebooks, a helpful receptionist, or a tourist information office will direct you to the restaurants where local people go for a really good meal. These will often specialize in grilled meat, fish, or chicken and pigeon. Lower-priced restaurants specialize in a range of meatless dishes, served at tiny tables on tin plates; they are inexpensive and friendly places where you are likely to be engaged in conversation by your neighbors.

Do you know a good restaurant?	*ti^c-raf maT-^cam kway-yis?*	هل تعرف مطعماً جيداً؟
I want to eat <u>local</u> food.	*^ca-wiz [^caw-za] 'eh-kul 'akl ma-Hal-lee.*	أريد أن آكل اكلاً محلياً.
▪ Oriental	▪ *shar-"ee*	شرقي
▪ Western-style	▪ *ghar-bee*	غربي
I am looking for a <u>French</u> restaurant.	*ba-daw-war ^ca-la maT-^cam fa-ran-seh-wee*	أبحث عن مطعم فرنسي
▪ Italian	▪ *ee-Tal-yeh-nee*	إيطالي
▪ Indian	▪ *hin-dee*	هندي
I want to have lunch at —.	*^ca-wiz [^caw-za] at-ghad-da fi —.*	أريد الغداء في — .
I want to dine at —.	*^ca-wiz [^caw-za] at-^cash-sha fi —.*	أريد العشاء في — .
Is it expensive?	*da gheh-lee?*	هل هو غال ؟
How much (roughly) for two people?	*"ad-di 'eyh (ta"-ree-ban) li shakh-Seyn?*	بكم تقريبا لشخصين ؟

AT THE RESTAURANT

My name is —.	*'is-mee —.*	اسمي —
I have (haven't) a reservation.	*^can-dee (ma-^can-deesh) Hagz.*	(ليس) لي حجز
I'd like a table for <u>four</u> please.	*^ca-wiz [^caw-za] Ta-ra-bey-za li 'ar-ba-^ca min faD-lak.*	أريد طاولة لأربعة من فضلك

■ for two	■ *li-'it-neyn*	لشخصين
Waiter!	*mitr!*	جرسون !
Could I have the menu, please.	*id-**dee**-nee il-**min**-yu min **faD**-lak.*	أعطني قائمة الطعام من فضلك
What do you recommend?	*'eyh '**aH**-san 'aT-**baa**" ʿan-**du**-kum?*	ماذا تقترح؟
Is it fresh?	*da **Taa**-za?*	هل هو طازج ؟
Is it spicy?	*da **Heh**-mee?*	هل هو متبل (حار) ؟
I am a <u>vegetarian.</u>	*a-na <u>na-**beh**-tee [na-ba-**tee**-ya]</u>*	أنا نباتي
■ vegan	■ *ma-ba-**kulsh** 'ay-yi man-tu-**geht** Ha-ya-wa-**nee**-ya*	لا أكل أية منتجات حيوانية

SOMETHING TO DRINK

In Saudi Arabia and some of the countries in the Gulf, alcohol is prohibited; in others the sale of alcohol is strictly limited in Ramadan. But in most countries in the Middle East, beer, wine, and spirits are available. In North Africa, Egypt, and Lebanon, wine is produced locally, the best-known labels being Gianaclis in Egypt and Ksara in Lebanon. Local beers tend to be light lagers.

International hotels will have a wide range of alcoholic drinks, and open-air *casinos* or cafés catering to a middle-class clientele will probably serve beer. Many neighborhood restaurants will, however, be "dry."

Do you have — ?	^{c}an-**du**-kum — ?	؟ — هل عندكم
◼ beer	◼ **bee**-ra	بيرة
◼ wine	◼ ni-**beet**	نبيذ
◼ whiskey	◼ **wis**-kee	ويسكي
◼ arak	◼ ^{c}**a**-ra″	عرق
◼ soft drinks	◼ **Ha**-ga sa″-^{c}a	مشروبات غير روحية
◼ fruit juice	◼ ^{c}a-**Seer**	عصير
◼ mineral water	◼ **may**-ya ma^c-da-**nee**-ya	
		مياه معدنية

Do you have any (fresh) <u>fruit juice</u>?	^{c}an-**du**-kum ^{c}a-seer (**Taa**-za)?	هل عندكم عصير طازج ؟
◼ orange juice	◼ ^{c}a-**Seer** bur-tu-″**aan**	عصير برتقال

We'd like some red/white wine.	^{c}aw-**zeen** ni-beet ′aH-mar/′ab-yaD.	نريد نبيذاً أحمر / أبيض

What is the best local wine?	′eyh ′**aH**-san ni-beet ma-**Hal**-lee?	ما هو أفضل نبيذ محلي؟

a bottle (two bottles) of wine	″i-**zeh**-zit(″i-**zehz**-teyn) ni-**beet**.	زجاجة (زجاجتين) نبيذ

◼ of beer	◼ **bee**-ra	بيرة
cold beer	**bee**-ra sa″-^{c}a	بيرة مثلجة
a glass	kub-**bay**-ya	كأس
a glass of wine	kub-**bay**-yit ni-**beet**	كأس نبيذ
with ice	bi **talg**	بثلج
without ice	min **gheyr** talg	بدون ثلج

TRAVEL TIP

Mineral water is inexpensive and easily obtainable throughout the Middle East. It is better not to risk the tap water, though tempting glasses of iced water will be served automatically with almost any order in a café or restaurant. Remember, the ice will be made from tap water, even in many international hotels.

Tea — especially mint tea — is both safe and more thirst-quenching than sweet carbonated drinks.

GENERAL REQUESTS

Please bring some bread.	min **faD**-lak **gib**-lee ᶜeysh/khubz.	أرجوك احضر لي خبزا
▓ Oriental bread	▓ khubz **ba**-la-dee	خبز عربي
▓ a napkin	▓ man-**deel**	منديل
▓ a glass	▓ kub-**bay**-ya	كأس
▓ butter	▓ **zib**-da	زبدة
▓ a plate	▓ **Ta**-ba″	طبق
▓ a spoon	▓ maᶜ-**la**-″a	ملعقة
▓ a knife	▓ sik-**kee**-na	سكينة
▓ a fork	▓ **shoh**-ka	شوكة
▓ toothpicks	▓ sal-la-**keht**	أعواد لتنظيف الاسنان
▓ salt and pepper	▓ malH wi **fil**-fil	ملح وفلفل
We'd like more —.	ᶜaw-**zeen** — ka-**mehn**.	نريد — أكثر

Please bring —.	*min faD-lak*	— أرجوك احضر لي
	gib-lee —.	
What desserts do you have?	*ʿan-du-kum Hal-la-wee-yeht 'eyh?*	ماهي انواع الحلوى عندكم ؟

If you're not satisfied try these phrases:

I didn't order this.	*ma Ta-lab-toosh.*	لم أطلب هذا
This isn't properly cooked.	*da mish mis-ti-wee.*	هذا ليس ناضجاً
This is overdone (dry).	*da neh-shif.*	هذا زائد النضج
This is cold.	*da beh-rid.*	هذا بارد
I want to speak to the headwaiter.	*ʿa-wiz [ʿaw-za] a-kal-lim il-mitr.*	أريد أن أكلم مدير غرفة الطعام
■ the manager	■ *il-mu-deer*	المدير
Do you have any appetizers?	*ʿan-du-kum maz-za?*	هل عندكم مزة؟

UNDERSTANDING THE MENU

Appetizers

The Middle East is famous for the variety of its *mezza*, snacks such as dips, pickles, cheese, and olives served either as appetizers to the main course or with drinks.

The best-known creamy dips, a specialty of Middle East cuisine, are:

dips (in general)	*sa-la-**Taat***	سلطات
tahina (pureed chick-peas and sesame seed paste)	*Ta-**Hee**-na*	طحينة
hummus (pureed chick-peas)	***Hum**-muS*	حمص
baba rannouj (roast eggplant [aubergine] with tahina)	*ba-ba ghan-**noog***	بابا غنوج
foul (broad beans, pureed and seasoned)	*fool*	فول
yogurt and cucumber dip with garlic	*la-ban za-**beh**-dee bil-khi-**yaar***	لبن زبادي بالخيار

The best way of eating these is with Oriental bread (*khubz **ba-la**-dee*).

Other appetizers include:

stuffed vine leaves	***wa**-ra" ⁨ᶜ⁩**i**-nab*	ورق عنب
fish roe	*ba-**Taa**-rikh*	بطارخ
olives	*zey-**toon***	زيتون
herring	***rin**-ga*	رنجة

cracked wheat with with parsley, onion, and tomato	*tab-**boo**-la*	تبولة
pickles	***Tur**-shee, ma-**khal**-lil*	طرشي/مخلل

Soups

soup	***shur**-ba*	شربة
vegetable soup	***shur**-bit khu-**Daar***	شربة خضار
onion soup	***shur**-bit ba-Sal*	شربة بصل
lentil soup	***shur**-bit ᶜads*	شربة عدس
fish soup	***shur**-bit sa-mak*	شربة سمك
consommé with noodles	***shur**-bit shiᶜ-**ree**-ya*	شربة شعرية
mulukhiyya (spinach-like vegetable soup served with rice and meat)	*mu-lu-**khee**-ya*	ملوخية

Salads

salad	*sa-la-Ta*	سلطة
mixed salad	*sa-la-Ta **khaD**-ra*	سلطة خضراء
tomato salad	*sa-la-Tit Ta-**maa**-Tim*	سلطة طماطم
potato salad	*sa-la-Tit ba-**Taa**-Tis*	سلطة بطاطس
beet salad	*sa-la-Tit **ban**-gar*	سلطة بنجر

Meat Dishes

meat	**laH**-ma	لحم
kebab (grilled marinated meat)	ka-**behb**	كباب
kibba (baked minced meat with cracked wheat and spices)	**kib**-ba	كبة
kufta (minced grilled meat)	**kuf**-ta	كفتة
meat and vegetable casserole	**Taa**-gin	طاجن
(roast) lamb	**Daa**-nee (**rus**-too)	ضاني (رستو)
veal	bi-**til**-loo	بتلو
veal cutlets	is-ka-**loop** bi-**til**-loo	اسكالوب بتلو
lamb cutlets	kus-ta-**ley**-ta	شرائح ضاني/كستلية
beefsteak	fi-**ley**, steyk	بفتيك
■ well done	■ mis-**ti**-wee	■ مستوي/تام النضج
■ medium	■ nuS-Si **si**-wa	■ نصف ناضج
■ rare (unusual in the Middle East)	■ ya **doh**-bak maH-**TooT** ^can-**naar**	قليل النضج
liver	**kib**-da	كبدة
kidneys	ka-**leh**-wee	كلاوي
brains	mukh	مخ

spiced grilled meat, served in fine slices	*sha-**wir**-ma*	شاورمة
fatta (mutton stewed in broth with bread and rice)	***fat**-ta*	فتة

Poultry and Game

(grilled) chicken	*fi-**rehkh**/da-**jehj** (**mash**-wee)*	دجاج (مشوي)
(stuffed) pigeon	*Ha-**mehm** (**maH**-shee)*	حمام (محشي)
duck	*baTT*	بط
rabbit	*'**ar**-nab*	أرنب
quail	*sim-**mehn***	سمان
turkey	*deek **roo**-mee*	ديك رومي

Because pork is forbidden to Muslims it is found only (occasionally) in international hotels and tourist restaurants:

ham, pork	*khan-**zeer***	خنزير

You may want to know how the dish is prepared:

roast	***rus**-too*	رستو
fried	***ma**"-lee*	مقلي
grilled	***mash**-wee*	مشوي
boiled	*mas-**loo**"*	مسلوق
stuffed	***maH**-shee*	محشي
baked	*fil-**furn***	في الفرن
minced (ground)	*maf-**room***	مفروم

Fish Dishes

What kind of fish do you have?	*ᶜan-**du**-kum 'as-**mehk** 'eyh?*	ما هي أنواع السمك عندكم؟
fish	*sa-mak*	سمك
prawns	*gam-**ba**-ree*	جمبري
squid	*ka-la-**mar**-ya*	أم الحبر، حبار
octopus	*okh-Tu-**booT***	أخطبوط
swordfish	*a-boo-**seyf***	أبو سيف
crab	*a-boo ga-**lam**-boo, ka-**boor**-ya*	كابوريا، أبو جلمبو
lobster	*is-ta-**koh**-za*	سرطان بحري ، استاكوزا
tuna	***too**-na*	تونة
sardines	*sar-**deen***	سردين
sole	***sa**-mak **moo**-sa*	سمك موسى

Vegetables

What vegetables do you have?	*ᶜan-**du**-kum khu-**Daar** 'eyh?*	ما هي أنواع الخضروات عندكم؟
artichokes	*khar-**shoof***	خرشوف
beans •	*fa-**Sul**-ya*	فاصوليا
carrots	***ga**-zar*	جزر
cauliflower	*"ar-na-**beeT***	قرنبيط
cucumber	*khi-**yaar***	خيار

lettuce	*khass*	خس
mixed vegetables	*khu-Daar mi-shak-kil*	خضروات مشكلة
okra ("ladies' fingers")	*bam-ya*	بامية
onions	*ba-Sal*	بصل
(fried) potatoes	*ba-Taa-Tis (ma"-lee-ya)*	بطاطس (مقلية)
peas	*bi-sil-la*	بسلة
radishes	*figl*	فجل
rice	*ruzz*	أرز
spinach	*sa-beh-nikh*	سبانخ
sweet potatoes	*ba-Taa-Ta*	بطاطا
tomatoes	*Ta-maa-Tim*	طماطم

The following vegetables are often served stuffed (**maH**-*shee*) with rice and herbs and sometimes minced meat:

aubergines, eggplants	*bi-din-gehn*	باذنجان
cabbage	*ku-rumb*	كرنب
zucchini, squash	*koh-sa*	كوسة
green peppers	*fil-fil 'akh-Dar*	فلفل اخضر

Dishes may be served or cooked with:

garlic	*bit-toom*	بالثوم

mint	*bi ni^c-neh^c*	بالنعناع
lemon	*bi la-moon*	بالليمون
olive oil	*bi zeyt zey-toon*	بزيت الزيتون

Side Dishes

macaroni (and pasta generally)	*ma-ka-roh-na*	مكرونة
(fried) eggs	*beyD (ma"-lee)*	بيض (مقلي)
lentils	*^cads*	عدس
(cheese) omelette	*om-leet (big-gib-na)*	اومليت (بالجبنة)
eggs baked with onions, tomatoes, and green peppers	*^cig-ga*	عجة
spiced sausages	*su-gu""*	سجق
pastrami	*bas-Tir-ma*	بسطرمة
hard, mild cheese	*gib-na roo-mee*	جبنة رومي
soft white salty cheese	*gib-na bey-Da*	جبنة بيضاء
yogurt	*la-ban za-beh-dee*	لبن زبادي

Some North African Dishes

couscous	*kus-ku-see*	كسكسي
peppery fish soup	*mar-qa*	مرقة

paper-thin pancakes filled with egg and deep fried	*breek*	بريك
spiced sausages	*mer-gez*	مرجاز

Desserts

Though Western-style restaurants will offer a range of desserts, it is not customary to end a meal with an elaborate sweet course, and many local restaurants may list only ice cream, crème caramel, or fruit.

ice cream	*ays-kreem*	أيس كريم
■ chocolate	■ *sho-ko-laa-Ta*	شكولاتة
■ vanilla	■ *va-nil-ya*	فانيلا
mixed ice cream	*ays-kreem mi-shak-kil*	أيس كريم مشكل
crème caramel	*kreym ka-ra-mel*	كريم كرامل
rice pudding	*ruzz bi la-ban*	أرز بلبن
vanilla blancmange	*ma-hal-la-bee-ya*	مهلبية
Umm Ali (pastry and milk pudding with raisins)	*'umm ^ceh-lee*	أم علي
qamar eldin (apricot jelly, sometimes served as a drink)	*"a-mar id-deen, mish-mi-shee-ya*	قمر الدين، مشمشية
fatir (large baked pancakes often served with jam or honey)	*fi-Teer Hilw*	فطير

Fruit

English	Transliteration	Arabic
fruit	*fak*-ha	فاكهة
apples	tuf-*fehH*	تفاح
apricots	*mish*-mish	مشمش
bananas	mohz	موز
dates	*ba*-laH	بلح
figs	teen	تين
grapefruit	*greyp* froot	جريبفروت
grapes	⁽i-nab	عنب
guava	ga-*weh*-fa	جوافة
lemon	la-*moon*	ليمون
mangoes	*man*-ga	مانجو
melon	sham-*mehm*	شمام
oranges	bur-tu-"*aan*	برتقال
peaches	khohkh	خوخ
pears	kom-*mit*-ra	كمثرى
plums	bar-"*oo*"	برقوق
pomegranates	rom-*maan*	رومان
strawberries	fa-*raw*-la	فراولة
tangerines	yu-sa-*fan*-dee	يوسف افندي
watermelon	baT-*Teekh*	بطيخ

Oriental Pastries

Every visitor must experience the delights of the Oriental pastry shop (*il-Ha-la-weh-nee*). Pastries are rich and very sweet, made with clarified butter and steeped in syrup, often stuffed with different kinds of nuts. A dollop of chilled cream ("*ish-Ta*) is an optional extra. You can eat your pastry on the spot, usually at a marble-topped bar, or buy a selection to take with you (they are generally sold by weight). Give a small tip to the person who deftly ties up your package with ribbon tape.

basbousa (semolina baked in the oven, often with nuts, and steeped in syrup)	*bas-boo-sa*	بسبوسة
baclava (layers of paper-thin pastry and crushed nuts, with syrup)	*ba"-leh-wa*	بقلاوة
kunafa (fine-spun pastry stuffed with nuts)	*ku-neh-fa*	كنافة
qatayif (tiny pancakes, layered with nuts, syrup, and cream)	"*a-Taa-yif*	قطايف
with cream	*bil-"ish-Ta*	بالقشطة
Turkish delight	**mal**-ban/lu-**koom**	ملبن، حلقوم

AFTER THE MEAL

The bill (check), please.	*il-Hi-**sehb**, min **faD**-lak.*	الحساب، من فضلك
Can I pay by credit card?	***mum**-kin ad-fa^c bi **kri**-dit kard?*	هل أستطيع أن ادفع ببطاقة اعتماد؟
Is service included?	*da bil-**khid**-ma?*	هل هذا يشمل الخدمة؟
That's for you.	*da ^ca-la-**sheh**-nak.*	تفضل، هذا لك
The food was excellent.	*il-'**akl** kehn mum-**tehz**.*	كان الاكل ممتازاً
We will come again.	*ha-**nee**-gee **teh**-nee.*	سناتي مرة ثانية

AT THE CAFÉ

Street cafés usually serve only tea, Turkish coffee, and soft drinks. They are excellent places to sit and rest and watch the world go by. Traditionally, men go there to chat and smoke a water pipe (***shee**-sha*) or play backgammon. Tourists are welcome, though a woman on her own might feel uncomfortable.

If you order a coffee you will automatically be given a small black Turkish coffee and a glass of water. Tea is usually served black, sometimes already sweetened.

In the big cities elegant tearooms or tea gardens, such as the famous Groppi's in Cairo, also serve light meals and pastries. Service may be leisurely, because most people go there to spend an hour or two.

coffee	"**ah**-wa	قهوة
tea	shayy	شاي
fruit juice	^{c}a-**Seer**	عصير
soda	**Soh**-da	صودا
soft drinks	**Ha**-ga sa"-^{c}a	مشروبات غير روحية

| Do you have French (i.e., filter) coffee? | ^{c}an-**du**-kum "**ah**-wa fa-ran-**seh**-wee? | هل عندكم قهوة فرنسية؟ |
| ■ instant coffee | ■ nes-ka-**fey** | نسكافيه |

I'd like a Turkish coffee without sugar.	^{c}a-**wiz** [^{c}**aw**-za] "ah-wa **seh**-da.	أريد قهوة سادة
■ medium sweet	■ maZ-**booT**	مضبوط
■ very sweet	■ suk-kar zee-**yeh**-da	سكر زيادة

| Do you have mineral water? | fee **may**-ya ma^c-da-**nee**-ya? | هل عندكم مياه معدنية؟ |

tea with lemon	shayy bi la-**moon**.	شاي بالليمون
■ with milk	■ bi **la**-ban	باللبن
■ with mint	■ bi ni^c-**neh**^{c}	بالنعناع
■ without sugar	■ min gheyr **suk**-kar	بدون سكر

| Some sugar, please. | **suk**-kar, min **faD**-lak. | سكر من فضلك |

sahlab (a hot milky drink topped with chopped nuts and shredded coconut)	*saH-lab*	سحلب
hot chocolate	*sho-ko-laa-Ta, ka-kaw*	شكولاتة، كاكاو
Do you have anything to eat?	*ʿan-du-kum 'akl?*	هل عندكم أكل؟
Do you have sandwiches?	*ʿan-du-kum sand-wit-sheht?*	هل عندكم سندويتشات؟

Some cafés and fruit juice bars sell chilled Middle Eastern drinks:

tamarind juice	*ta-mar hin-dee*	تمر هندي
karkaday (hibiscus drink)	*kar-ka-dey*	كركدية

SNACKS IN THE STREET

The Middle East is famous for the variety of its "street food": fried and grilled snacks sold from tiny kiosks and brightly decorated mobile stalls to be found on every street corner in cities such as Cairo. The flat "Oriental" bread (*khubz ba-la-dee*) is stuffed with fried bean cakes, grilled meat, or cheese. Fruit juice bars will squeeze oranges or puree bananas while you wait.

bean purée	*fool*	فول
ta'miyya (fried balls of ground beans or chickpeas)	*Taʿ-mee-ya, fa-leh-fil*	طعمية، فلافل

kushary (macaroni or rice with noodles, lentils, fried onion, and a hot tomato sauce)	*ku-sha-ree*	كشري
shawirma, doner kebab (spiced lamb or veal grilled on a vertical spit)	*sha-wir-ma*	شاورمة
sandwiches	*sand-wit-sheht*	سندويتشات
a <u>cheese</u> sandwich	*sand-witsh gib-na.*	سندويتش جبنة
■ liver	■ *kib-da*	كبدة
■ ta'miyya	■ *Taᶜ-mee-ya*	طعمية
peanuts	*fool su-deh-nee*	فول سوداني
popcorn	*fi-shaar*	فشار

TRAVEL TIP

The visitor should naturally be cautious of what and where he or she eats; anything freshly fried or grilled is likely to be safe, whereas the usual rules about avoiding salads — even garnishes on sandwiches — and fruit that cannot be peeled, should be strictly observed.

GETTING TO KNOW PEOPLE

GREETINGS

It is customary to shake hands when you are formally introduced to someone. When close friends or relations — men or women — haven't met for some time, they usually exchange kisses on both cheeks.

At Any Time of Day

Hello!	*is-sa-**leh**-mu* ^c*a-**ley**-kum!*	السلام عليكم!
(reply)	^c*a-**ley**-kum is-sa-**lehm***	عليكم السلام
Hi!/Welcome!	*ah-lan wa **sah**-lan!*	أهلا وسهلا
	ah-lan!	أهلا
(reply)	*ah-lan **beek** [**bee-kee**]*	أهلا بك
… to two or more	*ah-lan **bee-kum***	أهلا بكم
Welcome!	*mar-**Ha**-ba!*	مرحباً
(reply)	*mar-**Hab beek** [**bee-kee**]*	مرحباً بك
… to two or more	*mar-**Hab bee-kum***	مرحباً بكم
Good-bye!	*ma-^ca s-sa-**leh**-ma!*	مع السلامة
Remember me to —.	*sal-**lim**-lee ^ca-la —.*	سلم لي على —.
Nice to have met you.	*fur-**Sa** sa-^c**ee-da gid**-dan.*	فرصة سعيدة جداً
(reply) I am (even) happier.	*a-na 'as-^cad.*	أنا أسعد

In the Morning

Good morning.	*Sa-baH il-kheyr.*	صباح الخير
(reply)	*Sa-baH in-noor*	صباح النور

In the Afternoon/Evening

Good evening.	*mi-seh' il-kheyr.*	مساء الخير
(reply)	*mi-seh' in-noor*	مساء النور

At Night

Good night.   *tiS-baH [tiS-ba-Hee] ᶜa-la-kheyr.*

تصبح [تصبحي] على خير

. . . to two or more   *tiS-ba-Hoo ᶜa-la kheyr*

تصبحون على خير

How are you?	*iz-zay-yak? [iz-zay-yik?]*	ازيك ؟
or	*keyf Heh-lak? [keyf Heh-lik?]*	
		كيف حالك ؟
. . . to two or more	*iz-zay-yu-kum?*	ازيكم ؟
I'm fine, thanks.	*bi kheyr, il-Ham-du lil-leh.*	
		بخير، الحمد لله
or	*kway-yis [kway-yi-sa],*	كويس [كويسة]،
	il-Ham-du lil-leh.	الحمد لله
or	*il-Ham-du lil-leh*	الحمد لله
	("praise be to God")	
	may be used	
	by itself	

Have a good trip!	*riH-la kway-yi-sa!*	أتمنالك رحلة بهيجة
Welcome back!	*Ham-dil-la ᶜas-sa-leh-ma!*	
		حمد الله على السلامة!

CONSERVATIVE ETIQUETTE

In Saudi Arabia and some of the countries of the Gulf, very conservative traditions are maintained. Women are still secluded and rarely appear at social gatherings, though this is changing gradually. It is impolite to ask after someone's wife, although a general inquiry about the family is acceptable. In more orthodox circles it is not appropriate for a man and a woman who are not related to shake hands. Presenting the soles of one's feet to someone is considered ill-mannered. If you are being entertained in traditional style, seated on carpets and cushions, leave your shoes at the door and sit cross-legged or with your feet tucked under you. Showing a lot of arm or leg, whether you are a man or a woman, is to be avoided. During a meal, interest is focussed on the food, and conversation drops to a minimum level.

Show deference to someone by insisting that they pass through a door in front of you. Always offer a drink or a snack to a visitor, however casual the visit. In other countries there are fewer social constraints, but when in doubt it is always safest to err on the side of conservatism.

NAMES AND POLITE
FORMS OF ADDRESS

When talking to someone directly, the word *ya* is usually put in front of the name or title.

How are you, Ahmad?	*iz-**zay**-yak, ya '**aH**-mad?*
	ازيك، يا أحمد ؟
Good morning, madam.	*Sa-**baH** il-**kheyr**, ya ma-**dehm**.*
	صباح الخير، يا مدام

When talking to an elderly person whose name you don't know, it's polite to address them as

يا حاج [يا حاجة]

ya Hagg

or (to a woman) *ya **Hag**-ga*

which is the title given to anyone who has been on the pilgrimage to Mecca.

In Egypt especially, you will find yourself being addressed as

ya beyh	<div dir="rtl">يا بيه</div>
*ya **fan**-dim*	<div dir="rtl">يا افندم</div>
*ya **beh**-sha*	<div dir="rtl">يا باشا</div>

— all honorific titles of Turkish origin, used mostly to men.

INTRODUCTIONS

May I introduce to you —.	***mum**-kin a-"ad-**dim**-lak [a-"ad-**dim**-lik]* —.	<div dir="rtl">هل يمكن ان اقدم لك ـــ.</div>
■ Mr. —	■ *is-**say**-yid* —	<div dir="rtl">السيد ـــ</div>
■ Mrs. —	■ *ma-**dehm**/is-say-**yi**-da* —	<div dir="rtl">مدام، السيدة ـــ</div>
■ Miss —	■ *il-'eh-**ni**-sa* —	<div dir="rtl">الآنسة ـــ</div>
■ Dr. —	■ *id-duk-**toor** [id-duk-**too**-ra]* —	<div dir="rtl">الدكتور [الدكتورة] ـــ</div>
■ Professor —	■ *il-'us-**tehz** [il-'us-**teh**-za]* —	<div dir="rtl">الاستاذ [الاستاذة] ـــ</div>

My name is — .	*'is*-mee — .	إسمي — .
This is <u>my husband</u>.	da **goh**-zee.	هذا زوجي
▤ my father	▤ *'a-**boo**-ya*	أبي
▤ my brother	▤ *'a-**khoo**-ya*	أخي
▤ my son	▤ *'ib*-nee	ابني
▤ my fiancé	▤ kha-**Tee**-bee	خطيبي
▤ my friend	▤ **SaH**-bee	صديقي
This is <u>my wife</u>.	dee mi-**raa**-tee.	هذه زوجتي
▤ my mother	▤ *'um*-mee, wal-**di**-tee	أمي
▤ my sister	▤ *'ukh*-tee	أختي
▤ my daughter	▤ **bin**-tee	بنتي
▤ my fiancée	▤ kha-**Tib**-tee	خطيبتي
▤ my friend (fem)	▤ SaH-**bi**-tee	صديقتي
These are my children.	dohl 'aw-**leh**-dee.	هؤلاء اولادي
This is my family.	dee ᶜeyl-tee/'us-**ri**-tee.	هذه اسرتي

MAKING FRIENDS

People will want to know all about you — and it's quite polite to ask them questions about their family and their work in return. Family are very important, so why not take a couple of snapshots with you — of your family and home.

Where are you from?	*in*-ta [*in*-tee] mi-**neyn**?	من أين أنت؟
I am from —.	*a*-na min —.	أنا من —
■ America	■ am-**ree**-ka	أمريكا
■ Britain	■ bri-**Taan**-ya	بريطانيا
■ Canada	■ **ka**-na-da	كندا
■ Australia	■ os-**tral**-ya	استراليا
What is your name?	'*is*-mak ['*is*-mik] 'eyh?	ما اسمك؟
Pleased to meet you. (lit., "a happy occasion")	*fur*-Sa sa-**ee**-da.	فرصة سعيدة
The pleasure's mine.	*a*-na '*as*-**ad**	أنا أسعد
What's your job?	bi-tish-**ta**-ghal [bi-tish-**ta**-gha-lee] 'eyh?	ماذا تعمل؟
Are you married?	*in*-ta mit-**gaw**-wiz? [*in*-tee mit-gaw-**wi**-za?]	هل انت متزوج [متزوجة]؟
Do you have any children?	*an*-dak [*an*-dik] '*aw*-lehd?	هل عندك اطفال؟
Are you here on holiday?	*in*-ta [*in*-tee] fee '*a*-**geh**-za?	هل أنت هنا في عطلة؟
Where are you staying?	*in*-ta **neh**-zil [*in*-tee **naz**-la] feyn?	أين تقيم؟
I'm staying at —.	*a*-na **neh**-zil [**naz**-la] fee —.	أنا اقيم في —
Yes, I'm married.	'*ay*-wa, *a*-na mit-**gaw**-wiz [mit-gaw-**wi**-za].	نعم، انا متزوج [متزوجة]

| No, I'm not married. | *la'*, *a-na **mish** mit-**gaw**-wiz* [*mit-gaw-**wi**-za*]. | لست متزوجا [متزوجة] |

OCCUPATIONS

| I am a <u>businessman</u>. | *a-na **raa**-gil 'a^c-**mehl** / teh-gir.* | أنا رجل اعمال، تاجر |

▪ a businesswoman	▪ *say-**yi**-dit 'a^c-**mehl***	سيدة اعمال
▪ a student	▪ ***Taa**-lib* [*Taa-**li**-ba*]	طالب [طالبة]
▪ a teacher	▪ *mu-**dar**-ris* [*mu-dar-**ri**-sa*]	مدرس [مدرسة]، معلم [معلمة]
▪ a doctor	▪ *duk-**toor*** [*duk-**too**-ra*]	دكتور [دكتورة]، طبيب [طبيبة]
▪ a farmer	▪ *mu-**zeh**-ri^c*	مزارع
▪ an engineer	▪ *mu-**han**-dis* [*mu-han-**di**-sa*]	مهندس [مهندسة]
▪ a secretary	▪ *si-kir-**teer*** [*si-kir-**tee**-ra*]	سكرتير [سكرتيرة]
▪ a company director	▪ *mu-**deer*** [*mu-**dee**-rit*] *shir-ka*	مدير [مديرة] شركة
▪ a consultant	▪ *mus-ta-**shaar*** [*mus-ta-**shaa**-ra*], *kha-**beer*** [*kha-**bee**-ra*]	مستشار [مستشارة]
▪ a housewife	▪ ***sit**-ti beyt*	ربة منزل
▪ a nurse	▪ *mu-mar-**ri**-Da*	ممرضة

■ a journalist	■ **Sa**-Ha-fee [Sa-Ha-**fee**-ya]	صحفي [صحفية]
■ a lawyer	■ mu-**Heh**-mee [mu-Heh-**mee**-ya]	محامي [محامية]
I'm in <u>import/export.</u>	a-na fil-'is-ti-raad wit-taS-**Deer**.	أعمل بالاستيراد والتصدير
■ manufacturing	■ fiS-Si-**naa**-ᶜa	في الصناعة
■ banking	■ fi bank	في بنك
■ computing	■ fis-tiᶜ-**mehl** il-kom-**byoo**-tar	في استعمال الكمبيوتر
■ publishing	■ fi daar nashr	بالنشر
He is (is he?) — .	**huw**-wa — (?)	(هل) هو —
She is (is she?) —.	**hee**-ya — (?)	(هل) هي —

GENERAL CONVERSATION

Whenever you meet and talk with people, for example, when discussing a purchase or making a routine business call, you are likely to be presented with coffee or tea or a soft drink.

I'm here for <u>a few days.</u>	**ha**"-ᶜud **ka**-za yohm.	سابقى هنا عدة ايام
■ a week	■ 'is-**booᶜ**	اسبوع
■ (about) a month	■ (Ha-**weh**-lee) shahr	مدة شهر (تقريبا)

It's the first time
I've been to Egypt.

*dee 'aw-wil **mar**-ra 'eh-gee maSr.*

إنها المرة الاولى لي في مصر

I hope to visit — .

*ᶜa-wiz [ᶜaw-za] a-**zoor** —.*

أريد أن ازور —

I'm traveling
by myself.

*a-na mi-**seh**-fir [mi-**saf**-ra]
li **waH**-dee.*

انا مسافر [مسافرة] وحدي

I am with friends.

*a-na ma-ᶜa 'aS-**Haab**.*   انا مع اصدقاء

I'm waiting
for someone.

*a-na mis-**tan**-nee
[mis-tan-**nee**-ya] Hadd.*

انا منتظر [منتظرة]
واحداً

I love the country.

*ba-**Hibb** il-ba-lad.*   احب البلد

I love the
people here.

*ba-**Hibb** in-nehs hi-na.* احب الناس هنا

The people are
very kind.

in-nehs Tay-yi-been gid-dan.

الناس طيبون جداً

◾ generous

◾ *ku-ra-ma*   كرماء

I've had no
problems.

*ma-ᶜan-**deesh** ma-**sheh**-kil
khaa-liS.*

ليس عندي مشاكل

It is rather
hot.

*ig-**gaww** Harr shway-ya.*

الطقس حار الى حد ما

It is very humid.

*fee ru-**Too**-ba ki-teer.* الطقس رطب جداً

Do you speak
English?

*bi-tit-**kal**-lim [bi-tit-kal-**li**-mee]
in-gi-**lee**-zee?*   هل تتكلم الانجليزية؟

You speak English
very well!

*bi-tit-**kal**-lim [bi-tit-kal-**li**-mee]
in-gi-**lee**-zee kway-yis gid-dan!*

تتكلم الانجليزية بطلاقة !

I have learned a little <u>Arabic</u>.	*da-**rast** ^c**a**-ra-bee **shway**-ya.*	أنا تعلمت قليلا من العربية
■ Egyptian Arabic	■ ^c*a-ra-bee **maS**-ree*	اللهجة المصرية
It's very difficult!	*da Sa^cb **gid**-dan!*	هذه اللغة صعبة جداً
Please join us.	*it-**faD**-Dal [it-faD-**Da**-lee]*.	تفضل [تفضلي]
. . . to two or more	*it-faD-**Da**-loo*	تفضلوا

(*it-**faD**-Dal* can also mean "please take this," "do come in," "have a seat," etc.)

What will you have to drink?	***tish**-rab [tish-**ra**-bee] 'eyh?*	ماذا تريد أن تشرب ؟
. . . to two or more	*tish-**ra**-boo 'eyh?*	ماذا تشربون؟
May I take a picture of you?	***mum**-kin a-Saw-**wa**-rak? [a-Saw-**wa**-rik]?*	هل يمكن أن اصورك؟
Would you take a picture of me (us)?	***mum**-kin ti-Saw-**war**-nee (ti-Saw-**war**-na)?*	هل يمكن أن تصورني؟
Many thanks!	*'**al**-fi shukr!*	شكراً جزيلا!
I will send you the photos.	*hab-^c**at**-lak iS-**So**-war.*	سأرسل لك الصور

ARRANGING TO SEE SOMEONE AGAIN

When will I see you?	*a-shoo-fak [a-shoo-fik] 'im-ta?*	متى أراك ثانية؟
Can I see you tomorrow?	*a-shoo-fak [a-shoo-fik] buk-ra?*	هل ساراك غداً؟
I'll see you <u>here</u>.	*a-shoo-fak [a-shoo-fik] hi-na.*	ساراك هنا
■ at the hotel	■ *fil-fun-du", fil-'u-teel*	■ في الفندق
■ at the office	■ *fil-mak-tab*	■ في المكتب
At what time?	*is-seh-ᶜa kam?*	متى؟
Do join us for lunch.	*it-faD-Dal [it-faD-Da-lee] tit-ghad-da [tit-ghad-dee] ma-ᶜeh-na.*	تفضل للغذاء معنا
Do join us for dinner.	*it-faD-Dal [it-faD-Da-lee] tit-ᶜash-sha [tit-ᶜash-shee] ma-ᶜeh-na.*	تفضل للعشاء معنا
May I call you?	*mum-kin a-kal-li-mak [a-kal-li-mik] bit-ti-li-fohn?*	هل استطيع الاتصال بك؟
What is your telephone number?	*nim-rit ti-li-foh-nak [ti-li-foh-nik] 'eyh?*	ما هو رقم تليفونك؟
This is my telephone number.	*dee nim-rit ti-li-foh-nee.*	هذا هو رقم تليفوني

This is my address (in Egypt).	*da ᶜin-**weh**-nee (fi maSr).*	هذا عنواني (في مصر)
Be seeing you!	*i-la li-**qaa**'!*	إلى اللقاء!

When making any plans for the future it's usual to add:

| God willing (i.e., I hope). | *'in **shaa**' al-**laah**.* | إن شاء الله |
| See you tomorrow, I hope. | *a-**shoo**-fak **buk**-ra, 'in **shaa**' al-**laah**.* | أراك غداً إن شاء الله |

VISITING SOMEONE'S HOME

There are only a few points of etiquette to remember. No gifts are expected, but a box of candy for the children or a small souvenir would be a thoughtful gesture. The host will probably choose the best pieces of meat and add these to your plate whenever it looks as though it needs replenishing. Protest politely *before* you are full, because you will definitely be urged to eat more!

In many country areas it is still customary to eat some dishes with the fingers. In this case use the right hand only.

To indicate you have finished, sit back with a satisfied *'il-**Ham**-du lil-**leh**!* ("praise be to God!").

In a village, a large bowl and jug of water will be brought after a meal so that you can wash your hands and rinse your mouth. A bottle of cologne may be passed around, so that guests may refresh themselves (cologne, scent, and aftershave are always welcome gifts).

Tea or coffee will be served, and, if it is lunchtime, you may be invited to have a rest. More usually, it is polite to leave when the tea or coffee cups have been removed.

If you come upon people eating a meal, they will, out of politeness, invite you to join them; but if you were not expected, you should refuse unless they absolutely insist.

It was a lovely party.	*keh-nit **Haf**-la mum-teh-za.*	كان الحفل ممتازاً
The food was delicious.	*il-'**akl** kehn la-**zeez** gid-dan.*	كان الأكل لذيذاً جداً
(lit.) Blessings on your hands (to the hostess).	*tis-lam 'ee-**dey**-kee.*	تسلم يديك
Thank you so much.	*'**al**-fi shukr, mu-ta-**shak**-kir gid-dan.*	متشكر جداً
It's been lovely meeting you.	*it-shar-**raf**-na.*	تشرفت بلقائك
Can I give you a lift?	*mum-kin a-waS-**Sa**-lak [a-waS-**Sa**-lik]?*	هل اوصلك؟
. . . to two or more	*mum-kin a-waS-**Sal**-kum?*	هل اوصلكم؟

SHOPPING

Opening times of shops, offices, and banks vary from country to country and season to season; in summer, business may start and end early to avoid the heat of the day. Many shops close in the middle of the day and reopen in the late afternoon. In Saudi Arabia and some Gulf countries business comes to a halt briefly with the call to prayer; shops are either closed or simply left unattended while the shopkeeper goes to the local mosque or prays in a quiet back room.

In some countries businesses and institutions tend to close on Fridays, whereas in others the Western custom of Sunday closing has been retained.

The traditional *souk* (market or bazaar) — a maze of streets and tiny alleyways where you can buy everything from a frying pan to a silk carpet — is a fascinating place to visit, even if you don't want to buy. Because goods of a particular kind — jewelry, spices, hardware, clothing, and so on — are sold in one area of the souk, it's easy to compare prices when you are buying a major item. This incidentally is considered the sensible way to shop, so there will be no hard feelings if you decide to "come back later." The most famous souks are perhaps the Hamidiyya in Damascus and the Khan ElKhalili in Cairo. Because these are both at the heart of the old cities, you can explore some of the early mosques and palaces at the same time.

GENERAL EXPRESSIONS

I'd like to go shopping.	*ᶜa-wiz [ᶜaw-za] ash-ti-ree Ha-geht.*	اريد الذهاب للتسوق

Can I see that?	***mum*-kin a-*shoof* da?**	
		هل يمكن أن أرى هذا؟
I prefer this one.	*ba-*faD*-Dal da.*	أفضل هذا
How much is it?	*bi* ***kam*?**	بكم؟
That's (a bit) expensive.	*da* ***gheh*-lee (*shway*-ya).**	هذا غال الى حد ما
Do you have anything cheaper?	***ʿan*-dak *Ha*-ga 'ar-*khaS*?**	هل عندك شيء أرخص؟
Do you have anything better?	***ʿan*-dak *Ha*-ga 'aH-*san*?**	هل عندك شيء أفضل؟
I owe you —.	***ʿan*-dee — lak[lik]**	لك على —
You owe me —.	***ʿan*-dak [*ʿan*-dik] — lee-ya**	
		لي عليك —
Where can I find a —?	*a-*leh*-"ee — feyn?*	أين أجد —

- bakery
- bank
- barber
- beauty parlor
- bookshop
- butcher
- pharmacy (chemist)

▪	*furn,* ***makh*-baz**	مخبز
▪	*bank*	بنك
▪	*Hal-leh"*	حلاق
▪	*Sa-*lohn* tag-*meel**	صالون تجميل
▪	*mak-*ta*-ba*	مكتبة
▪	*gaz-*zaar**	جزار
▪	*'ag-za-*kheh*-na,* *Say-Da-*lee*-ya*	اجزاخانة، صيدلية

■ clothing store —	■ *ma-Hall ma-leh-bis* —	
		محل ملابس —
for men's clothes	*lir-rig-geh-la*	للرجال
for women's clothes	*li s-sit-teht*	للسيدات
for children's clothes	*li l-'aT-faal*	للاطفال
■ confectioner	■ *Ha-la-weh-nee*	حلواني
■ department store	■ *ma-Hall ki-beer*	محل كبير
■ dressmaker	■ *khay-yaa-Ta*	خياطة
■ drugstore	■ *'ag-za-kheh-na, Say-Da-lee-ya*	اجزخانة، صيدلية
■ dry cleaner	■ *ma-Hall tan-Deef*	
		محل تنظيف جاف
■ flower shop	■ *ma-Hall zu-hoor*	محل زهور
■ greengrocer	■ *khu-Da-ree*	محل خضروات
■ grocery store	■ *ba"-"ehl*	محل بقالة
■ hairdresser	■ *kwa-feer*	كوافير، مصفف الشعر
■ hardware store	■ *ma-Hall 'a-da-weht man-zi-lee-ya*	محل ادوات منزلية
■ jewelry store	■ *ga-wa-hir-gee*	جواهرجي
■ laundry	■ *magh-sa-la*	مغسلة
■ newsstand	■ *kushk ga-reh-yid*	كشك جرائد
■ optician	■ *naD-Da-raa-tee*	محل نظارات
■ pastry shop	■ *Ha-la-weh-nee*	حلواني

■ shoemaker	■ *gaz-**ma**-gee*	محل تصليح احذية
■ shoe store	■ *ma-**Hall** gi-zam*	محل احذية
■ shops	■ *da-ka-**keen**, ma-Hal-**leht***	محلات
■ stationer	■ *mak-**ta**-ba*	مكتبة
■ tailor	■ *tar-**zee**, khay-**yaaT***	خياط

BOOKS

Where can I buy English-language books?	*ash-**ti**-ree **ku**-tub in-gi-**lee**-zee feyn?*	أين استطيع شراء كتب بالانجليزية؟
I would like — .	*ᶜa-wiz [ᶜaw-za] —.*	أريد —
■ a guidebook	■ *da-**leel** si-yeh-Hee*	دليل سياحي
■ a map	■ *kha-**ree**-Ta*	خريطة
■ a map of the city	■ *kha-**ree**-Ta lil-**ba**-lad*	خريطة للمدينة
Do you have any books in English?	*ᶜan-**du**-kum **ku**-tub bi-lin-gi-**lee**-zee?*	هل عندكم كتب بالانجليزية؟
Do you have books about Egypt?	*ᶜan-**du**-kum **ku**-tub ᶜan maSr?*	هل عندكم كتب عن مصر ؟
■ about the Middle East	■ *ᶜan ish-**sharq** il-'**aw**-SaT?*	عن الشرق الاوسط
Do you have any novels?	*ᶜan-**du**-kum ri-wa-**yeht**?*	هل عندكم روايات؟

■ detective stories	■ *qi-SaS boo-li-See-ya*	قصص بوليسية
■ short stories	■ *qi-SaS qa-See-ra*	قصص قصيرة
■ dictionary	■ *qa-moos*	قاموس
■ English-Arabic dictionary	■ *qa-moos in-gi-lee-zee-ᶜa-ra-bee*	قاموس إنجليزي – عربي
■ a pocket dictionary	■ *qa-moos geyb*	قاموس جيب

I'll take these books. *heh-khud ik-ku-tub dee.*

سآخذ هذه الكتب

CLOTHING

I'm looking for — .	*ba-daw-war ᶜa-la —.*	أريد —
■ a belt	■ *Hi-zehm*	حزام
■ a blouse	■ *bloo-za*	بلوزة
■ a bra	■ *soot-yehn*	حملة صدر
■ briefs (men)	■ *kee-lott*	سروال داخلي
■ a cardigan	■ *ja-kitt tree-koh*	جاكيت (تريكو)
■ a coat	■ *bal-Too*	معطف
■ a dress	■ *fus-tehn*	فستان
■ handkerchiefs	■ *ma-na-deel*	مناديل
■ a hat	■ *bur-ney-Ta*	قبعة
■ a jacket	■ *ja-kit-ta*	جاكيت، سترة

■ jeans	■ *jeenz*	بنطلون جينز
■ a necktie	■ *ka-ra-**vat**-ta*	ربطة عنق
■ a nightgown	■ *"a-**meeS** nohm*	قميص نوم
■ panties	■ *kee-**lott***	سروال داخلي نسائي
■ pantyhose, tights	■ *koo-**lohn***	جوارب طويلة
■ a robe, dressing gown	■ *rohb*	ثوب، روب
■ sandals	■ ***san**-dal*	صندل
■ a scarf	■ *'i-**sharb**, ku-**fee**-ya*	كوفية
■ a shawl	■ *shehl*	شال
■ a shirt	■ *"a-**meeS***	قميص
■ shoes	■ ***gaz**-ma*	حذاء
■ a skirt	■ *gu-**nil**-la*	جيبة، جونلة
■ a slip	■ *kom-bi-ney-**zohn***	قميص داخلي
■ slippers	■ ***shib**-shib*	شبشب
■ socks, stockings	■ *sha-**raab***	جوارب
■ a suit (man's)	■ ***bad**-la*	بدلة
■ a suit (woman's)	■ *tay-**yeer***	طاقم حريمي
■ a sweater	■ *bu-**loh**-var*	بلوفر، كنزة صوفية
■ a swimsuit	■ *ma-**yoh***	مايو، لباس بحر
■ a T-shirt	■ *fa-**nil**-la*	فانلة، قميص نصف كم
■ a tracksuit	■ *libs tad-**reeb***	بدلة تدريب

trousers, pants	*ban-Ta-lohn*	بنطلون، سروال
an undershirt, vest	*fa-nil-la*	فانلة، قميص داخلي
underwear	*ma-leh-bis dakh-lee-ya*	ملابس داخلية

You may find it comfortable to wear the long loose robe (usually made of cotton) that is still traditional dress in many parts of the Middle East — the *galabiyya* (*gal-la-bee-ya*) (known in the Arab countries further east as the *thawb* or the *dish-da-sha*) — or the more widely cut version, with broad sleeves — the *kaftan* (*"uf-Taan*). A long cloak, the *abaya* (*ᶜa-beh-ya*) — may be worn over these; or, in North Africa especially, the woolen *burnous* (*bur-noos*).

Colors, Styles, Fabrics

I want something in —.	*ᶜa-wiz [ᶜaw-za] lohn —.*	أريد لون —
black	*'is-wid*	أسود
blue	*'az-ra"*	أزرق
red	*'aH-mar*	أحمر
green	*'akh-Dar*	أخضر
yellow	*'aS-far*	أصفر
white	*'ab-yaD*	أبيض
brown	*bun-nee*	بني
gray	*ra-maa-dee*	رمادي
beige	*beyj*	بني فاتح

■ pink	■ *war-*dee	وردي
■ purple	■ *ba-naf-si-gee*	بنفسجي
I don't like this color.	*ma-ba-**Hib**-bish il-**lohn** da.*	لا أحب هذا اللون
I prefer this one.	*ba-**faD**-Dal da.*	أفضل هذا
I'd like something lighter (in color).	*ᶜa-wiz **Ha**-ga 'af-**taH**.*	أريد لوناً أفتح
■ darker	■ *'agh-ma"*	أغمق
■ plain	■ *seh-da*	سادة
■ patterned	■ *mu-shag-ga-ra, man-"oo-sha*	منقوش
■ striped	■ *mu-khaT-**Ta**-Ta*	مخطط
■ (hand) embroidered	■ *mash-**ghool** (bil-**yadd**)*	مطرز (شغل يد)
Do you have anything else?	*ᶜan-du-kum **Ha**-ga **tan-ya**?*	هل يوجد شيء آخر؟
■ better	■ *'aH-san*	أفضل
■ cheaper	■ *'ar-khaS*	أرخص
■ larger	■ *'ak-bar*	أكبر
■ fuller	■ *'aw-saᶜ*	أوسع
■ smaller	■ *'aS-ghar*	أصغر
■ longer	■ *'aT-wal*	أطول
■ shorter	■ *'a"-Sar*	أقصر

Do you have anything in (pure) — ?	*°an-**du**-kum **Ha**-ga — (**Saa**-fee)?*	هل عندكم شيء — خالص ؟
■ cotton	■ *"uTn*	قطن
■ wool	■ *Soof*	صوف
■ silk	■ *Ha-**reer***	حرير
■ polyester	■ *pul-**yis**-tir*	ألياف صناعية
■ leather	■ *gild*	جلد
I'd like something heavier (i.e., warmer)	*°a-wiz [°aw-za] **Ha**-ga 'at-"al.*	أريد شيئاً أثقل
■ lighter (i.e., cooler)	■ *'a-**khaff***	أخف
■ for the evening	■ *swa-**reyh***	لحفلة ساهرة
Is this handmade?	*da shughl **yadd**?*	هل هذا صنع يد ؟

Trying It On

Can I try this on?	***mum**-kin al-**bi**-soo?*	هـل استطيـع لبس هذا؟
I take size —.	*ma-"**eh**-see — .*	مقاسي — .
Could you measure me?	***mum**-kin ti-"**ees**-nee?*	خذ مقاسي من فضلك
This is too — .	*da — °a-l**ɛh**-ya.*	هذا — جداً
■ long	■ *Ta-**weel***	طويل
■ short	■ *"u-**Say**-yar*	قصير

■ loose	■ **weh**-si^c	واسع
■ tight	■ **day**-ya"	ضيق

Can you alter
this for me?

mum-kin tuZ-buT-**heh**-lee?

هل يمكنك تغيير هذا لي ؟

When will it
be ready?

hat-**koon gah**-za 'im-ta?

متى ستكون جاهزة ؟

The zipper doesn't
work.

is-**sus**-ta mak-**soo**-ra.

السوستة
مكسورة

ELECTRICAL APPLIANCES

Most countries in the Middle East use 220 volts, but
there are exceptions; so check before you go, or take an
adapter with you.

I want to buy — . ^{c}a-wiz [^{c}**aw**-za] ash-**ti**-ree — .

أريد شراء — .

■ an adapter	■ mu-**Haw**-wil	محول
■ a battery	■ baT-Ta-**ree**-ya	بطارية
■ a blender	■ khal-**laaT**	خلاط
■ a CD player	■ gi-**hehz** li 'is-Ti-wa-**naat** ley-zar	جهاز لاسطو انات ليزر
■ a calculator	■ 'eh-la **Has**-ba	آلة حاسبة
■ a cassette player	■ gi-**hehz** ka-**sitt**	جهاز كاسيت
■ a cassette recorder	■ gi-**hehz** ka-**sitt** mu-**sag**-gil	مسجل كاسيت
■ a shaver	■ **ma**-ka-nit Hi-**leh**-"a	آلة حلاقة

■ a hair dryer	■ *sish-**waar**, mu-**gaf**-fif li sh-**sha**^c**r***	مجفف للشعر
■ a microcasette player	■ ***wok**-man, gi-**hehz** ka-**sitt** Su-**ghay**-yar*	ووكمان، جهاز كاسيت صغير
■ a plug	■ ***fee**-sha*	فيشة
■ a (portable) radio	■ ***rad**-yo (Su-**ghay**-yar)*	راديو (صغير)
■ a television	■ *ti-li-viz-**yohn***	تليفزيون
■ a videorecorder	■ *gi-**hehz** **vid**-yo*	جهاز فيديو

What voltage does this take?   *kam il-**volt**?*   ما هو الفولت الذي تستخدمه ؟

Could you demonstrate it for me?   ***mum**-kin ti-**shagh**-ghal-**hoo**-lee?*   هل يمكن أن تشغله لي ؟

It doesn't work.   *mab-yish-ta-**ghalsh**.*   لا يعمل

FOOD AND HOUSEHOLD ITEMS

(See p. 79–88 for food words.)

I'd like — .   *^c**a**-wiz [^c**aw**-za] — .*   أريد — .

■ a bar of soap	■ *Sa-**boo**-na*	صابونة
■ breakfast cereal	■ *korn fleyks*	كورن فلاكس
■ a can of sardines	■ *^c**il**-bit sar-**deen***	علبة سردين
■ chocolate (candy)	■ *sho-ko-**laa**-ta*	شكولاتة

cocoa (hot chocolate)	*ka-**kaw***	كاكاو
(ground) coffee	*bunn*	بن
cookies (biscuits)	*bas-ka-**weet***	بسكويت
cooking oil	*zeyt Ta-**beekh***	زيت للطهي
a loaf	*ri-**gheef***	رغيف خبز
matches	*ka-**breet***	كبريت
milk	***la**-ban, Ha-**leeb***	حليب
paper tissues	*ma-na-**deel wa-**ra"*	مناديل ورق
salt	*malH*	ملح
soap powder	*Sa-**boon bud**-ra*	صابون بودرة
sugar	***suk**-kar*	سكر
tea	*shayy*	شاي
toilet paper	***wa**-ra" twa-**litt***	ورق تواليت
vinegar	*khall*	خل
liquid detergent	*Sa-**boon seh**-yil*	صابون سائل
yogurt	***la**-ban za-**beh**-dee*	لبن زبادي

Containers

a bottle	*"i-**zeh**-za*	زجاجة
a bottle of —	*"i-**zeh**-zit —*	زجاجة —
a packet	***beh**-koo*	كيس
a tin, a can, a carton	*ᶜil-ba*	علبة

| a can of — | *ᶜil-bit* — | — علبة |
| a jar | *bar-Ta-maan* | برطمان |

THE SPICE MARKET

Oriental spices are increasingly popular in the West. A selection bought from the great sacksful on display in the spice section of the bazaar makes an unusual gift for adventurous cooks back home. (Label them at once so that you know which is which!) The most common are:

- cardamon (*Hab-ba-hehn* حبهان) Small pods of highly aromatic seeds, used in both sweet and savory dishes and to flavor Turkish coffee.
- cumin (*kam-moon* كمّون) Sold as whole seeds or in powdered form, adds interest to simple foods like lentils and beans. It is often used in combination with coriander.
- coriander (*kuz-ba-ra* كسبرة), either its ground seeds or leaves, which look like flat-leaved parsley and can also be used as a garnish.
- saffron (*zaᶜ-fraan* زعفران) Gives rice a subtle, slightly earthy flavor and delicate yellow color. (Turmeric is a cheaper substitute.)
- harissa (*ha-ree-sa* شطة), or ground red chilies, also sold as a paste, is an important ingredient in many North African dishes.

Nutmeg, cinnamon, and cloves — used for centuries in the West as ingredients in desserts, punches, and milk drinks — are also used in savory dishes in the Middle East, and can be bought there for a fraction of the price.

Every region has its own preferred mixture of ground spices. In North Africa the mixture known as *raas il-ha-noot* usually includes red pepper, coriander, and cumin.

Unless you are buying a ready-made mixture, buy the whole seeds, to be freshly ground when needed. In the spice bazaar you will also find dried fruit and nuts, again great bargains compared with the cost in Europe or the United States.

Quantities

The metric system is generally used, that is, kilos, grams, and liters. These words don't change in the plural in Arabic:

a kilo	*(X)* **kee**-loo —	— كيلو
(X kilos of) — .		
a gram	*(X) grehm —*	— جرام
(X grams) of —		
a liter	*(X) litr —*	— لتر
(X liters) of —		
half a kilo	*nuSS* **kee**-loo	نصف كيلو
a quarter of a kilo	*rub^c* **kee**-loo	ربع كيلو

The traditional measure of one pound — about half a kilo — is still widely used:

a pound (of —)	*raTl (—)*	رطل
That's enough.	*ki-**feh**-ya **ki**-da.*	هذا يكفي
A little more.	*ka-**mehn shway**-ya.*	أكثر قليلًا
A little less.	*'a-"all shway*-ya.*	أقل قليلًا
Can I see that, please?	***mum**-kin a-**shoof** da, min **faD**-lak?*	هل يمكن أن أرى هذا من فضلك ؟
Is it fresh?	*da **Taa**-za?*	هل هو طازج ؟

AT THE JEWELER'S

I'd like to see —.	^{c}a-wiz [^{c}aw-za] a-**shoof** —.	. — أريد أن أرى
■ a bracelet	■ ghi-**wey**-sha	سوار
■ a brooch	■ brohsh	دبوس
■ a chain	■ sil-**si**-la	سلسلة
■ a charm, medallion	■ ^{c}ul-**li**-"a	مدالية، تعليقة
■ some earrings	■ **Ha**-la″	حلق
■ a necklace	■ ^{c}u″d	عقد
■ prayer beads	■ sib-Ha	سبحة
■ a ring	■ **kheh**-tim	خاتم
■ a wristwatch	■ seh-^{c}it yadd	ساعة يد
■ an alarm clock	■ mi-**nab**-bih	منبه
■ a watch with an alarm	■ seh-^{c}it yadd bi mi-**nab**-bih	ساعة يد بها منبه
Is this — ?	da — ?	هل هذا — ؟
■ gold	■ **da**-hab	ذهب
■ platinum	■ bleh-**teen**	بلاتين
■ silver	■ **faD**-Da	فضة
■ stainless steel	■ **steyn**-lis steel	صلب لا يصدأ
■ solid gold	■ **da**-hab **Saa**-fee	ذهب صافي

■ gold plated   ■ *maT-lee da-hab*   مطلي ذهب

Gold jewelry is often sold by weight, with a sum added for the workmanship involved. The price of gold is published daily in the newspapers.

How many carats is it?	*da kam "i-raaT?*	كم قيراط هذا ؟
How much is it per carat?	*il-"i-raaT bi kam?*	بكم القيراط ؟
Is this new or antique?	*da gi-deed wal-la "a-deem?*	هل هذا جديد أم قديم ؟
What is this stone?	*'eyh il-Ha-gar da?*	ما هذا الحجر ؟

Precious and Semiprecious Stones

amethyst	*ga-masht*	جمشت
aquamarine	*za-bar-gad*	زبرجد
coral	*mur-gehn*	مرجان
diamond	*al-maaz*	ماس
emerald	*zu-mur-rud*	زمرد
ivory	*ᶜehg, sinn il-feel*	عاج
jade	*jehd*	يشب
onyx	*ᶜa-"ee"*	عقيق
pearls	*lu'-lu'*	لؤلؤ
ruby	*ya-"oot*	ياقوت
sapphire	*ya-"oot 'az-ra"*	زفير ، ياقوت أزرق

topaz	*to-**behz***	توباز
turquoise	*fey-**rooz***	فيروز

MUSIC, DISCS, AND CASSETTES

Is there a record shop around here?	*fee ma-**Hall** is-Ti-wa-**naat** "u-**ray**-yib?*	هل هناك محل أسطوانات قريب ؟
Do you have — ?	*ᶜan-**du**-kum — ?*	هل عندكم — ؟
▓ cassettes	▓ *ka-sit-**teht***	شرائط كاسيت
▓ compact discs	▓ *is-Ti-wa-**naat** ley-zar*	أسطوانات ليزر
▓ records	▓ *is-Ti-wa-**naat***	أسطوانات
▓ tapes	▓ *sha-**raa**-yiT*	شرائط
▓ videocassettes	▓ *'af-**lehm** vid-yo*	شرائط فيديو
I'd like — .	*ᶜa-wiz [ᶜaw-za] — .*	أريد — .
▓ Western music	▓ *mu-**see**-qa ghar-**bee**-ya*	موسيقى غربية
▓ classical music	▓ *mu-**see**-qa kla-see-**kee**-ya*	موسيقى كلاسيكية
▓ folk music	▓ *mu-**see**-qa shaᶜ-**bee**-ya*	موسيقى شعبية
▓ jazz	▓ *jazz*	جاز
▓ light music	▓ *mu-**see**-qa kha-**fee**-fa*	موسيقى خفيفة

- opera
- '**u**-bi-ra
- أوبرا

- oriental music
- mu-**see**-qa shar-"**ee**-ya
- موسيقى شرقية

Can I listen to this?   **mum**-kin **as**-ma^c da?

هل يمكن أن أسمع هذا ؟

NEWSPAPERS AND MAGAZINES

Do you have an
English-language
<u>newspaper</u>?

^{c}**an**-dak ga-**ree**-da in-gi-**lee**-zee?

هل عندكم جريدة بالإنجليزية ؟

- magazine
- ma-**gal**-la
- مجلة

Do you have
stamps?

^{c}**an**-dak Ta-**waa**-bi^c?

هل عندك
طوابع ؟

- postcards
- ku-**root** bus-**tehl**
- بطاقات بريدية

- a map of
  the town
- kha-**ree**-Ta lil-**ba**-lad
- خريطة للمدينة

- a guidebook
- da-**leel** si-**yeh**-Hee
- دليل سياحي

PHOTOGRAPHIC SUPPLIES

Is there a camera
shop near here?

fee ma-**Hall** ka-me-**reht** "u-**ray**-yib?

هل يوجد محل آلات تصوير قريب ؟

I'd like a
<u>good</u> camera.

^{c}**a**-wiz [^{c}**aw**-za]
ka-me-ra kway-**yi**-sa.

أريد آلة تصوير
جيدة

- inexpensive
- ri-**khee**-Sa
- رخيصة

- video
- **vid**-yo
- فيديو

Do you have <u>color</u> film?	*ᶜan-**du**-kum film mu-**law**-win?*	هل عندكم أفلام ملونة ؟
■ black and white	■ *'**ab**-yaD **wis**-wid*	أبيض وأسود
I'd like <u>20</u> exposures.	*ᶜa-wiz [ᶜaw-za] ᶜish-**reen** **Soo**-ra.*	أريد فلم ٢٠ صورة
■ 36	■ *sit-ta wa-ta-la-**teen***	٣٦ صورة
What is the expiration date?	*'eyh ta-**reekh** il-'in-ti-heh'?*	ما هو تاريخ إنتهاء الصلاحية؟
Do you develop film?	*bit-Ham-**ma**-Doo 'af-lehm?*	هل تحمض الأفلام ؟
I'd like a roll of film for slides.	*ᶜa-wiz [ᶜaw-za] film slaydz.*	أريد فلم شرائح
A print with <u>glossy</u> finish.	***Soo**-ra lam-**mee**-ᶜa.*	أريد طباعة لامعة
■ matte	■ *maT, maT-**fee**-ya*	مطفية
I want an <u>enlargement</u> of this one.	*ᶜa-wiz [ᶜaw-za] a-**kab**-bar dee.*	أريد تكبير هذه
■ another print	■ *nus-kha **tan**-ya min dee*	نسخة أخرى من هذه
When will they be ready?	*hat-**koon** **gah**-za 'im-ta?*	متى ستكون جاهزة ؟
Do you have flashbulbs?	*ᶜan-dak lam-**beht** flash?*	هل عندكم لمبات فلاش ؟

SOUVENIRS

The Middle East is famous for ceramics, carpets, jewelry, copper and brassware, leather goods, and fine inlay work in metal and wood. There is no problem in having goods shipped or air-freighted home, though there are likely to be restrictions on the export of antiques. If you are considering buying an antique, make sure you get a government guarantee of authenticity.

Bargaining is a normal practice in traditional markets and bazaars, though not in modern shops or supermarkets. The basic technique is to express mild shock and disbelief at the price suggested, propose a sum well below that, then gradually work up to a compromise between the two. Often the shopkeeper will make you a "final offer" as you are about to leave the shop. It is quite all right to shop around and compare prices, then return to a shop where you have already bargained strenuously. You will always be welcome!

Arabic has many elaborate phrases for use on such occasions. Some of the most useful are:

Be generous!	*khal-**leek** ka-**reem**!*	كن كريما !
You're putting me off (with the price)!	*khaD-**Deyt**-nee!*	أفزعتني !
Come down a bit.	*naz-zil shway-ya.*	أخفض لي السعر
Let's split the difference.	*ni"-sim il-ba-lad nuS-Seyn.*	نقسم البلد نصفين
Here's the money.	*it-faD-Dal.*	تفضل

When you do buy something, the shopkeeper — and friends, too — will congratulate you with:

| Congratulations! | mab-**rook!** | مبروك ! |

To which the reply is: al-**laah** yi-**beh**-rik **feek** [**fee**-kee]

الله يبارك فيك

Do you have leather goods?	^can-**du**-kum <u>maS-nu-^c**aat**</u> <u>gil-**dee**-ya?</u>	هل عندكم مصنوعات جلدية ؟
■ jewelry	■ mu-gaw-ha-**raat**	مجوهرات
■ pottery, ceramics	■ fukh-**khaar**	فخار ، خزف
■ carpets	■ sa-ga-**geed**	سجاجيد
■ (long narrow) rugs	■ mash-sha-**yeht**	مشايات
■ woven rugs	■ 'ak-**li**-ma	أكلمة
■ caftans	■ "a-fa-**Teen**	قفاطين
■ galabiyyas (Arab robe)	■ gal-la-bee-**yeht**	جلاليب
■ brassware	■ muS-nu-^c**aat** ni-**Hehs**	مصنوعات نحاس أصفر
■ copperware	■ maS-nu-^c**aat** ni-**Hehs** 'aH-mar	مصنوعات نحاس أحمر
■ glassware	■ maS-nu-^c**aat** "i-**zehz**	مصنوعات زجاجية
I am looking for a brass tray.	^ca-**wiz** [^c**aw**-za] <u>Sa-**nee**-ya ni-**Hehs**.</u>	أريد صينية نحاس

▥ a tray with inlay	▥ *Sa-**nee**-ya mu-Ta^c-^ca-ma*	صينية مطعمة
▥ a tray with a stand	▥ *Sa-**nee**-ya bi **kur**-see*	صينية بكرسي
▥ a box with inlay	▥ *san-**doo**" mu-Ta^c-^cam*	صندوق مطعم
▥ a coffee set	▥ *Ta"m lil-"**ah**-wa*	طاقم للقهوة
▥ a chess set	▥ *sha-Ta-**rang***	طاقم شطرنج
▥ a coffeepot	▥ *'ab-**ree**" "**ah**-wa*	إبريق قهوة
▥ an ashtray	▥ *Ta"-**Too**-"a*	طفاية
▥ slippers	▥ ***shib**-shib*	شبشب
▥ sandals	▥ ***san**-dal*	صندل
▥ a leather bag	▥ ***shan**-Ta gild*	حقيبة جلدية
▥ a leather cushion (pouffe)	▥ *boof gild*	حشية جلدية
▥ a water (hubble bubble) pipe	▥ ***shee**-sha*	نارجيلة ، شيشة
▥ a vase	▥ *zuh-**ree**-ya*	زهرية
▥ prayer beads	▥ ***sib**-Ha*	سبحة

Do you sell Oriental perfumes?	*^can-**du**-kum ^cu-**Toor** shar-"**ee**-ya?*
	هل عندكم عطور شرقية ؟
▥ jasmine	▥ *yas-**meen***	ياسمين

rose	*ward*	ورد
sandalwood	**san**-dal	صندل

Is this handmade?	*da shughl* **yadd**?	هل هذا شغل يد ؟
Please wrap these for me.	*lif-fu-***hum***-lee, min* **faD**-lak.	أرجو أن تلف هذا لي
Will you air freight this for me?	**mum**-kin tib-**c**at-**hoo**-lee *bil-ba-***reed** il-gaw-**wee**?	هل ترسل لي هذا بالبريد الجوي ؟
Please send it by surface mail.	*ib-**c**at-**hoo**-lee bil-ba-***reed** il-**c**eh-dee.*	أرجو أن ترسل لي هذا بالبريد العادي

STATIONERY ITEMS

I want — .	**c**a-wiz [**c**aw-za] — .	اريد — .
a ballpoint pen	"a-lam **gaff**	قلم جاف
envelopes	Zu-**roof**	ظروف
an eraser	as-**tee**-ka	ممسحة
glue	Samgh	صمغ
a notebook	**noh**-ta	دفتر جيب
a pencil	"a-lam ru-**SaaS**	قلم رصاص
a pencil sharpener	bar-**reh**-ya	مبراة
a ruler	mas-**Ta**-ra	مسطرة
Scotch tape	**wa**-ra" laz-**zeh**"	شريط لاصق

▓ string	▓ du-**baa**-ra	حبل دوبارة
▓ typing paper	▓ wa-ra″ li l-'**eh**-la l-**kat**-ba	
		ورق آلة كاتبة
▓ wrapping paper	▓ wa-ra″ gal-**lehd**	ورق لف طرود
▓ a writing pad	▓ blok noht	دفتر

TOBACCO

Do you have (American) cigarettes?	ᶜan-**du**-kum sa-**geh**-yir (am-ree-**keh**-nee)?	هل عندكم سجائر (أمريكية) ؟
I'd like a pack of <u>filter</u> cigarettes.	ᶜa-wiz [ᶜaw-za] ᶜil-bit sa-**geh**-yir <u>fil-tar.</u>	أريد علبة سجائر بالفلتر
▓ unfiltered	▓ bi-**doon** fil-tar	بدون فلتر
▓ menthol	▓ min-**tool**	بالمنتول
▓ king size	▓ king sayz	كنج سايز
▓ mild	▓ kha-**fee**-fa	خفيفة
What brands do you have?	ᶜan-dak 'aS-**naaf** 'eyh?	ما هي الأنواع عندكم ؟
Do you have — ?	ᶜan-**du**-kum — ?	هل عندكم — ؟
▓ cigars	▓ see-**gaar**	سيجار
▓ pipe tobacco	▓ dukh-**khehn** bee-ba	دخان غليون
▓ a lighter	▓ wal-**leh**-ᶜa	ولاعة

■ lighter fluid ■ *ban-**zeen**/ghehz wal-**leh**-ᶜa*

بنزين / غاز ولاعة

■ matches ■ *kab-**reet*** كبريت

TOILETRIES

Is there a pharmacy (chemist) near here? *fee 'ag-za-**kheh**-na "u-ray-**yi**-ba min **hi**-na?*

هل توجد أجزخانة قريبة ؟

Do you have — ? *ᶜan-**du**-kum — ?* هل عندكم — ؟

■ aftershave ■ *los-**yohn** baᶜd il-Hi-**leh**-"a*

سائل بعد الحلاقة

■ bobby pins ■ *bi-nas* دبابيس للشعر

■ a brush ■ *fur-sha* فرشاة

■ cleansing cream (makeup remover) ■ *kreym li-'i-**zeh**-lit il-mak-**yaj*** كريم لازالة المكياج

■ cologne ■ *ko-**lon**-ya* كولونيا

■ a comb ■ *mishT* مشط

■ depilatory cream ■ *kreym li-'i-**zeh**-lit ish-**sha**ᶜr*

كريم لازالة الشعر

■ a deodorant ■ *mu-**zeel** lil-ᶜa-ra"* مزيل لرائحة العرق

■ diapers ■ *ka-wa-**feel*** أحفضة للأطفال

■ emery boards ■ *mab-rad wa-ra" liD-Da-**waa**-fir* مبرد ورق للأظافر

▪ eyebrow pencil	▪ *"a-lam Ha-weh-gib*	قلم حواجب
▪ eyeliner	▪ *ay-lay-nar, kuHl*	قلم كحل
▪ eye shadow	▪ *Dill lil-ᶜu-yoon*	ظل جفون
▪ washcloth (face flannel)	▪ *foo-Ta lil-wishsh*	فوطة/منشفة وجه
▪ gargle	▪ *ghar-gha-ra*	غرغرة
▪ hairspray	▪ *is-brey lish-shaᶜr*	مثبت للشعر
▪ lipstick	▪ *rooj*	أحمر شفاه
▪ makeup	▪ *mak-yaj*	مكياج
▪ mascara	▪ *mas-ka-ra*	ماسكره
▪ mirror	▪ *mi-reh-ya*	مرآة
▪ mouthwash	▪ *gha-seel lil-famm*	غسيل للفم
▪ nail clippers	▪ *"aS-Saa-fa liD-Da-waa-fir*	قصافة للأظافر
▪ a nail file	▪ *mab-rad Da-waa-fir*	مبرد للأظافر
▪ nail polish	▪ *ma-nee-keer*	طلاء أظافر
▪ nail polish remover	▪ *a-see-tohn*	مزيل طلاء الأظافر
▪ nail scissors	▪ *ma-"aSS liD-Da-waa-fir*	مقص أظافر
▪ night cream	▪ *kreym lil-leyl*	كريم لليل
▪ razor blades	▪ *'am-wehs Hi-leh-"a*	أمواس حلاقة
▪ sanitary napkins	▪ *fo-waT SiH-Hee-ya*	فوط صحية

■ shampoo	■ *sham-**poo***	شامبو
■ shaving soap	■ *Sa-**boon** Hi-**leh**-"a*	صابون حلاقة
■ soap	■ *Sa-**boon***	صابون
■ a sponge	■ *sa-**fin**-ga*	إسفنجة
■ suntan lotion	■ *los-**yohn** li Hi-**meh**-yit il-**bash**-ra*	سائل حماية البشرة
■ suntan oil	■ *zeyt li Hi-**meh**-yit il-**bash**-ra*	زيت حماية البشرة
■ talcum powder	■ ***bud**-rit talk*	بودرة تلك
■ tampons	■ ***tam**-paks*	صمامات قطنية ، تامبونات
■ tissues	■ *ma-na-**deel** wa-ra"*	مناديل ورق
■ toilet paper	■ ***wa**-ra" twa-**litt***	ورق تواليت
■ a toothbrush	■ ***fur**-shit 'as-**nehn***	فرشاة للأسنان
■ toothpaste	■ *ma^c-**goon** lil-'as-**nehn***	معجون أسنان
■ tweezers	■ *mul-"**aaT***	ملقاط

PERSONAL CARE AND SERVICES

AT THE BARBER

Does the hotel have a barber shop?	*fee Hal-**leh**" fil-**fun**-du"?* هل يوجد حلاق بالفندق ؟
Where is there a good barber shop?	*feyn a-**leh**-"ee Hal-**leh**" kway-yis?* أين أجد حلاقاً جيداً ؟
Do I have to wait long?	***leh**-zim as-**tan**-na ki-**teer**?* هل يجب أن انتظر فترة طويلة ؟
I want a shave.	*^c**aw**-zak tiH-**la**"-lee id-**da**"n.* أريد أن أحلق ذقني
▪ a haircut	▪ *ti-"uS-**Si**-lee sha^c-ree* أقص شعري
▪ just a trim	▪ *ti-"aS-Sar-**hoo**-lee shway-ya* مجرد تهذيب
Trim it at the front.	*khif-fu-**hoo**-lee min"ud-**dehm**.* قصه قليلاً من الأمام
▪ at the back	▪ *min **wa**-ra* — من الخلف
▪ at the sides	▪ *min ig-gi-**nehb*** — على الجوانب
Leave it long.	*khal-**lee** Ta-**weel** shway-ya.* اتركه طويل
I'd like it very short.	*"aS-Sar-**hoo**-lee **khaa**-liS.* أريده قصير جداً

English	Transliteration	Arabic
I'd like a razor cut.	*"uS-Soo bil-moos.*	قصه بالموسى
Please trim my — .	*min faD-lak uZ-buT-lee — .*	من فضلك قص قليلًا — .
■ beard	■ *id-da"n*	ذقني
■ mustache	■ *ish-sha-nab*	شاربي ، شنبي
■ sideburns	■ *is-sa-weh-lif*	سوالفي
I want to have <u>my beard</u> shaved off.	*°a-wiz aH-la" da"-nee.*	أريد أن احلق ذقني
■ my mustache	■ *sha-na-bee*	شاربي ، شنبي
I part my hair <u>on the left.</u>	*af-ri" sha°-ree °ash-shi-mehl.*	أفرق شعري من اليسار
■ on the right	■ *°al-yi-meen*	من اليمين
■ in the middle	■ *fil-wuST*	من الوسط
A little more here.	*'ak-tar shway-ya hi-na.*	أكثر قليلًا من هنا
That's enough.	*ki-feh-ya ki-da.*	هذا يكفي
That's fine.	*kway-yis ki-da.*	هذا حسن
I (don't) want — .	*(mish) °a-wiz — .*	(لا) أريد —
■ shampoo	■ *sham-poo*	شامبو
■ tonic	■ *ko-lon-ya*	كولونيا
■ hair oil	■ *zeyt sha°r*	زيت شعر
■ hairspray	■ *is-brey*	مثبت الشعر

| Can I see it in the mirror? | *mum*-kin a-*shoo*-foo fil-mi-*reh*-ya? | أريد أن انظر في المرآة |
| How much do I owe you? | *ᶜa*-wiz kam? | كم الحساب ؟ |

AT THE BEAUTY PARLOR

[For cutting and trimming terms, see "At the Barber"]

Is there a <u>beauty parlor</u> near here?	*fee* Sa-*lohn* tag-*meel* "u-*ray*-yib?	هل يوجد صالون تجميل قريب ؟
▓ hairdresser	▓ kwa-*feer*	مصفف شعر ، كوافير
Can I make an appointment — ?	*mum*-kin a*H*-giz ma-ᶜ*ehd* — ?	أريد حجز موعد
▓ this afternoon	▓ baᶜd iD-**Duhr**	بعد الظهر
▓ tomorrow	▓ *buk*-ra	غداً
Can you give me — ?	*mum*-kin tiᶜ-*mil*-lee — ?	أريد — ؟
▓ a color rinse	▓ sham-*poo* bil-*lohn*	شامبو تلوين
▓ a facial massage	▓ tad-*leek*	تدليك وجه
▓ a steam massage	▓ tad-*leek* bil-bu-*khaar*	تدليك بالبخار
▓ a manicure	▓ ma-nee-*keer*	مانيكير
▓ a pedicure	▓ pi-di-*keer*	باديكير
▓ a permanent	▓ ber-ma-*nant*	برماننت
▓ a shampoo	▓ sham-*poo*	شامبو

■ a tint	■ **Sab**-gha	صبغة
■ a touch up	■ **Sab**-gha lig-gu-**zoor**	صبغة الجزور
■ a wash and set	■ **mee**-zam plee	غسيل وتصفيف
■ a wash and blow dry	■ gha-**seel** wi sish-**war** bass	غسيل وتجفيف

I (don't) want hairspray.	(mish) ʿ**aw**-za is-**brey**.	(لا) أريد مثبت للشعر
Just a little.	**shway**-ya bass.	قليل فقط
I'd like to see a color chart.	ʿ**aw**-za a-**shoof** da-**leel** ʾal-**wehn**.	أريد أن أرى دليل الألوان
I want this color.	ʿ**aw**-za il-**lohn** da.	أريد هذا اللون
■ the same color	■ nafs il-**lohn**	نفس اللون
■ a darker color	■ lohn ʾ**agh**-ma"	لون أغمق
■ a lighter color	■ lohn ʾ**af**-taH	لون أفتح

THE HAMMAM

Known in the West as the "Turkish bath," the Ham-**mehm** is in fact a general Middle East development of the Roman communal bath house — a social as well as a hygienic institution. Gossip, intrigue, and sometimes serious debate were as important to the clientele as the steaming, bathing, and massage that took place.

Many hammams still function; if you decide to use their services establish first what you want and how much it will cost. The price quoted may well not include tips to whoever hands out the towels, minds the clothes, and so on.

LAUNDRY AND DRY CLEANING

———

You may see the *mak-wa-gee* working in a tiny shop open to the street. He will press clothing and bed linens and have them delivered to your door within 24 hours if you are staying in the neighborhood. Note that the quality of dry cleaning services is highly variable. It is safest to take clothes with you that can be washed.

Is there a <u>laundry service</u> in the hotel?	*fee gha-**seel** wi **mak**-wa fil-**fun**-du"?*	هل يوجد غسيل ومكواة في الفندق ؟
▪ a dry cleaning service	▪ *tan-**Deef** neh-shif*	تنظيف جاف
Is there a <u>laundry</u> near here?	*fee magh-sa-la "u-ray-**yi**-ba?*	هل توجد مغسلة قريبة
▪ an ironer	▪ *mak-**wa**-gee*	مكوجي ، محل للكي
I want to have these — .	*dee — .*	هذه — .
▪ washed	▪ *lil-gha-**seel***	للغسيل
▪ dry cleaned	▪ *lit-tan-**Deef** in-neh-shif*	للتنظيف الجاف
▪ mended	▪ *lit-taS-**leeH***	للتصليح
▪ ironed	▪ *lil-**mak**-wa*	للكي
Here's the list.	*it-**faD**-Dal il-"ay-ma.*	هذه هي القائمة

[See Shopping section for clothes words.]

When will it/they be ready?	*Hat-**koon gah**-za 'im-ta?*	متى ستكون جاهزة؟
I need them for tonight.	*a-na miH-**tehg**-ha [miH-ta-**geh**-ha] bil-**leyl***	أريدهم الليلة
■ tomorrow	■ ***buk**-ra*	غداً
■ the day after tomorrow	■ *ba^c-di **buk**-ra*	بعد غد
I am leaving soon.	*a-na mi-**seh**-fir [mi-**saf**-ra] "u-**ray**-yib.*	سأسافر قريبا
■ tomorrow	■ ***buk**-ra*	غداً
Is my laundry ready?	*il-gha-**seel** bi-teh-^cee **geh**-hiz?*	هل غسيلي جاهز ؟
This isn't my laundry.	*dee mish bi-**ta**^c-tee.*	هذه ليست لي
There's something missing.	*fee **Ha**-ga **na"**-Sa.*	ينقص شيء ما
There's a button missing.	*fee zu-**raar naa**-"iS.*	ينقص زر
This is silk.	*da Ha-**reer**.*	هذا حرير

SHOE REPAIRS

| Can you repair these shoes for me? | ***mum**-kin ti-Sal-**laH**-lee ig-**gaz**-ma dee?* | هل يمكن أن تصلح هذه الأحذية لي ؟ |

They need new heels.	*leh*-zim *ka^cb* gi-**deed**.	تحتاج لكعب جديد
▨ soles	▨ *na^cl*	لنعل
Can you fix it while I wait?	*mum*-kin ti-Sal-**laH**-ha **Heh**-lan?	هل يمكن تصليحها حالا ؟
Would you polish them too?	*mum*-kin ti-lam-ma^c-**heh**-lee ka-**mehn**?	هل يمكن أن تلمعها ايضاً؟
I need them tomorrow.	*a*-na miH-**tehg**-ha [miH-ta-**geh**-ha] buk-ra.	احتاجها غداً

WATCH REPAIRS

Can you fix this watch for me?	*mum*-kin ti-Sal-**laH**-lee is-**seh**-^ca dee?	هل تستطيع إصلاح هذه الساعة لي ؟
▨ this alarm clock	▨ il-mi-**nab**-bih da?	هذا المنبه
It needs a new strap.	^c*aw*-za 'us-**teek** gi-**deed**	تحتاج لأوستيك جديد
▨ crystal (glass)	▨ "i-**zehz**	لزجاج
▨ hour hand	▨ ^c*a*"-rab sa-^c**eht**	لعقرب ساعات
▨ minute hand	▨ ^c*a*"-rab da-"**eh**-yi"	لعقرب دقائق
▨ second hand	▨ ^c*a*"-rab sa-**weh**-nee	لعقرب ثواني
▨ battery	▨ baT-Ta-**ree**-ya	لبطارية
It's stopped.	*wi*"-fit.	توقفت

It's fast.	*bit-"ad-dim.*	تقدم
It's slow.	*bit-'akh-khar.*	تؤخر
It needs cleaning.	*ᶜaw-za tan-Deef.*	تحتاج لتنظيف
When will it be ready?	*hat-koon gah-za 'im-ta?*	متى ستكون جاهزة ؟
May I have a receipt?	*mum-kin tid-dee-nee waSl?*	أرجوك أعطني إيصالاً

CAMERA REPAIRS

Can you fix this camera?	*mum-kin ti-Sal-laH-lee ik-ka-me-ra dee?*	
		هل يمكن تصليح آلة التصوير هذه ؟
There's a problem with — .	*fee mush-ki-la ma-ᶜa — .*	
		هناك مشكلة في — .
▪ the exposure counter	▪ *ᶜad-dehd iS-So-war*	عداد الصور
▪ the film winder	▪ *di-rehᶜ it-tagh-yeer*	ذراع التغيير
▪ the light meter	▪ *gi-hehz it-taᶜ-reeD/ miq-yehs iD-Doh'*	مقياس الضوء
▪ the rangefinder	▪ *Daa-bit il-ma-seh-fa*	ضابط المسافة
▪ the shutter	▪ *il-gheh-li", ish-sha-tar*	الغالق

| How much will it cost to fix it? | *it-taS-**leeH** hay-**kal**-lif kam?* | كم يكلف تصليحها ؟ |

| When can I come and get it? | *as-ti-**lim**-ha 'im-ta?* | متى أحضر لاستلامها ؟ |

| I need it as soon as possible. | *ᶜa-**wiz**-ha [ᶜaw-**zeh**-ha] fi ' **a**"-rab wa"t **mum**-kin.* | احتاجها في أقرب وقت ممكن |

MEDICAL CARE

AT THE PHARMACY

Where is the nearest <u>pharmacy</u>?	*feyn 'a"-rab 'ag-za-kheh-na/ Say-Da-lee-ya?*	أين أقرب أجزخانة/ صيدلية؟
■ all-night pharmacy	■ *'ag-za-kheh-na ley-lee-ya*	■ أجزخانة ليلية
At what times does it open (close)?	*bi-yif-taH (bi-yi"-fil) is-seh-ʿa kam?*	متى تفتح (تغلق)؟
I need something for — .	*ʿa-wiz [ʿaw-za] Ha-ga li — .*	أريد دواء —
■ asthma	■ *ir-rabw*	■ للربو
■ a cold	■ *zu-kehm, il-bard*	■ للبرد
■ constipation	■ *il-'im-sehk*	■ للامساك
■ a cough	■ *kuH-Ha*	■ للسعال
■ diarrhea	■ *il-'is-hehl*	■ للاسهال
■ a fever	■ *su-khu-nee-ya*	■ للحمى
■ hay fever	■ *Ha-seh-see-ya ra-bee-ʿee-ya*	■ للحساسية الربيعية
■ headache	■ *Su-daaʿ*	■ للصداع
■ indigestion	■ *soo'il-haDm*	■ لسوء الهضم
■ insomnia	■ *ʿa-dam in-nohm*	■ للأرق
■ nausea	■ *gham-ma-mehn*	■ لغثيان النفس

▓ sunburn	▓ *Hu-roo" ish-shams*	حروق الشمس
▓ toothache	▓ *wa-ga^c fiD-Dirs*	لألم الأسنان
▓ an upset stomach	▓ *ta-^cab fil-mi^c-da*	لاضطراب المعدة

Do I need a
prescription for
this medicine?

leh-zim ru-shit-ta lid-da-wa da?

هل أحتاج لروشتة لهذا الدواء؟

Can you fill this
prescription for
me now?

*mum-kin tiS-rif-lee ir-ru-shit-ta dee
dil-wa'''-tee?*

هل يمكنك أن تصرف الروشتة لي الآن؟

Do you stock
this medicine?

^can-du-kum id-da-wa da?

هل عندكم هذا الدواء؟

It's an emergency.   *da Ta-waa-ri'.*   هذه طوارىء

Can I wait for it?   *as-tan-neh-ha?*   هل انتظره؟

How long will
it take?

ha-yeh-khud "ad-di 'eyh?

كم من الوقت يحتاج ؟

I would like — .   *^ca-wiz [^caw-za] — .*   أريد — .

▓ adhesive tape	▓ *mu-sham-ma^c laa-Siq*	شريط لاصق
▓ antacid	▓ *da-wa Didd il-Hu-moo-Da*	دواء ضد الحموضة
▓ an antiseptic	▓ *mu-Tah-hir*	مطهر
▓ aspirins	▓ *as-bi-reen*	أسبرين

■ bandages	■ *ru-baaT*	رباط
■ Band-Aids	■ *blaas-tir*	ضمادات لاصقة
■ corn plasters	■ *blaas-tir ʿa-shehn il-kal-loo*	
		ضمادات لاصقة للمسامير
■ (absorbent) cotton	■ *"uTn Tib-bee*	قطن طبي
■ cough drops	■ *bas-til-ya liz-zohr*	باستيليا طبية
■ cough syrup	■ *da-wa kuH-Ha*	دواء للسعال
■ ear (nose) drops	■ *nu-"aT lil-widn* (للأنف)	نقط للأذن
	(lil-ma-na-kheer)	
■ eye drops	■ *"aT-ra lil-ʿeyn*	نقط للعين
■ an inhaler	■ *bakh-kheh-kha*	جهاز للاستنشاق
■ insect repellent	■ *kreym Taa-rid lil-Ha-sha-raat*	
		كريم طارد للحشرات
■ iodine	■ *Sab-ghit yood*	يود
■ a (mild) laxative	■ *mu-lay-yin*	مسهل
■ milk of magnesia	■ *maH-lool il-magh-nee-sya*	
		محلول المغنيزيا
■ painkillers	■ *mu-sak-ki-neht*	مسكنات
■ potassium permanganate	■ *ber-min-ga-neht il-bu-tas-yoom*	
		برمنجنات البوتاسيوم
■ sanitary napkins	■ *fo-waT SiH-Hee-ya*	فوط صحية

▧ sleeping pills	▦ *Hu-**boob** mu-naw-**wi**-ma*	حبوب منومة
▧ suppositories	▦ *lu-**boos**, mu-**sah**-hil*	لبوس
▧ tampons	▦ ***tam**-paks*	تامبونات طبية
▧ a thermometer	▦ *tir-mo-**mitr**, mi-**zehn** Ha-**raa**-ra*	ثرمومتر
▧ tranquilizers	▦ *mu-had-di-'**eht***	مهدئات
▧ vitamins	▦ *vi-ta-mi-**neht***	فيتامينات

Do you have care products for <u>contact lenses</u>?	*^can-**du**-kum maH-**lool** lil-^ca-da-**seht** il-**laS**-qa?*	هل عندكم محلول عدسات لاصقة ؟
▧ hard lenses	▦ *li l-^ca-da-**seht** in-**nash**-fa*	عدسات صلبة
▧ soft lenses	▦ *li l-^ca-da-**seht** iT-Ta-**ree**-ya*	عدسات لينة

FINDING A DOCTOR

Most doctors you will come across in the Middle East are likely to have a good working knowledge of English, because English is used in the teaching of medicine in many Arab countries.

I need a doctor.	***a**-na miH-**tehg** [miH-**teh**-ga] Ta-**beeb**.*	أنا محتاج لطبيب

Do you know a doctor who speaks English?	**ti**^c-raf Ta-**beeb** bi-yit-**kal**-lim in-gi-**lee**-zee **kway**-yis?	هل تعرف طبيبا يتكلم الانجليزية بطلاقة ؟
Where is his office (his clinic)?	mak-**ta**-boo (^cee-**yat**-too) feyn?	أين مكتبه (عيادته) ؟
Where is the hospital?	il-mus-**tash**-fa feyn?	أين المستشفى ؟

TALKING TO THE DOCTOR

I don't feel well.	**a**-na ta^c-**behn** [ta^c-**beh**-na] .	أشعر بتعب
I feel sick.	**nif**-see **gham**-ma ^ca-**leh**-ya.	أشعر بغثيان النفس
I feel dizzy.	**a**-na **deh**-yikh [**day**-kha].	أشعر بدوخة.
It hurts me here.	bi-yiw-**ga**^c-nee **hi**-na.	الألم هنا
My <u>ear</u> hurts.	<u>**wid**</u>-nee bi-tiw-**ga**^c-nee.	اذني تؤلمني
▪ eye	▪ ^c**ey**-nee	عيني
▪ foot	▪ **rig**-lee	قدمي
▪ hand	▪ '**ee**-dee	يدي
▪ head	▪ **raa**-see	رأسي
▪ neck	▪ ra-"**ab**-tee	عنقي
▪ knee	▪ ruk-**bi**-tee	ركبتي
▪ leg	▪ **rig**-lee	رجلي

■ wrist	■ *khun-"it 'ee-dee*	رسغي
My <u>arm</u> hurts.	<u>di-**reh**-^cee</u> *bi-yiw-**ga**^c-nee.*	ذراعي يؤلمني
■ ankle	■ *ka^c-bee*	كعب القدم
■ back	■ *Dah-ree*	ظهري
■ chest	■ *Sid-ree*	صدري
■ elbow	■ *koo-^cee*	كوعي
■ finger	■ *Su-**baa**-^cee*	أصبعي
■ heart	■ *"al-bee*	قلبي
■ hip	■ *ra-da-fee*	ردفي
■ mouth	■ *bu"-"ee*	فمي
■ shoulder	■ *kit-fee*	كتفي
■ tooth	■ *Dir-see*	ضرسي
■ throat	■ *zoh-ree*	حنجرتي
I've broken my — .	*ka-**sart** — .*	— مكسور
My whole body aches.	*kul-li **gis**-mee bi-yiw-**ga**^c-nee.*	كل جسمي يؤلمني
I feel feverish.	*^can-dee su-khu-**nee**-ya.*	أشعر بحمى
I'm constipated.	*^can-dee 'im-sehk.*	عندي إمساك
I have <u>a cold</u>.	*^can-dee zu-**kehm**.*	عندي برد
■ an abscess	■ *khur-**raag***	خراج

▪ something in my eye	▪ *Ha*-ga fi ^c*ey*-nee	شيء في عيني
▪ an infection	▪ 'il-ti-**hehb**	إلتهاب
▪ diabetes	▪ *ma*-raD is-**suk**-kar	مرض السكر
▪ diarrhea	▪ 'is-**hehl**	إسهال
▪ dysentery	▪ du-sin-**tar**-ya	دوسنتاريا
▪ hepatitis	▪ 'il-ti-**hehb** ka-bi-dee	إلتهاب كبدي
▪ a stomachache	▪ ta^c-ab fil-**mi**^c-da	ألم في المعدة

I am pregnant.	*a*-na **Heh**-mil.	أنا حامل
I'm (not) allergic to — .	^c*an*-dee (ma-^c*an*-**deesh**) Ha-sa-**see**-ya min — .	(ليس) عندي حساسية ــ .
▪ antibiotics	▪ mu-Da-**Daat** ha-ya-**wee**-ya	للمضادات الحيوية
▪ penicillin	▪ bi-ni-sil-**leen**	للبنسلين
I had a heart attack — years ago.	**gat**-lee 'az-ma qal-**bee**-ya min — si-**neen**.	أصبت بأزمة قلبية من ــ سنة .
I have high (low) blood pressure.	^c*an*-dee **Daght** ^ceh-lee (**waa**-Tee).	عندي ضغط دم مرتفع (منخفض)
Do I have <u>appendicitis</u>?	^c*an*-dee <u>'il-ti-**hehb** iz-**zay**-da</u>?	هل عندي إلتهاب الزائدة ؟
▪ tonsillitis	▪ 'il-ti-**hehb** il-**li**-waz	إلتهاب اللوز
▪ flu	▪ in-floo-**in**-za	إنفلونزا
Do I have to go to hospital?	**leh**-zim **ad**-khul il-mus-**tash**-fa?	هل يجب أن اذهب للمستشفى ؟

What can I eat and drink?	***mum*-kin 'eh-kul wash-rab 'eyh?**	ماذا أستطيع أن آكل وأشرب ؟

Doctor's Instructions

Open your mouth.	***if*-taH bu"-"ak/fum-mak.**	إفتح فمك
Stick out your tongue.	***Tal*-laᶜ li-seh-nak.**	أخرج لسانك
Cough.	*kuHH.*	إسعل
Breathe deeply.	khud ***na*-fas Ta-weel.**	خذ نفساً طويلاً
Take off your clothes (to the waist).	**i"-laᶜ hu-doo-mak (il-lee foh").**	إخلع ملابسك (حتى الوسط)
Lie down <u>on your back</u>.	nehm ᶜa-la ***Dah*-rak.**	ارقد على ظهرك
▪ on your stomach	ᶜa-la ***baT*-nak**	على بطنك
Get dressed.	***il*-bis [il-bi-see].**	إلبس

Patient

Are you going to give me a prescription?	ha-tid-***dee*-nee ru-shit-ta?**	هل ستعطني روشتة ؟
How often should I take this?	a-***khud*-ha kul-li "ad-di 'eyh?**	كم مرة في اليوم سآخذ من هذا ؟
(How long) do I have to stay in bed?	**leh-zim a"-ᶜud fis-si-reer ("ad-di 'eyh)?**	(حتى متى) سأبقى بالسرير؟
Do you need <u>a blood sample</u>?	**in-ta ᶜa-wiz <u>ᶜay-yi-nit damm</u>?**	هل تحتاج لعينة دم ؟
▪ a urine sample	▪ ᶜay-***yi*-nit bool**	عينة بول

Will you test my blood pressure?	*hat-**shoof** DakhT id-**damm**?*	هل ستقيس ضغط الدم ؟
Should I have X rays taken?	*ha-ti^c-**mil**-lee 'a-**shi**^{c}-^{c}a?*	هل أقوم بعمل أشعة ؟
What is your fee?	***kam** 'at-^{c}**eh**-bak?*	كم أتعابك ؟
I have medical insurance.	*^{c}**an**-dee ta'-**meen** SiH-Hee.*	عندي تامين صحي
Thank you very much.	*'al-fi shukr.*	شكراً جزيلاً

ACCIDENTS AND EMERGENCIES

Help!	*il-Ha-"**oo**-nee!*	النجدة !
Quickly, get a doctor!	*u**T**-lub Ta-**beeb** **Heh**-lan!*	أطلب الطبيب بسرعة
Call an ambulance!	*heht il-'is-^{c}ehf*	أطلب سيارة الاسعاف
We must go to the hospital.	***leh**-zim ni-**rooH** il-mus-**tash**-fa.*	يجب أن نذهب للمستشفى
I've (he's) lost a lot of blood.	*na-**zaft** (**na**-zaf) damm ki-**teer**.*	فقدت (فقد) دماً كثيراً
I've (he's) had a heart attack.	***gat**-lee (**gat**-loo) 'az-ma qal-**bee**-ya.*	اصبت (أصيب) بازمة قلبية
I think the bone is broken.	*a-**Zunn** inn il-^{c} **aDm** in-**ka**-sar.*	اعتقد أن العظم مكسور

I cut myself.	*in-ga-**raHt**.*	جرحت نفسي
I burned myself.	*it-Ha-**ra**"t.*	حرقت نفسي
I was (he was) knocked down.	*kha-ba-**Tit**-nee (kha-ba-**Ti**-too) ^ca-ra-**bee**-ya.*	صدمتني (صدمته) سيارة
I was (he was) bitten by a dog.	*kalb ^caD-**Di**-nee (^caD-**Doo**).*	عضني (عضه) كلب
rabies	*ma-raD il-**kalb***	مرض الكلب

AT THE DENTIST

Can you recommend a dentist?	***mum**-kin ti-"**ul**-lee ^ca-la Ta-beeb 'as-**nehn** kway-yis?*	هل تستطيع أن تقترح طبيب أسنان ؟
I'd like to make an appointment.	*^ca-wiz [^caw-za] aH-giz ma-^cehd.*	أريد أن أحجز موعداً
I must see him as soon as possible.	***leh**-zim a-**shoo**-foo fi 'a"-rab wa"t **mum**-kin.*	يجب أن أراه في أقرب وقت ممكن
I have an awful toothache.	*'as-**neh**-nee bi-tiw-**ga**^c-nee gid-dan.*	عندي ألم أسنان رهيب
I've lost a filling	*il-**Hashw** wi-"i^c.*	وقع الحشو
I've lost a crown.	*iT-Tar-**boosh** wi-"i^c.*	وقع الطربوش
I've broken a tooth.	*fee **sin**-na in-**ka**-sa-rit.*	عندي سن مكسور
My gums hurt me.	*il-**li**-sa bi-tiw-**ga**^c-nee.*	لثتي تؤلمني

| Is there an infection? | *fee "il-ti-**hehb**?* | هل هناك إلتهاب ؟ |

| Will it have to be extracted? | ***leh**-zim tit-**khi**-li^c?* | هل يجب أن تخلع السن ؟ |

Will you fill it — ?   *ha-tiH-**shee**-ha — ?*   هل ستحشوه — ؟

▨ temporarily	▨ *mu-'aq-**qa**-tan*	مؤقتاً
▨ with amalgam	▨ *bi Hashw ^c**eh**-dee*	بحشو عادي
▨ with gold	▨ *bi Hashw **da**-hab*	بذهب
▨ with silver	▨ *bi Hashw **faD**-Da*	بفضة
▨ with platinum	▨ *bi Hashw bla-**teen***	ببلاتين

I need a painkiller.   *^c**a**-wiz [^c**aw**-za] mu-**sak**-kin.*

أحتاج لمسكن

Can you fix ____?   ***mum**-kin ti-**Sal**-laH — ?*

هل تستطيع إصلاح — ؟

▨ this bridge	▨ *ik-**kub**-ree da*	هذا الكوبري
▨ this crown	▨ *iT-Tar-**boosh** da*	هذا الطربوش
▨ this denture	▨ *iT-**Ta**"-mi da*	هذا الطاقم

| When should I come back? | ***ar**-ga^c '**im**-ta?* | متى أعود ؟ |

| What is your fee? | *'**ug**-ri-tak kam?* | كم أتعابك ؟ |

WITH THE OPTICIAN

Is there an optician near here?	*fee na-Da-Da-**raa**-tee "u-**ray**-yib min **hi**-na?*	هل يوجد محل للنظارات قريب ؟
Can you repair these glasses for me?	***mum**-kin ti-Sal-**laH**-lee in-naD-**Daa**-ra dee?*	هل يمكنك إصلاح هذه النظارة لي ؟
Can you put in a new lens?	***mum**-kin ti-**rak**-kib Ha-gar gi-**deed**?*	هل تستطيع تركيب عدسة جديدة ؟
Can you repair the frame?	***mum**-kin ti-Sal-**laH**-lee ish-**sham**-bar?*	هل يمكنك أن تصلح الاطار ؟
I (don't) have the prescription.	*ᶜ**an**-dee (ma-ᶜan-**deesh**) il-ma-"ehs.*	(ليس) معي قياس النظر
Can you do an eye test now?	***mum**-kin tiᶜ-**mil**-lee ma-"ehs na-Zar dil-**wa**"-tee?*	هل يمكنك عمل قياس النظر الآن ؟
Do you sell contact lenses?	*ᶜan-**du**-kum ᶜa-da-**seht** laS-qa?*	هل تبيع عدسات لاصقة ؟
▨ hard	▨ ***nash**-fa*	صلبة
▨ soft	▨ *Ta-**ree**-ya*	لينة
I've lost a lens.	*Daa-ᶜit ᶜa-da-sa*	فقدت عدسة
Can you replace it right away?	***mum**-kin tid-**dee**-nee waH-da dil-**wa**"-tee?*	هل تستطيع إستبدالها حالاً ؟

COMMUNICATIONS

POST OFFICE

Where's the nearest post office?	*feyn 'a"-rab **mak**-tab ba-**reed**?* أين أقرب مكتب بريد ؟
Where's a mailbox?	*feyn san-**doo**" il-**bus**-Ta?* أين صندوق البريد ؟
What's the postage on — to America?	*'eyh '**ug**-rit il-ba-**reed** li 'am-**ree**-ka* *^ca-**shehn** — ?* كم أجرة البريد لأمريكا — ؟
▪ this letter	▪ *ig-ga-**wehb**-da* لهذا الخطاب
▪ an airmail letter	▪ *ga-**wehb** bil-ba-**reed*** خطاب *ig-**gaw**-wee* بالبريد الجوي
▪ a postcard	▪ *kart bus-**tehl*** لبطاقة بريدية
▪ this package	▪ *iT-**Tar**-di da* لهذا الطرد
I'd like to send this — .	*^ca-wiz [^caw-za]* — أريد إرسال هذا *ab-^cat da* — .
▪ by surface mail	▪ *bil-ba-**reed** il-^c**eh**-dee* بالبريد العادي
▪ by registered post	▪ *bil-ba-**reed** il-mu-**sag**-gal* بالبريد المسجل
▪ by special delivery (express)	▪ *bil-ba-**reed** il-mis-**ta**^c-gil* بالبريد المستعجل
▪ cash on delivery	▪ *id-**daf**^{c c} and it-tas-**leem*** الدفع عند التسليم

Is a customs declaration form necessary?	*leh-zim 'is-ti-maa-rit ig-gum-ruk?*	هل تلزم استمارة الجمرك ؟
Could you give me a receipt?	*mum-kin tid-dee-nee waSl?*	هل يمكنك أن تعطني إيصالاً ؟
When will it arrive?	*ha-yiw-Sal 'im-ta?*	متى ستصل ؟
Which is the window for — ?	*min an-hee shib-behk ash-ti-ree — ?*	أين شباك — ؟
▪ stamps	▪ *Ta-waa-bi^c*	الطوابع
▪ money orders	▪ *Ho-wa-leht meh-lee-ya*	الحوالات المالية
Do you have a photocopier?	*^{c}an-du-kum ma-ka-nit fo-to-ko-pee?*	هل عندكم آلة نسخ؟
I would like two copies.	*a-na ^{c}a-wiz [^{c}aw-za] nus-khi-teyn.*	أريد نسختين
Where is the general delivery (poste restante)?	*feyn mak-tab tas-leem ig-ga-wa-beht?*	أين مكتب تسليم الخطابات ؟
My name is — .	*'is-mee — .*	إسمي — .
Are there any letters for me?	*fee ga-wa-beht ^{c}a-sheh-nee?*	هل هناك خطابات لي ؟

TELECOMMUNICATIONS

ELECTRONIC COMMUNICATION
Most words relating to new technology have been borrowed from English (sometimes from French, in N. Africa). Equivalents in written, literary Arabic have usually been invented, but these are not always widely known or used.

Where is the telegram section?	feyn shib-**behk** it-til-ligh-ra-**feht**?	أين شباك التلغراف ؟
I'd like to send a telegram to — .	ᶜa-wiz [ᶜaw-za] **ab**-ᶜat til-li-**ghraaf** li — .	أريد إرسال تلغراف لـ —
How much is it per word?	ik-**kil**-ma bi kam?	كم سعر الكلمة ؟
May I have a form, please.	id-**dee**-nee 'is-ti-**maa**-ra min **faD**-lak.	اعطني إستمارة من فضلك
I want to send it collect.	ᶜa-wiz [ᶜaw-za] inn il-mus-**ta**-lim **yid**-faᶜ.	أريد أن يدفع المستلم
Do you have a fax machine?	ᶜan-dak **ma**-ka-nit faks?	هل عندكم آلة فاكس؟
I <u>want to send</u> three pages.	a-na ᶜ**a**-wiz [ᶜaw-za] **ab**-ᶜat ta-lat 'aw-**reh**"	أريد إرسال ثلاث أوراق.
▦ am expecting	mis-**tan**-nee [mis-tan-**nee**-ya]	مستني
I want to <u>send an e-mail.</u>	ᶜa-wiz [ᶜaw-za] **ab**-ᶜat ee-**meyl**	أريد إرسال رسالة إلكترونية.
▦ look at my e-mail	a-**shoof** il-ee-**meyl** bi-teh-ᶜee	قراءة رسائلي الإلكترونية.

Where is — ?	*feyn — ?*	أين — ؟
■ a public telephone	■ *ti-li-fohn ^camm*	تليفون عام
■ a telephone directory	■ *da-leel ti-li-foh-neht*	دليل التليفون
I'd like a phonecard	*^ca-wiz [^caw-za] kart ti-li-fohn*	أريد بطاقة تليفون.
I want to find this name.	*^ca-wiz [^caw-za] a-leh-"ee il-'is-mi da.*	أريد أن أجد هذا الاسم
May I use your phone?	*mum-kin as-ta^c-mil it-ti-li-fohn?*	هل أستطيع إستعمال هذا التليفون ؟
I have a mobile phone	*^can-dee mo-bayl*	عندي تليفون قابل للحمل.
Do you have an answerphone?	*^can-dak an-sir-fohn?*	هل عندك آلة تسجيل لرسائل تليفونية؟
I will send you an e-mail	*hab-^cat-lak ee-meyl*	سوف أبعث لك رسالة إلكترونية.
This is my e-mail address.	*it-faD-Dal ^cin-wehn il-ee-meyl bit-teh-^cee*	هذا عنواني الإلكتروني.
I want access to the internet	*^ca-wiz [^caw-za] at-far-rag ^cal-in-ter-net*	أريد قراءة الإنترنت.
I want to make a — .	*^ca-wiz [^caw-za] a^c-mil mu-kal-ma — .*	أريد عمل —
■ local call	■ *ma-Hal-lee-ya*	مكالمة محلية
■ person-to-person call	■ *shakh-See-ya*	مكالمة شخصية

Can I call direct?	*fee khaTT mu-**beh**-shir?*
	هل أستطيع الاتصال مباشرة ؟
I'd like to reverse the the charges.	*ᶜa-wiz [ᶜaw-za] inn ish-shakhS il-maT-**loob** yid-faᶜ.* أريد أن يدفع الشخص المطلوب
I'd like to book a call to — .	*ᶜa-wiz [ᶜaw-za] aH-giz mu-**kal**-ma li — .* أريد حجز مكالمة لـ ـــ .
How long will it take?	*ha-**yeh**-khud kam wa"t?* هل يجب أن أنتظر مدة طويلة ؟
I'd like to cancel the call.	*ᶜa-wiz [ᶜaw-za] al-ghee il-mu-**kal**-ma.* أريد إلغاء المكالمة
How much does it cost — ?	*— bi kam?* كم سعر — ؟
▪ per minute	▪ *id-da-"**ee**-"a* الدقيقة
▪ for three minutes	▪ *ta-lat da-"**eh**-yi"* الثلاث دقائق
Please give me Cairo 4810572.	*min **faD**-lak id-**dee**-nee il-qaa-**hi**-ra ar-**ba**-ᶜa ta-**man**-ya weh-Hid Sifr **kham**-sa sab-ᶜa it-**neyn*** من فضلك اعطني القاهرة ٤٨١٠٥٧٢ (see p. 17 for numbers)

(see p. 17 for numbers)

My number is — .	*nim-**ri**-tee — .* رقمي —
Is Mr. [Mrs.] — in?	*is-**say**-yid [ma-**dehm**/is-say-**yi**-da] — **maw**-good [maw-**goo**-da]?* هل السيد — موجود [السيدة — موجودة] ؟
— isn't in.	*— mish maw-**good**.* — ليس موجود

May I speak to — ?	*mum-kin a-kal-lim — ?*	هل يمكن أن أتكلم مع — ؟
Hello.	*'a-loh.*	آلو
This is — .	*a-na — .*	أنا —
Who is calling?	*meen bi-yit-kal-lim?*	من يتكلم ؟
One moment.	*laH-Za.*	لحظة
I can't hear.	*mish seh-mi^c [sam-^{c}a]*.	لا أسمع
Speak louder.	*ir-fa^c Soh-tak [ir-fa-^{c}ee Soh-tik]*.	إرفع صوتك
Don't hang up.	*khal-leek [khal-lee-kee] ma-^{c}eh-ya.*	لا تغلق
It's a bad line.	*il-khaTT wi-Hish.*	الخط سيء
I'll try again.	*ha-gar-rab khaT-Ti teh-nee.*	سأحاول مرة ثانية
There's no reply.	*ma-Had-dish bee-rudd.*	لا إجابة
The line is busy.	*il-khaTT mash-ghool.*	الخط مشغول
Wrong number.	*nim-ra gha-laT.*	الرقم خطأ
I was cut off.	*il-khaTT in-"a-Ta^c*	قطع الخط
Please dial it again.	*uT-lub in-nim-ra teh-nee min-faD-lak.*	أرجوك حاول ثانية
I want to leave a message.	*^{c}a-wiz [^{c}aw-za] a-seeb ri-seh-la.*	أريد أن أترك رسالة
How much was the call?	*keh-nit bi kam il-mu-kal-ma?*	كم كان سعر المكالمة ؟

DRIVING A CAR

SIGNS

No parking	*mam-**noo**^{c} il-'in-ti-**Zaar***	ممنوع الانتظار
No stopping	*mam-**noo**^{c} il-wu-"**oof***	ممنوع الوقوف
Caution	***iH**-dar*	إحذر
Stop	*qif*	قف
Slow	*hadd is-**sur**-^{c}a*	هدىء السرعة
Danger	***kha**-Tar*	خطر
Work in progress	*man-**Ti**-qit ^{c}**a**-mal*	منطقة عمل
School	*mad-**ra**-sa*	مدرسة
Hospital	*mus-**tash**-fa*	مستشفى
Motorway	*Ta-**ree**" sa-**ree**^{c}*	طريق سريع
One way	*it-ti-**geh** weh-Hid*	إتجاه واحد
No entry	*mam-**noo**^{c} id-du-**khool***	ممنوع الدخول
Detour	*taH-**wee**-la*	تحويلة
Dangerous bends	*mun-**Ha**-na kha-Tar*	منحنى خطر
Keep right (left)	***il**-zim il-yi-**meen*** (***ish**-shi-mehl*)	الزم اليمين (اليسار)

CAR RENTALS

Where can I rent a car?	*min feyn a-'**ag**-gar* <u>*^ca-ra-**bee**-ya/say-**yaa**-ra?*</u>	من أين استأجر سيارة ؟
▦ a motorcycle	▦ *mo-to-**sikl***	دراجة بخارية
▦ a bicycle	▦ *^ca-ga-la*	دراجة
▦ a scooter	▦ *skoo-tar*	دراجة صغيرة
I want a — car.	*^ca-wiz [^caw-za] ^ca-ra-**bee**-ya/ say-**yaa**-ra* — .	أريد سيارة — .
▦ small	▦ *Su-ghay-**ya**-ra*	صغيرة
▦ large	▦ *ki-**bee**-ra*	كبيرة
▦ sports	▦ *spoor*	سبور
▦ automatic	▦ *'u-tu-ma-**teek***	أوتوماتيكي
How much does it cost — ?	*bi kam* — ?	بكم — ؟
▦ per day	▦ *fil-**yohm***	في اليوم
▦ per week	▦ *fil-'us-**boo**^c*	في الاسبوع
Does that include full insurance?	*da bit-ta'-**meen** ik-**keh**-mil?*	هل هذا يشمل التأمين الكامل ؟
Is the gas included?	*da bil-ban-**zeen**?*	هل هذا يشمل البنزين ؟
Do you accept credit cards?	*bi-ti"-**ba**-loo **kri**-dit kard?*	هل تقبلوا بطاقات إعتماد ؟

احترس نوجد حيوانات

Caution: Animal Crossing

طريق غير ممهد

Bumpy Road

كوبري متحرك

Draw Bridge

طريق ضيق

Narrow Road

منحنى مزدوج
الأول للیسار

Double curves (S-curve)
(First one to the left)

منحدر خطر

Dangerous Incline

احترس

Caution

عبور المشاه

Pedestrian Crossing

مركز إسعاف

Ambulance Center

لافته تشير إلى الاتجاهات

Sign indicating directions

علامة نهاية المدينة

Sign indicating city limits

ممنوع الانتظار في الأيام الفردية
No standing on odd days

ممنوع الوقوف قطعاً
Absolutely no parking

كوبري بارتفاع منخفض
Low clearance bridge

ممنوع الانتظار للأيام الزوجية
No standing on even days

ممنوع الانتظار
No standing

المرور في اتجاهين
Passage in both directions

مزلقان مفتوح
Open crossing

طريق غير ممهد
Bumpy road (potholes)

ممنوع الدخول
No entry

أقصى عرض ٢ متر
Maximum Width 2 meters

انتهاء نطاقة تحديد الانتظار
End of no standing zone

Here's my driver's license.	*it-**faD**-Dal ir-**rukh**-Sa.*	تفضل ها هي الرخصة
Here's my passport.	*it-**faD**-Dal il-baS-**boor**/ga-**wehz** is-**sa**-far.*	تفضل ها هو جواز السفر
Do I have to leave a deposit?	***leh**-zim ad-fac car-**boon**?*	هل يجب ان اترك عربونا ؟
I want to rent the car here and leave it in — .	*ca-wiz [caw-za] a-'ag-gar il-ca-ra-**bee**-ya **hi**-na w a-**seeb**-ha fi — .. —*	أريد إستئجار السيارة هنا وتسليمها في — .. —
What kind of gas does it take?	*a-HuT-**Til**-ha ban-**zeen** 'eyh?*	ما نوع البنزين الذي تستخدمه السيارة ؟

Renting a car tends to be expensive, and facilities are usually rather limited; you may have little choice of drop-off points and if you break down it may take some time to repair or replace the car.

Driving techniques in the big cities can be hair-raising. You will encounter every kind of wheeled and four-legged transport, few of them respecting the highway code.

Bear in mind, too, that in the case of an accident, especially in Saudi Arabia and some of the Gulf countries, you could be involved in extremely lengthy legal proceedings, irrespective of who was at fault. You may well decide it is preferable to hire a driver for short periods of time or use public transportation, which is generally both cheap and efficient.

ON THE ROAD

[For more directions see Getting Around.]

Excuse me . . .	*law sa-**maHt** . . .*	بعد إذنك

Can you tell me . . . ?	***tis*-maH ti-"*ul*-lee . . . ?**	أرجوك ان تقول لي . . .
Which way is it to — ?	*min feyn iT-Ta-**ree**" li — ?*	ما هو الطريق إلى — ؟
We're lost.	***tuh*-na.**	ضللنا الطريق ، تهنا
Is this the road to — ?	*da Ta-**ree**" — ?*	هل هذا هو الطريق إلى — ؟
Where does this road go?	*iT-Ta-**ree**"da bee-**wad**-dee ᶜa-la **feyn**?*	إلى أين يؤدي هذا الطريق ؟
How far is it to the next town?	*'**a**"-rab **ba**-lad ᶜa-la **bu**ᶜd "ad-di '**eyh**?*	كم نبعد عن البلدة القادمة ؟
What's the next town called?	*'eyh 'ism il-**ba**-lad ig-**gay**-ya?*	ما هو إسم البلدة القادمة ؟
Can you show me on the map?	***mum*-kin ti-war-ri-**heh**-lee ᶜal-kha-**ree**-Ta?**	هل ممكن أن توضح لي الطريق على الخريطة ؟
Is the road in good condition?	*is-**sik**-ka kway-**yi**-sa?*	هل حالة الطريق جيدة ؟
Is the road to — open?	*iT-Ta-**ree**" li — maf-**tooH**?*	هل الطريق إلى — مفتوح ؟
How far is the next filling station?	*feyn '**a**"-rab ma-**HaT**-Tit ban-**zeen**?*	أين أقرب محطة بنزين ؟

AT THE SERVICE STATION

English	Transliteration	Arabic
I need gas.	*^ca-wiz [^caw-za] ban-zeen.*	أريد بنزينا
Fill her up with — .	*im-la l-khaz-zehn bi —.*	إملأها ب — .
■ diesel	■ *dee-zil*	ديزل
■ regular	■ *ban-zeen ^ceh-dee*	بنزين عادي
■ super	■ *soo-bar/mum-tehz*	سوبر / ممتاز
Give me — liters.	*HuT-Til-ha — litr.*	أعطني — لتر
Please check — .	*min faD-lak shoof-lee —.*	من فضلك إكشف على —
■ the battery	■ *il-baT-Ta-ree-ya*	البطارية
■ the brakes	■ *il-fa-raa-mil*	الفرامل
■ the carburetor	■ *ik-kar-bi-re-teer*	الكاربوراتير
■ the oil	■ *iz-zeyt*	الزيت
■ the spark plugs	■ *il-boo-jey-heht*	البوجيهات
■ the tires	■ *ik-ka-witsh*	الاطارات
■ the tire pressure	■ *DakhT ik-ka-witsh*	ضغط الاطارات
■ the water	■ *il-may-ya*	الماء
Change the oil.	*ghay-yar-lee iz-zeyt.*	غيّر الزيت
Grease the car.	*shaH-Ham-lee il-^ca-ra-bee-ya/ is-say-yaa-ra.*	شحّم السيارة

Charge the battery.	ish-**Hin**-lee il-baT-Ta-**ree**-ya.	
		إشحن البطارية
Change this tire.	ghay-**yar**-lee ik-ka-**witsh** da.	
		غيّر هذا الاطار
Wash the car.	igh-**sil**-lee il-ᶜa-ra-**bee**-ya/	
	is-say-**yaa**-ra.	إغسل السيارة
Where are the rest rooms?	it-twa-**litt** feyn?	
		أين التواليت / دورة المياه ؟
Do you have a phone?	ᶜan-**du**-kum ti-li-**fohn**?	
		هل عندكم تليفون ؟

ACCIDENTS, REPAIRS

My car has broken down.	il-ᶜa-ra-**bee**-ya/is-say-**yaa**-ra ᶜaT-**laa**-na.	سيارتي معطلة
It overheats.	bi-**tis**-khan.	هي تسخن
It doesn't start.	ma-bit-"**umsh**.	هي لا تقوم
I have a flat tire.	ik-ka-**witsh neh**-yim.	الاطار خال من الهواء
I have a puncture.	ik-ka-**witsh** makh-**room**.	الاطار مخروم
The radiator is leaking.	ir-rad-ya-**teer** bee-**khurr**.	الرادياتير يخر
The battery is dead.	il-baT-Ta-**ree**-ya **nay**-ma.	لا تعمل البطارية

English	Transliteration	Arabic
The keys are locked inside the car.	"a-**falt** il-ᶜa-ra-**bee**-ya ᶜa-la l-ma-fa-**teeH**.	أنا قفلت السيارة على المفاتيح
Is there a garage near here?	fee **war**-sha "u-**ray**-yib min **hi**-na?	هل توجد ورشة قريبة ؟
Do you know a good mechanic?	**ti**ᶜ-raf mi-ka-**nee**-kee **kway**-yis?	هل تعرف ميكانيكيا جيداً ؟
I need a mechanic (a tow truck).	**a**-na miH-**tehg** [miH-**teh**-ga] mi-ka-**nee**-kee (wintsh yis-**Hab**-nee).	احتاج ميكانيكي (شاحنة لسحب السيارة).
Do you have the spare part?	ᶜ**an**-dak **qiT**-ᶜit il-ghi-**yaar**?	هل عندك قطعة الغيار ؟
Do you have distilled water?	ᶜ**an**-dak **may**-ya mi-"aT-**Ta**-ra?	هل عندك ماء مقطر ؟
I (don't) have a spare wheel.	ᶜ**an**-dee (ma-ᶜan-**deesh**) is-**tab**-na/ ᶜ**a**-ga-la stibn.	ليس عندي إطار احتياطي
Can you — ?	**mum**-kin — ?	هل من الممكن أن — ؟
▪ help me	▪ ti-sa-ᶜ**id**-nee	تساعدني
▪ push me	▪ ti-zu"-"**i**-nee	تدفعني
▪ tow me	▪ ti-gur-**ri**-nee	تجرني
I don't have any tools.	ma-ᶜan-**deesh** ᶜ**i**-dad.	ليس معي أدوات
Can you lend me — ?	**mum**-kin ti-sal-**lif**-lee — ?	هل يمكن أن تسلفني — ؟
▪ a flashlight	▪ kash-**shehf**	كشاف كهربائي

▦ a hammer	▦ *sha-koosh*	مطرقة ، شاكوش
▦ a jack	▦ *ku-reek, jehk*	جك ، مرفاع
▦ a monkey wrench	▦ *muf-tehH ki-beer/in-gi-lee-zee*	
		مفتاح ربط
▦ a spanner	▦ *muf-tehH Sa-moo-la*	
		مفتاح صواميل
▦ pliers	▦ *zar-ra-dee-ya*	زردية
▦ a screwdriver	▦ *mu-fakk ma-sa-meer*	مفك مسامير

There's something
wrong with the — .

*fee **Ha**-ga **bay**-Za fi — .*

هناك مشكلة في — .

▦ directional signal	▦ *il-fla-shar*	الاشارة
▦ electrical system	▦ *ni-Zaam ik-kah-ra-ba*	الكهرباء
▦ exhaust	▦ *ish-shak-mehn*	أنبوبة العادم
▦ fan	▦ *il-mar-wa-Ha*	المروحة
▦ fan belt	▦ *seer il-mar-wa-Ha*	سير المروحة
▦ fuel pump	▦ *tu-rum-bit il-ban-zeen*	
		طلمبة البنزين
▦ gas tank	▦ *khaz-zehn il-ban-zeen*	
		خزان البنزين
▦ gears	▦ *in-na″-leht, it-tu-roos*	التروس
▦ gearshift	▦ *ᶜa-Sa il-fee-tehs*	ناقل السرعة
▦ horn	▦ *ik-ka-laks, in-ni-feer*	
		البوق ، الكلاكسون

■ ignition	■ *il-'ish-^{c}ehl*	الاشعال
■ radiator	■ *ir-rad-ya-teer*	الرادياتير
■ starter	■ *il-kon-takt*	مبدىء الحركة
■ steering wheel	■ *id-di-rik-syohn/^{c}a-ga-lit*	عجلة القيادة
	is-si-weh-"a	
■ transmission	■ *na"l il-Ha-ra-ka*	نقل الحركة
■ water pump	■ *tu-rum-bit il-may-ya*	طلمبة الماء

EXTERNAL PARTS

bumper	*il-'ak-Si-daam*	الاكصدام
door	*il-behb*	الباب
door handle	*il-'uk-ra*	ممسكة الباب
fender, wing	*ir-raf-raf*	الرفرف
headlights	*ik-kash-sha-feht*	النور الأمامي
hood, bonnet	*ik-kab-boot*	الكبوت
taillight	*il-fa-noos*	النور الخلفي
trunk, boot	*ish-shan-Ta*	صندوق
wheel	*il-^{c}a-ga-la*	عجلة
windshield	*"iz-zehz ish-shib-behk*	
		الحاجب الزجاجي
windshield wipers	*il-mas-sa-Heht*	المساحات

What's the matter?	*'eyh il-mush-**ki**-la?*	ما هي المشكلة ؟
Can you fix it today?	***mum**-kin ti-Sal-laH-**heh**-lee in-na-**har**-da/il-**yohm**?*	هل يمكن أن تصلحها لي اليوم ؟
How long will it take?	*ha-**yeh**-khud "ad-di 'eyh?*	متى ستكون جاهزة ؟
Can you give me a lift to — ?	***mum**-kin ti-waS-**Sal**-nee li — ?*	هل يمكن أن توصلني إلى — ؟
How much do I owe you?	*kam il-Hi-**sehb**?*	كم الحساب ؟

GENERAL INFORMATION

TELLING THE TIME

hour	*seh-ᶜa*	ساعة
half an hour	*nuS-Si seh-ᶜa*	نصف ساعة
a quarter of an hour	*rub-ᶜi seh-ᶜa*	ربع ساعة
twenty minutes	*til-ti seh-ᶜa*	ثلث ساعة
What time is it?	*is-seh-ᶜa kam?*	كم الساعة ؟
It is — .	*is-seh-ᶜa* — .	الساعة — .
12:00	*it-naa-shar*	١٢
1:05	*waH-da wi kham-sa*	١,٠٥
2:10	*it-neyn wi ᶜa-sha-ra*	٢,١٠
3:15	*ta-leh-ta wi rubᶜ*	٣,١٥
4:20	*ar-ba-ᶜa wi tilt*	٤,٢٠
5:25	*kham-sa wi kham-sa wi ᶜish-reen*	٥,٢٥
6:30	*sit-ta wi nuSS*	٦,٣٠
7:35	*sab-ᶜa wi kham-sa wi ta-la-teen*	٧,٣٥
7:40	*ta-man-ya il-la tilt*	٧,٤٠
8:45	*tis-ᶜa il-la rubᶜ*	٨,٤٥

9:50	ᶜ*a-sha-ra* **il-la** ᶜ*a-sha-ra*	٩,٥٠
10:55	*Hi-**daa**-shar* **il-la kham**-sa	١٠,٥٥
11:00	*Hi-**daa**-shar*	١١

EXPRESSIONS OF TIME

At what time (is) — ?	— *is-**seh**-ᶜa* **kam?**	في أي وقت — ؟
When?	'*im-ta?*	متى ؟
at — o'clock	*is-**seh**-ᶜa* —	في الساعة —
at exactly five o'clock	*is-**seh**-ᶜa* **kham**-sa *biZ-**ZabT***	في الساعة الخامسة بالضبط
in (i.e. after) 1 hour	**baᶜ**-di *seh-ᶜa*	بعد ساعة
in (i.e. within) 1 hour	*fi seh-ᶜa*	في خلال ساعة
in 2 hours	*baᶜd (or fi) saᶜ-**teyn***	بعد (في خلال) ساعتين
(not) before 3 o'clock	*(mish)* "*abl is-**seh**-ᶜa ta-**leh**-ta*	(ليس) قبل الساعة الثالثة
(not) after 4:30	*(mish) baᶜd is-**seh**-ᶜa ar-**ba**-ᶜa wi **nuSS***	(ليس) بعد الرابعة والنصف
at about 7 o'clock	*Ha-**weh**-lee is-**seh**-ᶜa sab-ᶜa*	في حوالي الساعة السابعة

between 8 and 9 o'clock	*beyn is-**seh**-ᶜa ta-**man**-ya wi **tis**-ᶜa*	بين الساعة الثامنة والتاسعة
until 6:30	*li **gheh**-yit is-seh-ᶜa sit-ta wi **nuSS***	حتى الساعة السادسة والنصف
I have been waiting — .	***a**-na mis-**tan**-nee* [*mis-tan-**nee**-ya*] — .	أنتظر — .
■ since 3 o'clock	■ *min is-**seh**-ᶜa ta-**leh**-ta*	من الساعة الثالثة
■ for half an hour	■ *ba-"**eh**-lee **nuS**-Si seh-ᶜa*	منذ نصف ساعة
■ for a quarter of an hour	■ *ba-"**eh**-lee **rub**-ᶜi seh-ᶜa*	منذ ربع ساعة
3 hours ago	*min **ta**-lat sa-ᶜeht*	منذ ثلاث ساعات
early	***bad**-ree*	مبكر
late	***wakh**-ree*	متأخر
late (in arriving)	*mut-'**akh**-khir*	متأخر
on time	*fil-ma-ᶜehd*	في الموعد
noon	*iD-**Duhr***	الظهر
midnight	*nuSS il-**leyl***	منتصف الليل
in the morning	*iS-**SubH***	في الصباح
in the afternoon	*baᶜd iD-**Duhr***	بعد الظهر
at night	*bil-**leyl***	بالليل

DAYS OF THE WEEK

What day is today?	*in-na-**har**-da 'eyh?*	أي يوم اليوم ؟
Today is — .	*in-na-**har**-da/il-**yohm** — .*	اليوم — .
Monday	*(yohm) lit-**neyn***	(يوم) الاثنين
Tuesday	*(yohm) it-ta-**leht***	(يوم) الثلاثاء
Wednesday	*(yohm) **lar**-ba^c*	(يوم) الاربعاء
Thursday	*(yohm) il-kha-**mees***	(يوم) الخميس
Friday	*(yohm) ig-**gum**-^{c}a*	(يوم) الجمعة
Saturday	*(yohm) is-**sabt***	(يوم) السبت
Sunday	*(yohm) il-**Hadd***	(يوم) الأحد
last Tuesday	*(yohm) it-ta-**leht** il-lee **feht***	(يوم) الثلاثاء الماضي
yesterday	*im-**beh**-riH/'ams*	أمس
the day before yesterday	*'aw-wil im-**beh**-riH/'ams*	أول أمس
tomorrow	***buk**-ra*	غداً
the day after tomorrow	***ba**^{c}-di **buk**-ra*	بعد غد
next Monday	*(yohm) lit-**neyn** ig-**gayy***	يوم الاثنين القادم
the same day	***nafs** il-**yohm***	نفس اليوم

two days	*yoh-**meyn***	يومان
three days	***ta**-lat ay-**yehm***	ثلاثة أيام
every day	***kul**-li yohm*	كل يوم
day off	*yohm 'a-**geh**-za*	يوم إجازة / عطلة
holiday	*'a-**geh**-za*	إجازة / عطلة
birthday	*ᶜeed mi-**lehd***	عيد ميلاد
from now on	*min **hi**-na wi **reh**-yiH*	في المستقبل
this week	*il-'is-**booᶜ** da*	هذا الأسبوع
last week	*il-'is-**booᶜ** il-lee **feht***	الأسبوع الماضي
next week	*il-'is-**booᶜ** ig-**gayy***	الأسبوع القادم
month	*shahr*	شهر
two months	*shah-**reyn***	شهران
three months	***ta**-lat shu-**hoor***	ثلاثة أشهر
this month	*ish-**shah**-ri da*	هذا الشهر
next month	*ish-**shahr** ig-**gayy***	الشهر القادم
during the month of —	*fi shahr —*	في خلال شهر —
■ Ramadan	■ *ra-ma-**Daan***	رمضان
since the month of —	*min shahr —*	منذ شهر —
every month	***kul**-li shahr*	كل شهر
per month	*fish-**shahr***	في الشهر

this year	is-sa-**neh** dee	هذه السنة
last year	is-**sa**-na il-lee **feh**-tit	السنة الماضية
next year	is-**sa**-na g-**gay**-ya	السنة القادمة
two years	sa-na-**teyn**	سنتان
three years	**ta**-lat si-**neen**	ثلاث سنوات
per year	fis-**sa**-na	في السنة
all year	**Tohl** is-**sa**-na	طوال السنة
every year	**kul**-li sa-na	كل سنة
during the year	fi khi-**lehl** is-**sa**-na	في خلال السنة

MONTHS OF THE YEAR

Western calendar

January	ya-**neh**-yir	يناير
February	fib-**reh**-yir	فبراير
March	**meh**-ris	مارس
April	ab-**reel**	أبريل
May	**may**-yoo	مايو
June	**yoon**-yoo	يونيو
July	**yool**-yoo	يوليو
August	a-**ghus**-Tus	أغسطس
September	sib-**tam**-bir	سبتمبر
October	uk-**too**-bar	اكتوبر

| November | *nu-**vim**-bir* | نوفمبر |
| December | *di-**sim**-bir* | ديسمبر |

Eastern calendar (used in Syria, Lebanon, Jordan, Iraq)

January	*ka-**noon** it-teh-nee*	كانون الثاني
February	*shu-**baaT***	شباط
March	*mart, 'a-**thaar***	مارت ، آذار
April	*ney-**sehn***	نيسان
May	***meh**-yis, 'ay-**yaar***	مايس ، أيار
June	*Ha-zee-**raan***	حزيران
July	*Tam-**mooz***	تموز
August	*'ehb*	آب
September	*'ay-**lool***	أيلول
October	*tish-**reen** il-'**aw**-wal*	تشرين الأول
November	*tish-**reen** it-teh-nee*	تشرين الثاني
December	*ka-**noon** il-'**aw**-wal*	كانون الأول

THE FOUR SEASONS

spring	*ir-ra-**bee**ᶜ*	الربيع
summer	*iS-**Seyf***	الصيف
autumn	*il-kha-**reef***	الخريف
winter	*ish-**shi**-ta*	الشتاء

WEATHER

The weather is fine.	ig-**gaww** kway-yis	الطقس جيد
It's (very) hot.	id-**din**-ya Harr (**gid**-dan)	الطقس حار (جداً)
It's chilly.	id-**din**-ya bard	الطقس بارد
It's cloudy.	ig-**gaww** mi-**ghay**-yim	الطقس مغيّم
It's windy.	id-**din**-ya reeH	الهواء شديد
It's foggy.	fee Da-**baab**	يوجد ضباب
There's a sandstorm.	fee ^caa-**Si**-fa ram-**lee**-ya	توجد عاصفة رمليـة
It's humid.	fee ru-**Too**-ba	الطقس رطب
It's raining.	bit-**maT**-Tar	الطقس ممطر
It's snowing.	bi-**yin**-zil talg	يسقط الثلج

COUNTRIES AND NATIONALITIES

Where are you from?	**in**-ta [**in**-tee] mi-**neyn**?	من أين أنت ؟
I am from — .	**a**-na min — .	أنا من —
I am — .	**a**-na — .	أنا —

COUNTRY	NATIONALITY
Note: When there is not an accepted adjective for the nationality, the expression would be "from (min)" + the country.	
Africa af-**reeq**-ya أفريقيا	af-**ree**-qee [af-**ree**-qee-ya] أفريقي

COUNTRY		NATIONALITY
America	*am-ree-ka*	*am-ree-kee/am-ree-**keh**-nee*
		*[am-ree-**kee**-ya/am-ree-ka-**nee**-ya]*
	أمريكا	أمريكي
Asia	*as-ya*	*as-**yeh**-wee [as-ya-**wee**-ya]*
	آسيا	آسيوي
Australia	*us-**tral**-ya*	*us-**traa**-lee [us-tra-**lee**-ya]*
	استراليا	استرالي
Austria	*in-**nim**-sa*	*nim-**seh**-wee [nim-sa-**wee**-ya]*
	النمسا	نمساوي
Belgium	*bal-**jee**-ka*	*bal-**jee**-kee [bal-jee-**kee**-ya]*
	بلجيكا	بلجيكي
Brazil	*ba-ra-**zeel***	*ba-ra-**zee**-lee [ba-ra-zee-**lee**-ya]*
	برازيل	برازيلي
Britain	*bri-**Tan**-ya*	*bri-**Taa**-nee [bri-Ta-**nee**-ya]*
	بريطانيا	بريطاني
Canada	*ka-na-da*	*ka-na-**dee** [ka-na-**dee**-ya]*
	كندا	كندي
China	*iS-**Seen***	*See-nee [See-**nee**-ya]*
	الصين	صيني
Denmark	*id-**di**-ni-mark*	*di-ni-**mar**-kee [di-ni-mar-**kee**-ya]*
	الدنمرك	دنمركي
England	*in-gil-**ti**-ra*	*in-gi-**lee**-zee [in-gi-lee-**zee**-ya]*
	انجلترا	انجليزي
Europe	*u-**rub**-ba*	*u-**rub**-bee [u-ru-**bee**-ya]*
	أوروبا	أوروبي
Finland	*fin-**lan**-da*	*fin-**lan**-dee [fin-lan-**dee**-ya]*
	فنلندا	فنلندي

COUNTRY		NATIONALITY
France	*fa-**ran**-sa* فرنسا	*fa-ran-**seh**-wee [fa-ran-sa-**wee**-ya]* فرنسي
Germany	*al-**man**-ya* المانيا	*al-**meh**-nee [al-ma-**nee**-ya]* الماني
Greece	*il-yu-**nehn*** اليونان	*yu-**neh**-nee [yu-na-**nee**-ya]* يوناني
Holland	*ho-**lan**-da* هولندا	*ho-lan-**dee** [ho-lan-**dee**-ya]* هولندي
Hungary	*il-**ma**-gar* المجر	***ma**-ga-ree [ma-ga-**ree**-ya]* مجري
India	*il-**hind*** الهند	***hin**-dee [hin-**dee**-ya]* هندي
Iran	*i-**raan*** ايران	*i-**raa**-nee [i-raa-**nee**-ya]* ايراني
Ireland	*ayr-**lan**-da* ايرلندا	*ayr-**lan**-dee [ayr-lan-**dee**-ya]* ايرلندي
Israel	*is-ra-'**eel*** اسرائيل	*is-ra-'**ee**-lee [is-ra-'ee-**lee**-ya]* اسرائيلي
Italy	*i-**Taal**-ya* ايطاليا	*i-**Taa**-lee/i-Tal-**yeh**-nee* *[i-Taa-**lee**-ya/i-Tal-ya-**nee**-ya]* ايطالي
Japan	*il-ya-**behn*** اليابان	*ya-**beh**-nee [ya-ba-**nee**-ya]* ياباني
Luxembourg	***luk**-sum-burg* لوكسمبرج	*min ...* من ...
Malaysia	*ma-**leyz**-ya* ماليزيا	*ma-**ley**-zee [ma-ley-**zee**-ya]* ماليزي

COUNTRY		NATIONALITY
New Zealand	*nyoo zee-lan-da* نيوزيلندا	*nyoo zee-lan-dee* [nyoo-zee-lan-dee-ya] نيوزيلندي
Norway	*in-nur-weyg* النرويج	*nur-wey-gee* [nur-wey-gee-ya] نرويجي
the Philippines	*il-fi-li-been* الفيليبين	*fi-li-bee-nee* [fi-li-bee-nee-ya] فيليبيني
Portugal	*il-bur-tu-ghehl* البرتغال	*bur-tu-gheh-lee* [bur-tu-gha-lee-ya] برتغالي
Russia	*roos-ya* روسيا	*roo-see* [roo-see-ya] روسي
Scotland	*is-kut-lan-da* اسكتلندا	*is-kut-lan-dee* [is-kut-lan-dee-ya] اسكتلندي
South America	*am-ree-ka l-ga-noo-bee-ya* من ... أمريكا الجنوبية .	*min ...*
Spain	*as-ban-ya* اسبانيا	*as-beh-nee* [as-ba-nee-ya] اسباني
Sweden	*is-su-weyd* السويد	*su-wey-dee* [su-wey-dee-ya] سويدي
Switzerland	*su-wis-ra* سويسرا	*su-wis-ree* [su-wis-ree-ya] سويسري
Turkey	*tur-kee-ya* تركية	*tur-kee* [tur-kee-ya] تركي

COUNTRY		NATIONALITY
United	*il-wi-lay-yeht*	*min ...*
States	*il-mut-ta-Hi-da*	
	من ...الولايات المتحدة	
Wales	*weylz*	***weyl**-zee [weyl-**zee**-ya]*
	ويلز	ويلزي
Yugoslavia	*yu-ghus-**laf**-ya*	*yu-ghus-**leh**-fee [yu-ghus-la-**fee**-ya]*
	يوغسلافيا	يوغسلاڧي

The Arab World

COUNTRY		NATIONALITY
Algeria	*al-ga-**zeh**-'ir*	*ga-**zeh**-'i-ree [ga-zeh-'i-**ree**-ya]*
	الجزائر	جزائري
Bahrain	*baH-**reyn***	*baH-**rey**-nee [baH-rey-**nee**-ya]*
	البحرين	بحريني
Djibouti	*ji-**boo**-tee*	*min . . .*
	جيبوتي	من . . .
Egypt	*maSr*	***maS**-ree [maS-**ree**-ya]*
	مصر	مصري
Iraq	*il-ᶜi-**reh**"*	*ᶜi-**reh**-"ee [ᶜi-ra-"**ee**-ya]*
	العراق	عراقي
Jordan	*il-'**ur**-dun*	*'ur-**du**-nee ['ur-du-**nee**-ya]*
	الأردن	أردني
Kuwait	*ik-ku-**weyt***	*ku-**wey**-tee [ku-wey-**tee**-ya]*
	الكويت	كويتي

COUNTRY		NATIONALITY
Lebanon	*lib-**nehn***	*lib-**neh**-nee [lib-na-**nee**-ya]*
	لبنان	لبناني
Libya	*lib-ya*	*lee-bee [lee-**bee**-ya]*
	ليبيا	ليبي
Mauritania	*mu-ri-**tan**-ya*	*mu-ri-**teh**-nee [mu-ri-teh-**nee**-ya]*
	موريتانيا	موريتاني
Morocco	*il-**magh**-rib*	*magh-**ri**-bee [magh-ri-**bee**-ya]*
	المغرب	مغربي
Oman	*ᶜu-**mehn***	*ᶜu-**meh**-nee [ᶜu-ma-**nee**-ya]*
	عمان	عماني
Palestine	*fa-laS-**Teen***	*fa-laS-**Tee**-nee [fa-laS-Tee-**nee**-ya]*
	فلسطين	فلسطيني
Qatar	*qa-tar*	*qa-Ta-ree [qa-Ta-**ree**-ya]*
	قطر	قطري
Saudi Arabia	*il-ᶜa-ra-**bee**-ya is-su-ᶜu-**dee**-ya*	*su-ᶜoo-dee [su-ᶜoo-**dee**-ya]*
	العربية السعودية	سعودي
Somalia	*iS-Su-**maal***	*Su-**maa**-lee [Su-maa-**lee**-ya]*
	الصومال	صومالي
Sudan	*is-su-**dehn***	*su-**deh**-nee [su-da-**nee**-ya]*
	السودان	سوداني
Syria	*soor-ya*	*soo-ree [soo-**ree**-ya]*
	سوريا	سوري
Tunisia	*too-nis*	*too-ni-see [too-ni-**see**-ya]*
	تونس	تونسي

COUNTRY		NATIONALITY
United Arab Emirates	il-'i-maa-**raat** الامارات	min . . . من . . .
Yemen	il-**ya**-man اليمن	**ya**-ma-nee [ya-ma-**nee**-ya] يمني

DIRECTIONS

north	ish-sha-**mehl**	الشمال
south	il-ga-**noob**	الجنوب
east	ish-**shar**"	الشرق
west	il-**gharb**	الغرب

COUNTING TIMES

once	**mar**-ra **waH**-da	مرة واحدة
twice	mar-ri-**teyn**	مرتان
three times	ta-lat mar-**raat**	ثلاث مرات
four times	ar-ba^c mar-**raat**	أربع مرات

FOR THE BUSINESS TRAVELER

[See also the sections on Banking and Money Matters and Telecommunications.]

Personal contacts and personal relationships will be a crucial factor in the success or failure of any business venture in the Middle East. There, one rarely finds the strict division between work and leisure so common in the West. Thus patience is needed to nurture a social/business relationship. Avoid a high-pressure approach, which may be perceived as crude and undignified. For instance, you may arrive for a business appointment to find other people in the office — friends, relations, or business associates. Be prepared for the exchange of quite lengthy social preliminaries before you can broach the topic you want to discuss.

So many stereotypes and prejudices have become associated with the Middle East that people will find it refreshing to do business with a foreigner who has actually taken the trouble to learn about the area. Read as much as you can about the social and political system of the countries you are going to visit, talk with people who know them well, and be ready to learn while you are there.

You will certainly be offered hospitality by business colleagues and should be ready to reciprocate enthusiastically on your home ground.

How you dress is important. Err on the side of formality — that means a jacket and tie despite high temperatures and humidity (you will understand the purpose of the traditional loose cotton robes of Saudi Arabia and the Gulf states!). It is rather unusual for women to do business in Saudi Arabia and the Gulf, though they are employed in high positions in hospitals, schools, universities, and so on. Being respectably dressed for a foreign woman means sleeves to below the elbow, skirts to below the knee, and not too much décolleté. In Saudi Arabia (except in Jedda) all women are expected to wear the voluminous *abaya* when they go out in the street.

It is best to try to schedule a business trip during the winter, spring, or autumn, because in the summer months there is a mass exodus from the big cities and the people you were hoping to contact may be at the seaside or vacationing in Europe.

Avoid traveling to the Middle East on business during the month of Ramadan (see p. 197), because the pace of life is so much slower. Don't expect to accomplish much during the two big religious festivals of the Muslim year (p. 198), which are national holidays and a time for family celebrations and reunions.

MINI-DICTIONARY FOR BUSINESS

account	*Hi-**sehb***	حساب
accounts, accounting	*Hi-seh-**beht***	حسابات
■ deposit account	■ *Hi-**sehb** 'i-**deh**ᶜ*	حساب إيداع
■ current account	■ *Hi-**sehb** geh-ree*	حساب جاري
amount	***mab**-lagh*	مبلغ
bank notes	*'aw-**reh**" na"d*	أوراق نقد
bill (noun)	*fa-**too**-ra*	فاتورة
bill of exchange	*kam-bee-**yeh**-la*	كمبيالة
bill of lading	*bu-**lee**-Sit shaHn*	بوليصة شحن
bill of sale	*ᶜa"d rahn il-man-"oo-**leht**,* *ᶜa"d il-**bee**ᶜ*	عقد رهن المنقولات ،عقد البيع

boycott	mu-"**aT**-ᶜa	مقاطعة
business operation	ᶜa-ma-**lee**-ya ti-ga-**ree**-ya	عملية تجارية
cash (noun)	na"d	نقد
cash on delivery	id-**daf** ᶜ ᶜand it-tas-**leem**	
		الدفع عند التسليم
cash payment	daf ᶜ **na**"-dee	دفع نقدي
I (you) cash a check	**aS**-rif (**tiS**-rif) sheek	أصرف (تصرف) شيكا
certified check	sheek ma"-**bool** id-**daf** ᶜ	
		شيك مقبول الدفع
chamber of commerce	il-**ghur**-fa it-ti-ga-**ree**-ya	الغرفة التجارية
company (companies)	**shir**-ka (sha-ri-**keht**)	شركة (شركات)
compensation (for damage)	ta ᶜ-**weeD** (ᶜan it-**ta**-laf)	تعويض (عن التلف)
competition	mu-**naf**-sa	منافسة
competitive price	si ᶜr mu-**neh**-fis	سعر منافس
contract	ᶜa"d	عقد
contractual obligations	il-ti-za-**meht** it-ta-ᶜ**eh**-qud	إلتزامات التعاقد
controlling interest	**HiS**-Sa mu-say-**Ti**-ra	حصة مسيطرة
co-owner	**meh**-lik mush-**ta**-rak	مالك مشترك

co-partner	sha-**reek** mush-**ta**-rik	شريك مشترك
credit	'i^c-ti-**mehd**	إعتماد
delivery	it-tas-**leem**	التسليم
discount	khaSm	خصم ، تخفيض
dishonored check	sheek mar-**fooD**	شيك مرفوض
distribution	it-taw-**zee**^c	التوزيع
down payment	**duf**-^ca mab-da-'ee-ya	دفعة مبدئية
duty	ru-**soom** gum-ru-**kee**-ya	رسوم جمركية
enterprise (project)	mash-**roo**^c	مشروع
enterprise (company)	**shir**-ka	شركة
expenses	maS-roo-**feht**	مصروفات
export	it-taS-**deer**	التصدير
free on board	it-tas-**leem** ^ca-la l-beh-**khi**-ra	التسليم على الباخرة
free trade zone	man-**Ti**-qit ti-**gaa**-ra **Hur**-ra	منطقة تجارة حرة
goods	il-ba-**Daa**-yi^c	البضائع
head office	il-**mak**-tab ir-ra-'**ee**-see	المكتب الرئيسي
import	il-'is-ti-**raad**	الاستيراد
infringement of patent rights	'ikh-**lehl** bi Ha"" il-'ikh-ti-**reh**^c	إخلال بحق الاختراع
insurance	ta'-**meen**	تأمين

insurance against all risks	*ta'-**meen** ^camm*	تأمين عام
international law	*il-qa-**noon** id-**daw**-lee*	القانون الدولي
lawful ownership	*mil-**kee**-ya qa-noo-**nee**-ya*	ملكية قانونية
lawsuit	*qa-**Dee**-ya*	قضية
lawyer	*mu-**Heh**-mee*	محامي
letter of credit	*ri-**seh**-lit i^c-ti-**mehd***	رسالة إعتماد
manager	*il-mu-**deer***	المدير
manufacturers	*iS-Si-**naa**-^ca*	الصنّاع
the Middle East market	*soo" ish-**sharq** il-'**aw**-SaT*	سوق الشرق الاوسط
market value	*il-**qee**-ma is-soo-**qee**-ya*	القيمة السوقية
owner of company	***Saa**-Hib ish-**shir**-ka*	مالك الشركة
partner	*sha-**reek***	شريك
past due	*mus-ta-**Hi**" " id-**daf** ^c*	مستحق الدفع
payment	*id-**daf** ^c*	الدفع
partial payment	***duf**-^ca guz-'**ee**-ya*	دفعة جزئية
we pay (you pay) customs	***nid**-fa^c (tid-**fa**-^coo) ig-ga-**meh**-rik*	ندفع (تدفعوا) الجمارك
percentage	***nis**-ba mi-'a-**wee**-ya*	نسبة مئوية
post office box	*san-**doo**" ba-**reed***	صندوق بريد
profit	*ribH*	ربح

profitable	**mur**-biH	مربح
property	'am-lehk	أملاك
purchasing agent	wa-**keel** mush-ta-ra-**yeht**	وكيل مشتريات
refund (noun)	'i-ᶜ**eh**-dit il-**mehl**	إعادة المال
sale	il-**bee**ᶜ	البيع
we (you) sell	ni-**bee**ᶜ (ti-bee-ᶜoo)	نبيع (تبيعوا)
we (you) send	**nib**-ᶜat (tib-**ᶜa**-too)	نرسل (ترسلوا)
shipment	**shiH**-na	شحنة
shipper	**sheh**-Hin	شاحن
spare parts	**qi**-Taᶜ gha-**yaar**	قطع غيار
supplier	mu-**war**-rid	مورّد
taxes	Da-**raa**-yib	ضرائب
sales tax	Da-**ree**-bit il-**bee**ᶜ	ضريبة البيع
luxury tax	Da-**ree**-bit il-'is-tih-**lehk**	ضريبة الاستهلاك
tax-exempt	**ma**ᶜ-fee min iD-Da-**raa**-yib	معفي من الضرائب
trade fair	**ma**ᶜ-raD ti-**geh**-ree	معرض تجاري
trade union	ni-**qaa**-ba	نقابة عمال
we (you) transfer	ni-**Haw**-wil (ti-Haw-**wi**-loo)	نحول (تحولوا)
transportation charges	'u-**goor** in-**na**"l	أجور النقل

via	^{c}an Ta-**ree**″	عن طريق
wholesale	il-**bee**^{c} bil-**gum**-la	البيع بالجملة

The Petrochemical Industry

crude oil	zeyt khehm	بترول خام
the price of crude	st^{c}r iz-**zeyt** il-**khehm**	سعر البترول الخام
per barrel	il-bar-**meel**	البرميل
drilling	il-**Hafr**	الحفر
exploratory drilling	Hafr is-tik-**sheh**-fee	حفر إستكشافي
local branch	far ^{c} ma-**Hal**-lee	فرع محلي
natural gas	ghehz Ta-**bee**-^{c}ee	غاز طبيعي
oil	bit-**rohl**	بترول
oil company	shir-kit bit-**rohl**	شركة بترول
oil fields	Hu-**qool** il-bit-**rohl**	حقول البترول
oil rig	gi-**hehz** il-**Hafr**	جهاز الحفر
offshore oil	bit-**rohl** baH-ree	بترول بحري
oil well	beer bit-**rohl**	بئر بترول
OPEC	**oh**-pek, mu-naZ-**Za**-mit il-bi-**lehd** il-mu-Sad-**di**-ra lil-bit-**rohl**	أوبك، منظمة البلدان المصدرة للبترول
pipeline	khaTT 'a-na-**beeb**	خط أنابيب
production	'in-**tehg**	إنتاج

(petroleum) products	*mun-ta-**geht** bit-ro-**lee**-ya*	منتجات بترولية
refined oil	*bit-**rohl** mu-**kar**-rir*	بترول مكرر
refinery	*ma^c-mal tak-**reer***	معمل تكرير

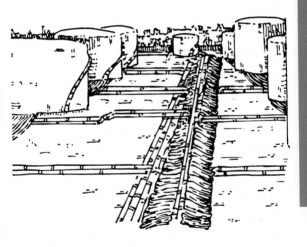

ISLAM

The Koran, the holy book of Islam, which contains the divine revelations received by the prophet Mohammed, is the cornerstone of the Muslim faith. The fundamental religious observances of Islam consist of the profession of faith, prayer, fasting, almsgiving, and the pilgrimage to Mecca in Saudi Arabia, birthplace of the prophet. Like Judaism and Christianity, Islam is monotheistic, believing in an omnipotent creator to whom all must answer.

A Muslim prays after ritual ablutions five times a day — at dawn, noon, in the afternoon, at sunset, and in the evening — facing the direction of Mecca. The call to prayer, or *a-thehn*, will become a familiar sound, as it is chanted or broadcast via loudspeakers from minarets all over town. A Muslim may pray in any quiet and secluded place, kneeling and prostrating himself on a small rug kept especially for that purpose. It is, however, considered important to attend midday prayers at the mosque on Fridays, when a sermon is preached. Sometimes the mosque is so full that the worshippers overflow onto the pavement outside.

There is no priesthood in Islam, no mediator between the worshipper and God. Prayers may be led by any Muslim well-versed in the ritual, though a sizeable community will appoint an Imam, or religious teacher, to officiate. Although there is no equivalent of an established church, schools of theologians and jurists (*c-u-la-ma*) evolved, differing in their precise interpretations of Muslim doctrine.

Dissension within the Islamic state has focussed mostly on the rights and duties of the successive Caliphs. These elected successors to the Prophet played an essentially political and administrative rather than religious role. The Caliphates were transformed into something more akin to traditional Middle Eastern dynasties, with the right to succession being violently disputed at many points in history. The last Caliphate of any real power was the Ottoman Empire based in Turkey, which finally collapsed in the early twentieth century, after a long period of decline.

The ancient Islamic state, stretching in Medieval times from Spain to China, has long since fragmented into independent states. These have been secularized to varying degrees. Saudi Arabia, an absolute monarchy, retains the sharia (*sha-ree-ᶜa*), or Islamic legal system, while others are republics and have adopted and adapted Western legal systems. Sometimes the two operate in parallel, depending on the nature of the legal matter at issue.

The Prophet Mohammed

Mohammed was born in Mecca in West Arabia in about 571 A.D., into an essentially nomadic, tribal society in which a variety of local gods were worshipped. The Koran was revealed to him when he was about 40 years old, by the angel Gabriel. As more and more conversions took place, Mohammed was obliged to leave Mecca, and was welcomed with his followers in Medina, where he became a ruler and military leader as well as a religious teacher. His influence gradually spread throughout the peninsula, until at his death he left an organized and well-armed state unified in its adherence to the new faith.

According to Islam, Mohammed is the last and greatest of the line of prophets in the Judeo-Christian tradition. Abraham, Moses, and Jesus are all venerated as bearers of God's word, but the Koran is seen as the last in this series of divine revelations, completing and superseding all previous scriptures. Christians and Jews, as "people of the pact," traditionally enjoyed certain rights and privileges within the Islamic state, including freedom of worship.

Islamic Civilization

The Arabs founded, but were by no means the exclusive contributors to, a rich civilization that lasted for over a thousand years. There were two great waves of conquest, one immediately following the death of Mohammed, which took the Muslim armies north into Syria, west into Egypt, across North Africa, and into Persia in the east. Two centuries later, most of Spain came under Muslim rule, as did northern India and parts of China. The Arabs assimilated and built upon the scientific and technical knowledge of their subject nations, translating into Arabic works on mathematics, philosophy, astronomy, and medicine from the ancient Greek, Persian, and Indian civilizations. During what were the Dark Ages in Europe, great advances were also being made in the fields of chemistry, anatomy, geography, optics, and mechanical engineering. Universities, libraries, and hospitals flourished, often in close association with the great mosques of the period.

So in the Middle Ages it was to the East that Europe looked for scientific knowledge. (Our system of numerals, for example, was borrowed from the Arabs, who had themselves borrowed and adapted the system from an Indian source.)

In the arts, Islamic civilization can be seen at its most impressive in its great architectural creations, from the Taj Mahal in India to the Alhambra palace in Spain. In both, formal gardens, pools, and fountains perfectly complement the graceful architecture. (Garden motifs as well as complex geometric patterns often recur in textiles, ceramics, and carpet designs.) The bold and elegant shapes of dome, minaret, and monumental gateway are generally left unadorned; decoration is concentrated on interior surfaces, in the form of tiling, mosaic, and elaborate plasterwork.

In the museums of the Arab world you will see examples of other great artistic achievements of Islamic civilization, in the form of pottery, glassware, pierced and inlaid metalwork, carpets, and textiles — art forms that continue to flourish today.

Since pre-Islamic times poetry had been the favored literary genre, and the themes and forms of Arabic poetry are clearly reflected in the work of the Medieval poets of southern Europe. Many believe that it was contact with this rich and varied culture that fostered new ideas in both the arts and sciences in Europe, culminating in the great flowering of the Renaissance.

The Muslim Calendar

The calendar is based on a key event in the history of the Islamic faith, the migration from Mecca to Medina by the Prophet and his followers in 622 A.D. This is therefore taken as the beginning of the Islamic era. In everyday conversation the years and months of the Western calendar are used, but for religious purposes and in published material of all kinds, Islamic dates are referred to. Both are used in newspapers.

The year is divided into 12 lunar months, each starting at the new moon, and consisting of about 29 days. This means that the Muslim year starts about 10 days earlier each year in relation to the Western calendar.

Here are the names of the months:

mu-**Har**-ram	محرّم
Sa-far	صفر
ra-**bee**^c il-'**aw**-wal	ربيع الأول
ra-**bee**^c it-**teh**-nee	ربيع الثاني
gu-**mehd** il-'**aw**-wal	جمادى الأولى
gu-**mehd** it-**teh**-nee	جمادى الآخرة
ra-**gab**	رجب
sha^c-**behn**	شعبان
ra-ma-**Daan**	رمضان
shaw-**wehl**	شوّال
zul-**qa**^c-da	ذو القعدة
zul-**Hig**-ga	ذو الحجة

Ramadan is the month of fasting, when Muslims neither eat, drink, nor smoke from dawn till sunset.

Special dishes are eaten at the evening meal known as *il-fi-Taar*, which breaks the fast. In the early hours before dawn a second meal — *is-su-hoor* — is taken, to see people through the hours of fasting ahead.

Fasting is considered both a spiritual discipline and a reminder of those less fortunate than oneself who are hungry all year round. So it is a time to give generously to poor people in one's neighborhood. Devout Muslims gather to read aloud from the Koran, and go to the mosque more frequently during Ramadan.

The pace of life tends to slow down, with many people sleeping during the morning hours. In the evening, and often late into the night, there is a holiday atmosphere in the downtown areas of the cities, where shops and cafés stay open and the streets are thronged with people.

Hotels and all places catering to tourists function normally, but many neighborhood restaurants and cafés are closed during daylight hours. Non-Muslims are certainly not expected to fast, but it is polite not to eat, smoke, or drink in the street.

Muslim Festivals

Ramadan ends in the Feast of the Breaking of the Fast or the Small Feast — *ᶜeed il-fiTr* or *il-ᶜeed iS-Sugh-ghay-yar*, which is associated with all kinds of local customs, such as providing one's children with new clothes. The culminating day of the pilgrimage to Mecca is on the tenth of *zul Hig-ga*. This is known as the Great Feast, or Feast of Sacrifice — *il-ᶜeed il-ki-beer* or *ᶜeed il-'aD-Ha*, when every family that can afford it slaughters a sheep, in remembrance of the story of Abraham and Isaac, and meat is distributed to the poor.

The prophet's birthday — *moo-lid in-na-bee* — on the twelfth of *ra-beeᶜ il-'aw-wal* — is also celebrated; for days in advance mosques are illuminated and ceremonies and festivities abound.

During Ramadan, and on the occasion of any religious or secular festival — including birthdays — the equivalent to "Merry Christmas," "Happy Birthday," and so on is:

kul-li sa-na win-ta Tay-yib [win-tee Tay-yi-ba]

To which the reply is:

win-ta Tay-yib [win-tee Tay-yi-ba]

Or the more formal greeting is:

kul-li ᶜehmm win-tum bi-kheyr

Saint's Days

In Egypt and North Africa especially there is a long tradition — probably dating back to pre-Islamic times — of venerating the memory of men and women of great piety and learning. Their tombs have become shrines, and even mosques have been founded to commemorate them, which may become places of pilgrimage. One of the liveliest public celebrations is a saint's day or *moo-lid*; miniature fairgrounds for children are set up, as well as street stalls selling food, toys, and souvenirs. Shops and cafés stay open till late at night, and bands of musicians and singers provide religious and secular music.

Secular Festivals

The Western New Year — *raas is-sa-na* — is celebrated wherever Western influence has made itself felt, but it is not generally an official holiday. May 1, Labor Day (May Day), is also accorded varying degrees of importance in different countries.

In Egypt an ancient spring festival, that of *shamm in-ni-seem*, is celebrated on Greek Orthodox Easter Monday throughout the country. Everyone flocks to the fields, parks, and gardens in their newest clothes, and huge amounts of spring onions and salted fish are consumed.

Christian Festivals

Large Christian communities are to be found throughout the Middle East; in Lebanon they constitute about half the population. Roughly 15 percent of Egyptians belong to the Greek Orthodox Church, one of the earliest established forms of Christianity, even today using the language of Ancient Egypt in its liturgy. The Greek Orthodox and Eastern Orthodox calendar does not coincide with the Western Christian calendar. The Eastern Christmas — *ᶜeed il-mi-lehd* (literally, "Feast of the Birth") — and Easter — *ᶜeed il-qi-yeh-ma* ("Feast of the Resurrection") — are celebrated about 12 days later than their Western equivalents.

THE ARAB WORLD TODAY

The Arab world has a degree of cultural unity, based on shared religious beliefs, a common literary language of great prestige, and many shared social institutions such as the extended family, with its elaborate system of rights and obligations. But within this framework there is great diversity — of race, of wealth, of political systems, of attitudes to the West, and to modern technology.

In the West the stereotypical Arab as an oil-rich sheikh jet-setting around the capitals of Europe has tended to replace the more romantic image of the keen-eyed son of the desert, ascetic, proud, and bound by a strict code of honor. Both exist, but only as tiny pieces in a much larger mosaic. They are both vastly outnumbered by the hardworking fellaheen (*fel-la-Heen*), or peasant farmers, who still provide the economic base of the more populous Arab countries.

Urban centers increasingly attract workers to the factories from country towns and villages. Cairo, the town planner's nightmare — or ultimate challenge — has exploded from being a sizeable city of 3 million to a vast agglomeration of 16 million in the space of 30 years. Armies of government clerks (*mu-waZ-Za-feen*) — often university graduates — find it hard to make ends meet on their slender salary, and will often take a second job in the afternoon or evening.

There has been a massive emigration of the working population from the poorer to the richer countries within the Arab world and beyond, with all the social and economic turmoil that entails.

In this shifting scene two factors at least remain constant, which favor the foreign visitor: the innate sociability of the Arab people, and their abiding tradition of hospitality to strangers.

Women in Islam

Saudi Arabia, as the birthplace of the prophet Mohammed, sees itself as the guardian of traditional values, accepting changes to the established order with extreme caution. Attitudes that seem reactionary to Westerners, such as requiring women to go heavily veiled in public places and forbidding them to drive, should be viewed against some truly dramatic social reforms, like the provision of education for women at all levels, within the space of one generation.

Throughout the Middle East the trend has been toward greater emancipation for women and their increasing participation in every area of public life. In many ways they have enjoyed fuller legal rights than their Western sisters, from the early days of Islam, since they have always had individual property rights and legal protection against ill-treatment by their husbands.

Polygamy is still practiced in most Arab countries, although it is unusual among the mass of the population — since wives must be treated equally in every respect, few men can afford more than one! A woman must enter freely into the marriage contract, though frequently social and family pressures may mean that personal preference is not a major factor in the arrangement for either partner.

TRADITION AND CHANGE

In recent years, even in countries like Egypt, which have been open to Western influences for more than a century, a profound reevaluation of social and religious attitudes is taking place. The West is no longer synonymous with progress and enlightenment. The strength and stability offered by traditional values is increasingly appreciated, particularly among the younger generation. Fashions in dress — like the adoption of the nunlike headcovering (the *Hi-gehb*) and long skirts by young women, and the chin-strap beard of the young men — are outward signs of these changing attitudes.

THE ARABIC LANGUAGE

THE ARABIC SCRIPT

This section explains the general principles on which the writing system works, and will help you to recognize the common signs and notices that you will see on any trip to an Arab country.

Arabic is written from right to left, and it is a "cursive" script — that is, the letters of the word are usually joined up, whether in print or handwriting.

Many different styles exist, just as many different typefaces are used to print the Roman alphabet. Calligraphy is one of the great art forms of Islamic civilization, and some highly elaborate styles have been evolved, which you will see incorporated in metalwork, ceramics, architectural decoration, and so on. The style used in this book is simple, and one of the most common in everyday use.

The table below shows the 29 letters of the alphabet as they would occur in isolation. Their order (from right to left) is that used traditionally in Arabic dictionaries. You will notice that the letters which are very similar in shape are grouped together.

The transcription of the letters follows that used in this book, although two extra sounds occur that are not found in Egyptian Arabic: **th** as in "thing" and **th** as in "this." In Egyptian the first **th** is pronounced either **s** or **t**, and the second **th** as either **z** or **d**.

←

kh	H	j or g	th	t	b	eh or aa	'
خ	ح	ج	ث	ت	ب	ا	ء

D	S	sh	s	z	r	th	d
ض	ص	ش	س	ز	ر	ذ	د

k	q	f	gh	c	Z	T
ك	ق	ف	غ	ع	ظ	ط

	y	w	h	n	m	l
	ي	و	ه	ن	م	ل

ي (**y**) and و (**w**) can also be used to represent the long vowels **ee** and **oo** respectively.

Besides these 29 letters there are three additional "vowel marks," two written above, and one below the consonant they follow:

فَ = fa   ف = fi   فُ = fu

بَ = ba   بِ = bi   بُ = bu

These short vowels are not generally written in, because Arabic speakers can recognize the word quite well without them (just as you don't usually need to put in the vowel marks in English shorthand).

Another "optional" symbol — ّ — is one used over a letter to indicate that letter is doubled, or long:

جزّار = gaz-**zaar**   شبّاك = shib-**behk**

The glottal stop symbol ء (') rarely occurs by itself but is usually "carried" by ا ، و ، or ي : أ ؤ يْ

In the "joining up" process letters tend to change their shape. Typically, letters coming at the end of a word (or occurring in isolation, as above) end in a flourish or "tail." They lose this tail if they occur at the beginning or in the middle of a word.

First the letters that *don't* join up with the letters that follow them, and therefore do *not* change their shape:

ا   د   ذ   ر   ز   و

The following lose their tails:

ب   ت   ث   ج   ح   خ   ص   ض

ع   غ   ف   ق   ل   م   ن   ي

So if we were to join up ت + ح + ت (taHt — "under, below"), this would give تحت with only the final **t** ending in a flourish. Notice that dots are placed above or below the middle of the flourish if there is one. The same is true for the two forms of ب (**b**) and ث (**th**):

باب = behb ("door")   and   ثلث = thilth ("third")

Final ي sometimes loses its two dots: ى

Here are a few more examples of letters written first in their "full" form, and then as they would look joined up into words:

ب ل د   ج م ي ل   ب ح ر

بلد (**ba-lad**)   جميل (ga-**meel**)   بحر (baHr)

ف و ل   ض ا ن ي   ش خ ص

فول (fool)   ضاني (**Daa**-nee)   شخص (shakhS)

k has *three* variant forms, depending on whether they are initial, medial, or final in a word:

	FINAL	MEDIAL	INITIAL
k	ك	كـ	كـ

Three other letters have initial, medial, and final shapes, the final one varying slightly if it is unjoined:

	FINAL Unjoined	FINAL Joined	MEDIAL	INITIAL
c	ع	ـع	ـعـ	عـ
gh	غ	ـغ	ـغـ	غـ
h	ه	ـه	ـهـ	هـ

This last letter may be written with two dots over it in final position: ة or ـة . Then it represents the feminine ending -a, as in طبيبة *Ta-bee-ba* — doctor (fem.) جميلة *ga-mee-la* — beautiful (fem.) Some examples of these last few letters in words:

(*ᶜan*-dee)	(*gum*-ruk)	(say-*yaa*-ra)
عندي	جمرك	سيارة
(*ma*-ᶜa)	(Say-da-*lee*-ya)	(maT-ᶜam)
مع	صيدلية	مطعم
(is-*seh*-ᶜa)	(ik-*kil*-ma)	(il-ᶜin-*wehn*)
الساعة	الكلمة	العنوان

The last three examples all begin with the definite article **il-** الـ (see Grammar Notes). Notice this is always written the same way, even if the **l** changes to match the following consonant in spoken Arabic.

You will occasionally come across three relatively new letters, which have been invented to cope with borrowed, foreign sounds. Arabic doesn't normally have a **v** sound, but this does occur in foreign borrowings such as "video." A variant of **f** with three dots is sometimes used: فيديو *vi-dyoo* Egyptian Arabic uses **g** rather than **j** in words like *ga-meel* جميل (beautiful) or *ga-mal* جمل *(camel)*, but **j** may occur in foreign words such as "jeans." To make the difference clear, three dots can again be used:

مكياج *mak-yaaj* (makeup)   چينز*jeenz*

A **p** in foreign borrowings is usually Arabized to a **b**, as in *bu-loh-var* (pullover). But it can be represented by a modification of the **b** symbol ب again using three dots:

پ. For example:

سڤن اپ Seven-Up

So you may find a word such as "jeep" being written

جيب or چيب , or چيپ جيپ !

DIALECTS OF THE ARAB WORLD

Considerable differences exist between the varieties of Arabic spoken throughout the Arab world; even within one country a good deal of local variation can be found. Although you will be able to make yourself understood very well with Egyptian Arabic, as the most widely known and prestigious form of the spoken language, if you are visiting other countries you may want to try to approximate the local dialect.

The differences lie in pronunciation and use of vocabulary rather than in grammatical structure. The following notes, indicating the most striking of these features, should help you "tune in" rapidly to another dialect. Dialects have been grouped together to simplify the picture, but it should be remembered that this simplification masks a lot of internal variation.

Egyptian Arabic

What identifies a speaker immediately as an Egyptian is his or her use of g as in *ga-**meel*** (beautiful), **gid-**dan (very), and so on; in virtually all other dialects (and in literary Arabic) this is a *j*, either as in "*jam*" or "*measure*": *ja-**meel***, **jid-**dan, and so on.

The other feature (shared by some of the more Eastern dialects) is the use of the glottal stop ″ to replace what is elsewhere a *q*. The *q* has only survived in Egyptian in relatively few (usually rather learned) words. So other dialects will differentiate between *qa-lam* (pen) and '*a-lam* (pain), whereas in Egyptian they are pronounced the same, both with a glotal stop: ″*a-lam* = '*a-lam*. Two slightly different symbols have been used for the Egyptian glottal stop, so that you will know where you should switch to *q* in another part of the Arab world. So ″*ul-lee* (tell me) will be pronounced ***qul**-lee* elsewhere, but '*is-**boo**ᶜ* (week) will stay the same.

South of Cairo a rather different dialect is spoken, in which *j* is used for *g* and *q* for ″. This Upper Egyptian, or '*sa-ᶜee-dee*', Arabic (sometimes made fun of by the educated city dweller) in fact has much in common with Sudanese.

Dialects of the Eastern Mediterranean (*Lebanon, Jordan, Syria, Palestine*)

Egyptian *g* = *j* (as in mea*s*ure, rather than *j*am)

Some unstressed vowels are dropped. For example, Egyptian *ki-**teer*** = EM *kteer* (much, many).

As in Egyptian, *q* is usually replaced by ″.

Here are some common expressions:

Not	*mish* or *ma*
Where?	*weyn?*
What?	*shoo?* or '*ehsh?*
Why?	*leysh?*
How much?	″*ad-**dehsh**?*
How?	*keyf?*

How are you? **key**-*fak [key-fik]?*

Thing, something *shey'*

Thus, so *heyk*

Yes *'eyh*

Nice, good *ma-leeH*

I want **bid**-*dee* or **bad**-*dee*

(You want . . . , etc.: the ending changes as after *"ud-dehm-* (in front of); see p. 220: **bid**-*dak*, **bid**-*dik*, **bid**-*doo,* (etc.).

Sudanese

Very similar to Egyptian, except than *j* (as in "jam") is used instead of *g*, so *gi-deed* = Sudanese *ja-deed*, and Egyptian *"* is either *q* or *g*; for example, Egyptian *"ah-wa* = Sudanese **gah**-*wa* (coffee), *"i-zeh-za* = *gi-zeh-za.*

Iraqi

Additional sounds: *th* as in "thing," corresponding to Egyptian *t* (hence *ka-theer* = *ki-teer*) or *s*, and <u>th</u> as in "this" corresponding to Egyptian *d* or *z*.

Egyptian *g* = Iraqi *j* (as in "jam").

Egyptian *"* = *q* or *g*: *Ta-ree"* = Iraqi *Ta-reeq*, *"ah-wa* = Iraqi **gah**-*wa.*

k next to *a* or *i* often becomes *tsh*: Egyptian *kam* = Iraqi *tshehm.*

Here are some common expressions:

What? *shi-**noo**?*

Who? *min?*

How? *keyf? shlohn?*

How much? *kehm? tshehm?*

Where? *weyn?*

Why? *leysh?*

When? **mi**-*ta?*

Fine, good *zeyn*

Bad *baT-**Taal***

Thus, so **hee**-*tshee*

This, that **heh**-<u>th</u>*a*

I want *a-**reed***

Not *moo, mush*

Dialects of Saudi Arabia and the Gulf

th and <u>*th*</u> are used (as in "think" and "this"): *tha-leh-tha* (three), **heh-<u>tha</u>** (this, that).

k often becomes *tsh* next to *a*, *e*, *i*: *kam = tshehm, keyf = tsheyf*. Egyptian ″ is usually *g*, occasionally *q*: **gah**-*wa*, **fun**-*dug*, *ga-leel*. Egyptian *g = j* (as in "jam").

Here are some common expressions:

What? *shoo?*
Where? *weyn?*
How? *keyf?, tsheyf?, shlohn?*
How are you? **shloh-nak [shloh-nik]?**
How much? *kehm?, tshehm?*
Much, very *ka-theer*
I want *a-reed, a-bee, ab-gha*
Good, fine *zeyn*
Yesterday *'ams*
This, that **heh-<u>tha</u> [heh-<u>thee</u>]**
Thanks *mash-koor*

North African Dialects
(Moroccan, Algerian, Tunisian, Libyan)

These are possibly the furthest from Egyptian, particularly Moroccan, where there is a strong Berber influence.
Egyptian *g = j*
Egyptian ″ = *q* or *g*: ″*alb = qalb*, ″*ah-wa = gah-wa*.

Many unstressed vowels are lost: Egyptian *ta-leh-ta =* NA **tleh**-*ta*, ″*a-deem = qdeem*.

Here are some common expressions:

Yes *yeh*
Thank you *ba-ra-kal-laa-hu feek*
What? *'ehsh? shnoo?*
Why? ^c*a-lehsh?*
When? *waq-tehsh? foh-gehsh?*
How much/many? *gad-dehsh? sh-hehl?*
How? *keyf? key-fehsh?*
Who? *shkoon?*
Good, well *la-behs, beh-hee*
Nice, pleasant *mleeH, miz-yehn*

Bad   *doo-nee*, *kheh-yib*
Much, very   *yeh-sir*, *biz-zehf*
I want   *ni-Hibb*, *heb-ghee [bagh-ya]*
Food   *mak-la*
Tomorrow   *ghud-wa*, *ghed-da*
To form a "yes/no" question, add -*shee* to the verb or adjective: *beh-hee-shee?* — (Is it) O.K.?

GRAMMAR NOTES

The rules outlined here are those of spoken Egyptian Arabic, but most apply to other spoken forms of Arabic as well. The differences between the modern dialects are ones of pronunciation and vocabulary rather than of grammar.

Consonantal Roots and Word Patterns

The most striking feature of Arabic, like other Semitic languages, is the way a series of (usually three) consonants is used as the basis for forming many closely related words. Take the series *d-r-s*; from this are formed the words *dars* — "lesson," *da-ras* — "he studied," *dar-ras* — "he taught," *mad-ra-sa*— "school," *mu-dar-ris* — "teacher," and many others, all related to the concept of study. Once you know the meaning of a root you can often guess at the meaning of a word containing it, because the addition of particular patterns of vowels, plus prefixes or suffixes, modifies the meaning of the root in predictable ways.

"Place" nouns often follow the patterns of either *mak-tab* (office) or *mak-ta-ba* (library or bookstore), i.e., the place where writing takes place or it is found. The verb "to write" is *yik-tib*. Just as *mad-ra-sa* (school) refers to a place where studying (*yud-rus*) occurs, so *magh-sa-la* (laundry) refers to washing (**yigh**-sil). On the same pattern we find **ma^c-bad** (temple), **maw-"af** (stop or station), **maS-na^c** (factory), **ma-Taar** (airport), **ma"-ba-ra** (tomb), **maH-fa-Za** (wallet), **makh-zan** (storehouse), **maT-^cam** (restaurant), and many more.

"Agent" nouns indicating people or machines engaged in specific activities follow the pattern of fal-lehH (farmer), with a doubled middle consonant followed by a long vowel. Further examples are ba-"ehl (grocer), **Tab-baakh** (cook), Hal-leh" (barber), Sar-raaf (cashier), khab-behz (baker), khal-laaT (mixer, blender).

Like "place" nouns, these sometimes end in the feminine -a: Tay-yaar is a pilot (someone who flies), whereas Tay-yaa-ra means both a female pilot and an airplane (a machine that flies).

"Causative" verbs are also created by doubling the middle consonant. While **yud**-rus means "to study," **yi-dar**-ris means "to teach," that is, to cause to study — and yi-naD-Daf (to clean or to cause to be clean) is from the adjective na-**Deef** (clean). Other causative verbs included in this book are yi-**wa"**-"af to (cause to) stop, yi-**ghay**-yar (to change), yi-**gad**-did (to renew), yi-**naZ**-Zam (to organize).

Nouns formed from these verbs follow the pattern of tag-**deed** (renewal) and tan-**Deef** (cleaning). If you check the entries beginning with ta- in the mini-dictionary, you can infer that there must be a verb yi-**waz**-za^c (to distribute), corresponding to the noun taw-**zee**^c (distribution), and a verb yi-**khaf**-faD (to reduce), corresponding to takh-**feeD** (reduction), and so on.

These are just a handful of the many productive patterns in the language. Once you know the basic meaning of a consonantal root, you will be able to predict quite confidently the form and meaning of a whole range of words associated with it.

In an Arabic dictionary that uses the Arabic script, words are entered alphabetically, not according to the first consonant of the word (which may be a prefix, e.g., *ma-* or *ta-*), but according to the first consonant of the root, so **yigh**-*sil* (to wash), *magh*-**sa**-*la* (laundry), and *gha*-**seel** (washing) will all be classed together under the heading *gh-s-l*. If you decide to tackle the script, you will be able to use a dictionary and see just how productive many of these roots are.

Word Order

The order of words in sentences is much the same as in English; the only major difference is that adjectives follow the nouns they modify:

*bint ga-**mee**-la*
                  lit, a girl beautiful
                  i.e., a beautiful girl

If a word such as *very* modifies the adjective, it too follows:

*bint ga-**mee**-la **gid**-dan*
                  lit., a girl beautiful very
                  i.e., a very beautiful girl

NOUNS

Nouns are either masculine or feminine. Feminine nouns usually end in *-a*:

*mu-**dar**-ris* a teacher (masc.)	*mu-dar-**ris**-sa* a teacher (fem.)

Notice the above nouns are *indefinite*. To make them *definite* ("the . . .") the prefix *il-* is put at the beginning of the word:

*il-mu-**dar**-ris* the teacher   *il-**bee**-ra* the beer

The *l* of this prefix sometimes changes to match the first consonant of the noun:

*is-**suk**-kar* (the sugar)   — not *il-**suk**-kar*
*in-**nehs*** (the people)   — not *il-**nehs***

The consonants that trigger this change are:
    t d n s z sh r T D S Z

For *k*, *g*, and *j* the change is optional. So:

*il-**kart*** (the card)   or *ik-**kart***

Plurals

Sometimes an ending is added to make a noun plural (as in English):

*mu-dar-ri-**seen*** (teachers)   *do-la-**raat*** (dollars)

-een and *-aat* are among the most common plural endings. But even more frequently, the whole shape of the word changes, with only the consonantal root remaining intact. There are over a dozen different plural "patterns"; the most common are:

SINGULAR	PLURAL	SINGULAR	PLURAL
1 **wa-ra**" (paper)	'**aw-reh**"	**wa**-lad (boy)	'**aw-lehd**
2 '*is-**boo**c* (week)	'*a-sa-**bee**c*	mif-**tehH** (key)	ma-fa-**teeH**
3 **mak**-tab (office)	ma-keh-tib	taz-**ka**-ra (ticket)	ta-**zeh**-kir
4 kart (card)	ku-**root**	Deyf (guest)	Du-**yoof**
5 **sik**-ka (road)	si-kak	nim-ra (number)	ni-**mar**

Unfortunately, most of the time you can't predict the plural from the singular; it just has to be learned. This is the hardest part of Arabic grammar, but if you use the wrong plural pattern or ending, people will probably still understand!

Duals

If two objects or people are being referred to, a special form of the noun is used. For masculine nouns the ending *-eyn* is added:

yohm	*yoh-**meyn***	*'alf*	*'al-**feyn***
(day)	(2 days)	(1000)	(2000)

For feminine nouns ending in *-a*, the *a* is removed and *-teyn* added:

seh-*ᶜa*	*saᶜ-**teyn***	**Ha**-*ga*	*Hag-**teyn***
(hour)	(2 hours)	(thing)	(2 things)

Noun + Noun

When one noun immediately follows another, it usually indicates possession or the notion "of":

*beyt mu-**Ham**-mad*	Muhammed's house
Saa-*Hib* **ley**-*la*	Leila's friend

When the first noun is feminine, the *-a* ending changes to *-it*:

shur-*ba* (soup)	but	**shur**-*bit* **ba**-*Sal* (onion soup)
"*i-**zeh**-za* (bottle)	but	"*i-**zeh**-zit* **bee**-*ra* (a bottle of beer)

If you want to say "*the* bottle of beer" or "*the* teacher's daughter" only the second noun carries the definite *il-*:

"*i-**zeh**-zit il-**bee**-ra*	*bint il-mu-**dar**-ris*

Numbers

The numbers are given on page 17. 1 is the only number to have separate masculine and feminine forms:

***weh*-Hid** and ***waH*-da:** *yohm* ***weh*-Hid** one day, *sa-na* ***waH*-da** one year

Numbers 3 to 10 are followed by a plural noun:

*ta-lat 'a-sa-**bee**^{c}* (3 weeks) ***ar**-ba^c si-**neen*** (4 years)

Notice the final *-a* has been dropped before these plural nouns.

With all higher numbers, a *singular* noun is used:

*ta-la-**teen** **sa**-na* (30 years) *it-**naa**-shar shahr* (12 months)

When ordering in a restaurant, however, or when currency is being referred to, the singular is *always* used:

*ta-**leh**-ta **bee**-ra* (3 beers) ***kham**-sa do-**laar*** (5 dollars)

When the hundreds are followed by a noun, ***mee**-ya* becomes *meet*:

| 300 dollars | *tul-tu-meet do-**laar*** |
| 500 pounds | *khum-su-meet gi-**ney*** |

ADJECTIVES

Like nouns, adjectives have three different forms — masculine, feminine, and plural:

| ***kway*-yis** (good) masc. | *kway-**yi**-sa* fem. |
| | *kway-yi-**seen*** pl. |

| ***Tay*-yib** (kind) masc. | *Tay-**yi**-ba* fem. |
| | *Tay-yi-**been*** pl. |

The feminine ending is always -a, but as with nouns, the plural may take many forms:

la-Teef (pleasant) masc. *la-Tee-fa* fem. *lu-Taaf* pl.

mag-noon (crazy) masc. *mag-noo-na* fem.
ma-ga-neen pl.

Adjectives agree with the nouns they modify:

wa-lad la-Teef (a nice *bint la-Tee-fa* (a nice girl)
boy)

Fortunately there is a strong tendency toward using the (regular!) feminine form with plural nouns as well. So you can say *either*

nehs lu-Taaf (nice people) **or** *nehs la-Tee-fa*

Adjectives also agree with the noun in being definite or indefinite, so the same definite prefix *il-* must be added to adjectives next to a definite noun:

wa-lad la-Teef **but** *il-wa-lad il-la-Teef*
(a nice boy)   (the nice boy —
                                         lit., the boy the nice)

Comparatives and Superlatives

To say "bigger, biggest," "cheaper, cheapest," and so on, a special pattern is used:

ki-beer (big) *'ak-bar* (bigger, biggest)
ri-kheeS (cheap) *'ar-khaS* (cheaper, cheapest)
ga-meel (beautiful) *'ag-mal* (more, most
beautiful)

When it means "the most . . ." it *precedes* the noun:

'ar-khaS si^cr	*si^cr 'ar-khaS*
(the cheapest price)	(a cheaper price)

Comparative/superlative adjectives are invariable:

'ak-bar wa-lad	(the biggest boy)
'ak-bar bint	(the biggest girl)
'ak-bar 'aw-lehd	(the biggest boys)

NONVERBAL SENTENCES

There is no equivalent in Arabic to "am, is, are"; the subject is just followed directly by the rest of the sentence:

mu-Ham-mad maS-ree	Muhammed is Egyptian.
a-na min lan-dan	I'm from London.

To make these negative, *mish* is placed after the subject:

mu-Ham-mad mish maS-ree	Muhammed isn't Egyptian.
a-na mish min lan-dan	I'm not from London.

PRONOUNS

Personal Pronouns

These pronouns take the following form as subject of a sentence:

a-na	I	*iH-na*	we
in-ta	you (masc.)	*in-tum-ma*	you (pl.)
in-tee	you (fem.)		
huw-wa	he		
hee-ya	she	*hum-ma*	they

As in Spanish and Italian, these pronouns are used optionally with verbs — usually only when you want to emphasize the subject:

(a-na) ᶜ*a-wiz* ʹ*eh-kul*   I want to eat.
(hee-ya) ᶜ*aw-za teh-kul*   She wants to eat.

Following a noun or preposition, they take the following forms:

-ee	″*ud-deh-mee*	in front of me
-ak	″*ud-deh-mak*	in front of you (masc.)
-ik	″*ud-deh-mik*	in front of you (fem.)
-oo	″*ud-deh-moo*	in front of him
-ha	″*ud-dehm-ha*	in front of her
-na	″*ud-dehm-na*	in front of us
-kum	″*ud-dehm-kum*	in front of you (pl.)
-hum	″*ud-dehm-hum*	in front of them

After a noun they have a possessive meaning:

bey-*tee* my house   ʹ**ukh**-*tak* your sister
(to a man)

After verbs, the same forms are used:

*yi-**shoof**-ha* he sees her   *ba-**Hib**-boo* I like him.

The only exception is the "me" form, which is -*nee* after verbs:

*yi-**shoof**-nee* he sees me.

Demonstrative Pronouns

To say "this one" or "that one," *da* or *dee* is used (depending on whether the noun referred to is masculine or feminine):

*da **kway**-yis*   *dee kway-**yi**-sa*
that (masc.) one is good   that (fem.) one is good

The plural "these" or "those" is *dohl*:

*dohl kway-yi-**seen***   those are good

da, *dee*, and *dohl* can be added to a definite noun to make it demonstrative:

*il-**wa**-lad* the boy   *il-**wa**-lad da* that boy
*il-**bint*** the girl   *il-**bint** dee* that girl

Possessive Particle

The word *bi-**teh**^{c}* means "belonging to." This particle can be used after a noun to indicate possession of the noun:

*il-**beyt** bi-**teh**^{c}*   the house belonging to
*mu-**Ham**-mad*   Mohammed, Mohammed's
                       house

It agrees with the noun it follows in number and gender. The feminine form is *bi-**teh**-^{c}it*:

*il-^{c}a-ra-**bee**-ya bi-**teh**-^{c}it*   Mohammed's car
*mu-**Ham**-mad*

The plural form is *bi-**too**^{c}*:

*il-bu-**yoot** bi-**too**^{c}*   Mohammed's houses
*mu-**Ham**-mad*

As with ordinary adjectives, the feminine singular may also be used after plural nouns:

*il-bu-**yoot** bi-**teh**-^{c}it*   Mohammed's houses
*mu-**Ham**-mad*

When the possessor is a pronoun — "me, you, him, etc." — the suffixed forms given on p. 220 are added:

*il-**beyt** bi-**teh**-^{c}ee*   the house belonging to me,
                         my house

Notice the feminine *bi-teh-ᶜit* gets shortened to *bi-taᶜt* if what follows begins with a vowel:

*il-ᶜa-ra-**bee**-ya bi-**taᶜ**-tee*   my car
*il-ᶜa-ra-**bee**-ya bi-**taᶜt***   the engineer's car
*il-mu-**han**-dis*

VERBS

Present Tense

In the dictionary the verbs are given in the third person form of the present ("he goes," "he sees," and so on), beginning with *y-*. All forms of a regular present tense verb are as follows:

ash-rab I drink	**nish**-rab we drink
tish-rab you (masc.) drink	tish-**ra**-boo you (pl.) drink
tish-**ra**-bee (fem.) drink	
yish-rab he drinks	yish-**ra**-boo they drink
tish-rab she drinks	

These are the forms of the verb that follow words such as **mum**-kin (it is/is it possible), **ᶜa**-wiz (I want), **leh**-zim (it is necessary), '*in shaa' al-laah* (I hope):

ᶜa-wiz **ash**-rab shayy   I want to drink tea.
leh-zim **tish**-rab ″**ah**-wa   You (masc.) must drink
coffee.   coffee.
mum-kin **yish**-rab   Can he drink some water?
may-ya?

If the verb is being used by itself to indicate an habitual or ongoing action, it is usually prefixed by *b(i)-*:

bi-**yish**-rab   he drinks, is drinking
bash-rab   I drink, am drinking

Imperatives

Take the second person and omit the initial *t-*:

ish-rab!	drink! (masc.)
ish-ra-bee!	drink! (fem.)
ish-ra-boo!	drink! (pl.)

Future Tense

h(a)- is prefixed to the basic present:

ha-yish-rab	he will drink
hash-rab	I will drink

Negatives

In the present tense, *ma-* is added to the beginning, and *-sh* to the end of the verb:

*ma-bi-yish-**rabsh***	he doesn't drink/ isn't drinking

With the future, *mish* is placed before the verb:

*mish **hash**-rab*	I shall not drink

Past Tense

This will not be widely used in situations expressing immediate needs and feelings. The same consonantal root is combined with a set of suffixes:

*shi-**ribt*** I drank	*shi-**rib**-na* we drank
*shi-**ribt*** you (masc.) drank	*shi-**rib**-too* you (pl.) drank
*shi-**rib**-tee* you (fem.) drank	
shi-rib* he drank	**shir**-boo they drank
shir-bit she drank	

The vowels separating the root consonants are either *i - i* (as in **shi-rib**) or *a - a* (as in **da-ras**: he studied).

As with the present tense, the negative is formed by placing *ma-* and *-sh* around the verb:

*ma-shi-**rib**-tish*	I did not drink, etc.

(See p. 7 for a note on the little "helping vowel" that avoids a heavy sequence of three consonants.)

"Want" and "Need"

"Verbs" such as *ᶜa-wiz [ᶜaw-za]* (want) and *miH-tehg [miH-teh-ga]* (need) in fact behave more like adjectives, because they have only masculine, feminine, and plural forms. The plurals are *ᶜaw-zeen* and *miH-teh-geen*. They are negated by *mish* before the verb:

(a-na) mish ᶜa-wiz   I don't want

"Have"

There is no verb "to have" in Arabic; a preposition "with" (*ᶜand* or *ma-ᶜa*) is used with the object pronouns given above:

ᶜan-doo fi-loos   lit., with him money, that is,
                        He has money
ᶜan-dee wa"t   lit., with me time,
                        that is, I have time

These are negated like verbs, with *ma-* and *-sh* around the word:

ma-ᶜan-doosh fi-loos   he has no money
ma-ᶜan-deesh wa"t   I have no time

QUESTIONS

Questions requiring "yes" or "no" as an answer have the same form as statements, but the voice rises at the end of the sentences.

mu-Ham-mad min   Muhammed is from Egypt
maSr ↓   (falling intonation)
mu-Ham-mad min   Is Muhammed from Egypt?
maSr? ↑   (rising intonation)

Questions beginning in English with "what," "where," "why," "how," and so on often have the question word at the beginning in Arabic too:

feyn il-'u-tu-**bees**?	Where is the bus?
iz-**zayy** il-'aw-lehd?	How are the children?

But many speakers put the question word at the end of the sentence:

il-'u-tu-**bees** feyn?	Where is the bus?
'is-mak 'eyh?	What is your name?
in-ta za^c-lehn leyh?	Why are you angry?

COMPLEX SENTENCES

Once you are confident about using simple sentences that contain just one verb, you may want to create more elaborate structures.

Relative Clauses

Relative clauses are those following a noun and beginning with "who," "which," "that," "on which," "from whom," etc. in English.

In Arabic, if the noun is definite (begins with *il-*), the relative word is *il-lee*:

ish-rab il-**bee**-ra il-lee fit-tal-**leh**-ga.
Drink the beer that is in the refrigerator.

If the definite noun does not correspond to the subject of the relative clause, a matching pronoun has to be added to the second verb:

ish-rab il-**bee**-ra il-lee ish-ta-**reyt**-ha im-**beh**-riH.
Literally: Drink the beer that I bought *it* yesterday.

If the noun being modified by a relative clause is indefinite (no *il-*), no *il-lee* is used either:

ti^c-raf bint mish ^caw-za tit-gaw-wiz?
Do you know a girl (who) doesn't want to get married?
hash-rab bee-ra ish-ta-reyt-ha im-beh-riH.
I will drink some beer that I bought yesterday.
(Literally: I will drink some beer I bought it yesterday.)

"That" Clauses

Clauses introduced by "that" usually begin with *inn* in Arabic:

a-Zunn inn seh-mi fil-beyt.
I think that Sami is at home.
at-man-na inn ley-la ha-tee-gee buk-ra.
I hope that Leila will come tomorrow.

Like verbs and prepositions (see above), *inn-* may carry a suffixed pronoun:

a-Zunn in-noo fil-beyt.
I think that he is at home.
at-man-na in-na-ha ha-tee-gee buk-ra.
I hope that she will come tomorrow.

While "that" can be dropped in English, *inn* should always be used in Arabic.

ENGLISH-ARABIC DICTIONARY*

The feminine form is given in square brackets. When a plural is given, it is preceeded by (pl.). Verbs are given in the third person singular present form ("he goes," etc.), beginning with *yi-*. For other forms of the verbs see the Notes on Grammar on page 222.

A

able "*eh-dir* ["*ad-ra*] قادر [قادرة]

about (approximately)
Ha-weh-lee حوالي، تقريباً

about (concerning)
^can عن

above *foh*" فوق

absent *gheh-yib* غائب

accident *Had-sa* حادثة

accidentally *Sud-fa* بالمصادفة

accompany *yi-waS-Sal* يرفق

account (financial) *Hi-sehb*
(pl.) *Hi-seh-beht* حساب، حسابات

accountant *mu-Heh-sib* محاسب

ache (noun) *wa-ga^c/'a-lam*
وجع / ألم

(verb) *yiw-ga^c* يوجع

head — *Su-daa^c* صداع

actor *mu-mas-sil* ممثل

actress *mu-mas-si-la* ممثلة

adapter plug *mu-Haw-wil*
محول، وصيلة

addicted (to) *mud-min (bi)*
مدمن (على)

address *^cin-wehn* عنوان

administration '*i-daa-ra* إدارة

advertisement '*i^c-lehn*
(pl.) '*i^c-leh-neht* إعلان، إعلانات

advice *na-See-Ha* نصيحة

advise *yin-SaH* ينصح

afraid *kheh-yif*
[*khay-fa*] خائف

Africa *af-reeq-ya* إفريقيا

African '*af-ree-qee* إفريقي

after *ba^cd* بعد

afternoon *ba^cd iD-Duhr* بعد الظهر

afterwards *ba^c-deyn* بعد ذلك

again *teh-nee* مرة أخرى، ثانية

against *Didd* ضد

agent *wa-keel*
(pl.) *wu-ka-la* وكيل، وكلاء

— ago *min* —   — منذ

agreed *mu-weh-fi"*   موافق

air conditioning *tak-yeef ha-wa*   مكيف، تكييف الهواء

airline *shir-kit Tay-ya-raan*   شركة طيران

(by) air mail *bil-ba-reed ig-gaw-wee*   بالبريد الجوي

airplane *Tay-yaa-ra*   طائرة

airport *ma-Taar*   مطار

Alexandria *is-kin-di-ree-ya*   إسكندرية

Algeria *'ig-ga-zeh-yir*   الجزائر

Algerian *ga-zay-ree*   جزائري

all *kull*   كل

allergy *Ha-sa-see-ya*   حساسية

all right *Tay-yib*   طيب

almonds *lohz*   لوز

almost *ta"-ree-ban*   تقريبا

also *ka-mehn/bar-Doo*   أيضاً

although *ma-ᶜa 'inn*   رغم أن

always *ta-mal-lee/day-man*   دائماً

ambassador *sa-feer* (pl.) *su-fa-ra*   سفير، سفراء

ambulance *il-'is-ᶜehf*   سيارة الإسعاف

America *am-ree-ka*   أمريكا

American *am-ree-keh-nee* (pl.) *'am-ree-kehn*   أمريكي

analysis *taH-leel*   تحليل

analyze *yi-Hal-lil*   يحلل

and *wi*   و

anesthetic *bing*   مخدر

angry (at) *zaᶜ-lehn (min)*   زعلان (من)

animal *Ha-ya-wehn* (pl.) *Ha-ya-weh-neht*   حيوان، حيوانات

ankle *kaᶜb*   كعب القدم

annual *sa-na-wee*   سنوي

another *teh-nee [tan-ya]*   آخر، أخرى

answer (noun) *radd*   رد، إجابة

(verb) *yi-rudd*   يرد

antiquities *'a-saar*   آثار

antiseptic *mu-Tah-hir*   مُطَهِّر

any *'ayy*   أي

anyone *Hadd*   أي شخص

anywhere *'ay-yi ma-kehn*   أي مكان

apartment *sha"-"a* (pl.) *shu-"a"*   شقة، شقق

appetite *sha-hee-ya*   شهية

appetizers *maz-za*   مزة

apples *tuf-fehH*   تفاح

appointment *ma-ᶜehd* (pl.) *ma-wa-ᶜeed*   موعد، ميعاد

apricots *mish-mish*   مشمش

April 'ab-**reel** — إبريل

Arab **^ca**-ra-bee
(pl.) **^ca**-rab — عربي، عرب

Arabic **^ca**-ra-bee — عربي

archeology ^cilm il-'a-**saar** — علم الآثار

architect mu-**han**-dis
mi^c-**maa**-ree — مهندس معماري

area man-**Ti**-"a — منطقة

arm di-**reh**^c — ذراع

army geysh — جيش

army officer **Zaa**-biT
(pl.) Zub-**baaT** — ضابط، ضباط

around (approximately)
Ha-**weh**-lee — تقريبا

arrival wu-**Sool** — وصول

arrive **yiw**-Sal — يصل

art fann (pl.) fu-**noon** — فن، فنون

artist fan-**nehn** — فنان

as soon as 'aw-wil ma — حالما

ashtray Ta"-**Too**-"a — طفاية، طقطوقة

ask **yis**-'al — يسأل

ask for **yuT**-lub — يطلب

asleep **neh**-yim [**nay**-ma] — نائم

aspirin as-bee-**reen** — أسبيرين

Aswan 'aS-**waan** — أسوان

at (place) fi — في / بـ

(not) at all **khaa**-liS — مطلقا

aubergine bi-din-**gehn** — باذنجان

August a-**ghuS**-Tus — أغسطس

aunt (paternal) **^cam**-ma — عمة

(maternal) **kheh**-la — خالة

Australia os-**tral**-ya — أستراليا

auto repair shop **war**-sha — ورشة

autumn kha-**reef** — خريف

average mu-ta-**was**-siT — متوسط

awake **Saa**-Hee — صاحي

awful fa-**Zee**^c — فظيع

B

baby Tifl (pl.) 'aT-**faal** — طفل، أطفال

back (noun) Dahr — ظهر

back (adj.) war-**raa**-nee — خلفي

back of, behind **wa**-ra — وراء

backgammon **Taw**-la — طاولة

backwards **wa**-ra — إلى الوراء

bad **wi**-Hish — سيئ، رديء

not — mish baT-**Taal** — مش بطال

bag **shan**-Ta
(pl.) **shu**-naT — حقيبة، حقائب

baggage **shu**-naT/
^cafsh — حقائب، أمتعة

baked fil-**furn** — في الفرن

bakery furn/**makh**-baz — فرن، مخبز

ball *koh-ra* كرة

ballpoint pen "*al-lam gaff* قلم جاف

bananas *mohz* موز

bandages *ru-baaT* رباط

bank *bank*
(pl.) *bu-nook* بنك، بنوك

bar *baar* بار

barber *Hal-leh"* حلاق

bargain (verb)
yi-faa-Sil يساوم

bargaining *fi-Saal* مساومة

basket *sa-bat* سلة

basketball *bas-kit-bohl* كرة السلة

bath *ban-yoo* بانيو

bathroom *Ham-mehm,* حمام، تواليت
twa-litt

bathe *yis-ta-Ham-ma* يستحم

battery *baT-Ta-ree-ya* بطارية

bazaar, market *soo"* سوق

beach *plehj/shaTT* شاطئ

beach umbrella *sham-see-ya* شمسية

beans *fa-Sul-ya,* فاصولية
fool فول

beard *da"n* لحية

beautiful *Hilw/ga-meel* جميل

beauty parlor *Sa-lohn tag-meel* صالون تجميل

because *ᶜa-shehn, li-'ann* لأن

become *yib-"a* يصبح

bed *si-reer* سرير، سراير
(pl.) *sa-reh-yir*

bedroom 'oh-Dit nohm غرفة نوم

beef *laH-ma ba-"a-ree* لحم بقر

beer *bee-ra* بيرة

before (prep) "*abl* قبل

beforehand "*ab-li ki-da* من قبل

begin *yib-ti-dee* يبدأ

behind *wa-ra* خلف

believe *yi-sad-da"* يصدق

bell *ga-ras* جرس

belly dancing *ra"S ba-la-dee* رقص شرقي

belt *Hi-zehm* حزام

bet (verb) *yi-raa-hin* يراهن

better, best '*aH-san/kheyr* أحسن، أفضل

between *beyn* بين

bicycle *ᶜa-ga-la* عجلة، دراجة

big *ki-beer* كبير

bigger, biggest '*ak-bar* أكبر

bill (check) *Hi-sehb* حساب، حسابات
(pl.) *Hi-seh-beht*

bills (currency) 'aw-reh" na"d
أوراق نقد

bird ᶜaS-foor
(pl.) ᶜa-Sa-feer طائر، طيور

birthday ᶜeed mi-lehd عيد ميلاد

biscuit bas-ka-weet بسكويت

black 'is-wid
[soh-da] [أسود [سوداء

blanket baT-Ta-nee-ya بطانية

blender khal-laaT خلاط

blind 'aᶜ-ma
[ᶜam-ya] [أعمى [عمياء

blocked mas-dood مسدود

blood pressure DakhT
id-damm ضغط الدم

blouse bloo-za بلوزة

blue 'az-ra" [zar-"a] [أزرق [زرقاء

board looH لوح

boat mar-kib (pl.) ma-reh-kib
سفينة/مركب، مراكب

bobby pins bi-nas دبابيس للشعر

body gism جسم

boiled mas-loo" مسلوق

bomb qum-bi-la
(pl.) qa-neh-bil قنبلة، قنابل

bone ᶜaDm عظم

book ki-tehb
(pl.) ku-tub كتاب، كتب

book (verb) yiH-giz يحجز

booking Hagz حجز

bookstore mak-ta-ba مكتبة

boring mu-mill مضجر

borrow yis-ti-lif يستلف

boss ray-yis رئيس

both lit-neyn الاثنان

bottle "i-zeh-za
(pl.) "a-zeh-yiz زجاجة، زجاجات

box san-doo" صندوق

boy wa-lad
(pl.) 'aw-lehd ولد، أولاد

bra soo-tyehn حمالة الصدر

bracelet ghi-wey-sha سوار

brain mukhkh مخ

brakes fa-raa-mil فرامل

branch farᶜ
(pl.) fu-rooᶜ فرع، فروع

brand mar-ka
(pl.) mar-keht ماركة، ماركات

brass na-Hehs 'aS-far نحاس أصفر

Brazil ba-ra-zeel برازيل

Brazilian ba-ra-zee-lee
[ba-ra-zee-lee-ya] برازيلي

bread ᶜeysh/khubz خبز

break (verb) yik-sar يكسر

broken mak-soor
[mak-soo-ra] مكسور

broken (out of order)
ᶜaT-laan [ᶜaT-laa-na] معطل

breakfast (noon) *fi-Taar* إفطار

(verb) *yif-Tar* يفطر

breathe *yit-naf-fis* يتنفس

bribe *rash-wa* رشوة

bride *ᶜa-roo-sa* عروسه

bridegroom *ᶜa-rees* عريس

bridge *kub-ree* كوبري، كباري

(pl.) *ka-beh-ree*

bring *yi-geeb* يحضر

Britain *bri-Tan-ya* بريطانيا

British *bri-Taa-nee* بريطاني
[*bri-Taa-nee-ya*]

broke (bankrupt) *mi-fal-lis* مفلس

brother *'akhkh* أخ، أخوة

(pl.) *'ikh-weht*

brown *bun-nee* بني

brown-skinned *'as-mar* [أسمر]
[*sam-ra*]

brush *fur-sha* فرشاة

buffet (dining) car *bu-feyh* بوفية، عربية الأ

bug *Ha-sha-ra* حشرة، حشرات
(pl.) *Ha-sha-reht*

building *ᶜi-maa-ra* عمارة، عمارات
(pl.) *ᶜi-maa-raat*

burial *dafn* دفن

burn *yiH-ra"* يحرق

burned *maH-roo"* محروق

bus *'u-tu-bees* اوتوبيس، اوتوبيسات
(pl.) *'u-tu-bee-seht*

bus stop *ma-HaT-Tit 'u-tu-bees* محطة اوتوبيس

business *ti-gaa-ra, 'aᶜ-mehl* تجارة، أعمال

businessman *teh-gir, raa-gil* رجل أعمال، تاجر
'aᶜ-mehl

busy *mash-ghool* مشغول

but *bass, leh-kin* لكن

butcher *gaz-zaar* جزار

butter *zib-da* زبده

button *zu-raar* زر، أزرار
(pl.) *za-raa-yir*

buy (verb) *yish-ti-ree* يشتري

by the hour *fis-seh-ᶜa* في الساعة

by the way... *ᶜa-la fik-ra* على فكرة

C

cabaret *ka-ba-rey* كابارية، عرض

cabbage *ku-rumb* كرنب

café *"ah-wa* مقهى

caftan *"uf-Taan* قفطان، قفاطين
(pl.) *"a-fa-Teen*

cake *ga-toh* كاتو
(pl.) *ga-to-heht*

Cairo *il-qaa-hi-ra, maSr* القاهرة

call (telephone) *mu-kal-ma* مكالمة

call (verb) *yi-**kal**-lim* يكلم

camel *ga-mal* جمل

camera *ka-me-ra* كاميرا، آلة تصوير

campsite *mu-**khay**-yam si-**yeh**-Hee* مخيم سياحي

can (noun) *ᶜil-ba (pl.) ᶜi-lab* علبة، علب

Canada *ka-na-da* كندا

Canadian *ka-na-dee [ka-na-dee-ya]* كندي [كندية]

cancel *yil-ghee* يلغي

cancer *sa-ra-**Taan*** سرطان

candles *shamᶜ* شمع

capital (finance) *ra's mehl* رأس مال

capital (city) *ᶜaa-**Si**-ma* عاصمة

car *ᶜa-ra-**bee**-ya/say-**yaa**-ra* سيارة

carat *"i-**raaT*** قيراط

card *kart (pl.) ku-**root**/bi-**Taa**-qa (pl.) bi-**Taa**-qaat* كارت، كروت/بطاقة، بطاقات

(be) careful! *Heh-sib! [Has-bee!]* إحذر

carpenter *nag-**gaar*** نجار

carpet *sig-**geh**-da (pl.) sa-ga-**geed*** سجادة، سجاجيد

carriage (horsedrawn) *Han-**Toor*** حنطور

carry *yi-**sheel**, yiH-mil* يحمل

cash (noun) *na"d* نقد

cashier *Sar-**raaf*** صراف

cassette *ka-sitt (pl.) kasit-**teht*** كسيت، كسيتات

cassette player *gi-hehz ka-**sitt*** جهاز كسيت

cause (noun) *sa-bab* سبب

ceiling *sa"f* سقف

cemetery *mad-fan* مدفن

center *wisT* وسط

center (institution) *mar-kaz* مركز

ceramics *fukh-khaar* فخار

certain (sure) *mit-'ak-kid [mit-'ak-ki-da]* متأكد [متأكدة]

certainly *Haa-Dir* حاضر، تحت أمرك

chain *sil-**si**-la* سلسلة

chair *kur-see (pl.) ka-reh-see* كرسي، كراسي

change (money) *yi-**Haw**-wil* يحول

change (verb. intr.) *yit-**ghay**-yar* يتغير

(verb. trans.) *yi-**ghay**-yar* يغير

change (remainder) *beh-"ee* باقي

small — *fak-ka* فكة

channel *qa-**naah*** قناة

chat (verb) *yi-**dar**-dish* يدردش

chauffeur *saw-weh"* سائق، سواق

cheap *ri-kheeS [ri-khee-Sa]* رخيص

    cheaper, *'ar-khaS* رخيص

    cheapest أرخص

cheat (verb) *yi-ghishsh* يغش

check, bill *Hi-sehb* حساب

check (personal) *sheek* شيك، شيكات
    (pl.) *shee-keht*

    traveler's checks *shee-keht* شيكات سياحية
    si-ya-Hee-ya

check (examine) *yi-shoof* يفحص

check in (baggage) *yi-sag-gil* يسجل

cheek *khadd* خد، خدود
    (pl.) *khu-dood*

cheese *gib-na* جبنة

chemist's (druggist's)
    'ag-za-kheh-na, أجزخانة، صيدلية
    Say-da-lee-ya

chess *sha-Ta-rang* شطرنج

chest (box) *san-doo"* صندوق

chest (body) *Sidr* صدر

chick peas *Hum-muS* حمص

chicken *fi-rehkh/da-jehj* فراخ/دجاج

chicken soup *shur-bit fi-rehkh* شربة فراخ/دجاج
    / *da-jehj*

child *Tifl* (pl.) *'aT-faal, wa-lad*
    (pl.) *'aw-lehd* طفل، أطفال/ولد، أولاد

China *iS-Seen* الصين

Chinese *See-nee [See-nee-ya]* صيني

chocolate *sho-ko-laa-ta* شكولاتة

choose *yikh-taar* يختار

Christian *ma-see-Hee* مسيحي

Christmas
    ᶜeed il-mi-lehd عيد الميلاد

church *ki-nee-sa* كنيسة

cigarette *si-gaa-ra* سيجارة، سجائر
    (pl.) *sa-geh-yir*

cinema *si-ni-ma* سينما

city *ba-lad/ma-dee-na* مدينة

class, classroom *faSL* فصل

clean (adj.) *ni-Deef* نظيف
    [ni-Dee-fa]

clean (verb) *yi-naD-Daf* ينظف

cleansing cream *kreym li* كريم لإزالة المكياج
    'i-zeh-lit il-mak-yaj

clever *shaa-Tir [shaT-ra]* شاطر

clock *seh-ᶜa* ساعة

    alarm clock *mi-nab-bih* منبه

close (verb) *yi"-fil* يغلق، يقفل

    closed *ma"-fool* مغلق، مقفول

cloth *"u-mehsh* قماش

clothes *hu-doom* ملابس

club *neh-dee* (pl.) *na-weh-dee* نادي، نوادي

coast *seh-Hil* ساحل

coffee *"ah-wa* قهوة

ground – *bunn* بن

coffee shop *"ah-wa* مقهى

cold (things, weather) *beh-rid* بارد

(people) *bar-dehn* [*bar-deh-na*] بردان

(in the head) *zi-kehm/bard* زكام/برد

colleague *zi-meel* (pl.) *zu-ma-la* زميل، زملا.

college *kul-lee-ya* كلية

cologne *ko-lon-ya* كلونيا

color *lohn* (pl.) *'al-wehn* لون، ألوان

color chart *da-leel 'al-wehn* دليل ألوان

comb *mishT* مشط

come *yee-gee* يجيئ

come! (imp.) *ta-ᶜeh-la!* [*ta-ᶜeh-lee!*] هيا بنا!

comfort (noun) *raa-Ha* راحة

coming *gayy* [*gay-ya*] قادم/جاي

commerce *ti-gaa-ra* تجارة

committee *lag-na* لجنة

communications *mu-waS-laat* مواصلات

company *shir-ka* (pl.) *sha-ri-keht* شركة، شركات

complete (entire) *keh-mil* [*kam-la*] كامل

computer *kom-byoo-tar* كمبيوتر

concert *Haf-la mu-si-qee-ya* حفلة موسيقية

confectioner's *Ha-la-weh-nee* حلواني

confectionery *Ha-la-wee-yeht* حلويات

conference *mu'-ta-mar* (pl.) *mu'-ta-ma-raat* مؤتمر، مؤتمرات

confirm *yi-'ak-kid* يؤكد

congratulations! *mab-rook!* مبروك!

constipation *'im-sehk* إمساك

consulate *qun-Su-lee-ya* قنصلية

contact (verb) *yiT-Ti-Sil (bi—)* يتصل (بـ)

contact lenses *ᶜa-da-seht* عدسات

soft — *Ta-ree-ya* — لينة

hard — *nash-fa* — صلبة

continue *yi-kam-mil* يستمر

contract *ᶜa"d* عقد

cook (verb) *yuT-bukh* يطبخ

cook (noun) *Tab-baakh* طباخ

cookies *bas-ka-weet* بسكويت

Coptic *"ib-Tee* قبطي

copy (noun) *nus-kha* نسخة

coral *mur-gehn* مرجان

corn (maize) *du-ra* ذرة

corner (of street) *naS-ya* ناصية

correct *maz-booT* مضبوط

corruption *fa-sehd* فساد

cosmetics *mak-yaj* مكياج

cost (noun) *ta-man/si^{c}r* ثمن/سعر

cost (verb) *yi-kal-lif* يكلف

cotton *"uTn* قطن

cough (verb) *yi-kuHH* يسعل، يكح

    (noun) *kuH-Ha* سعال، كحة

council *mag-lis* مجلس

country (nation) *ba-lad* بلد، بلاد
    (pl.) *bi-lehd*

countryside *reef* ريف

(of) course *Tab-^{c}an* طبعا

cows *ba-"ar* بقر

crab *'a-boo ga-lam-boo* أبو جلمبو

crazy *mag-noon* مجنون
    [*mag-noo-na*]

cream *"ish-Ta* قشطة

(cosmetic) cream *kreym* كريم

credit card *kri-dit kard/*
bi-Taa-qit i^c-ti-mehd كريدت كارد/بطاقة اعتماد

crisis *'az-ma* أزمة

crowded *zaH-ma* زحمة/مزدحم

crystal (watch) *"i-zehz* زجاج

cucumber *khi-yaar* قثاء، خيار

culture *sa-qaa-fa* ثقافة

cultured *mu-saq-qaf* مثقف

cup *fin-gehn* (pl.) *fa-na-geen* فنجان، فناجين

currency *^{c}um-la* عملة

    hard — *^{c}um-la Sa^c-ba* عملة صعبة

customer *zi-boon* زبون، زبائن
    (pl.) *za-beh-yin*

customs *ig-gum-ruk* الجمرك

cut *yi"-Ta^c* يقطع

D

dam *sadd* سد

damage *yi-baw-waZ* يضر

dance (verb) *yur-"uS* يرقص

dancing *ra"S* رقص

danger *kha-Tar* خطر

dangerous *kha-Teer* خطير

date *ta-reekh* تاريخ

date (appointment) *ma-^{c}ehd* موعد، ميعاد

dates (fruit) *ba-laH* بلح

daughter *bint* (pl.) *ba-neht* بنت، بنات

dawn *fagr* فجر

day *yohm* (pl.) *'ay-yehm* يوم، أيام

two days *yoh-***meyn**   يومان

day after tomorrow *ba^c-di*
buk-ra   بعد غد

dead *may-**yit**   ميت

deaf *'aT-rash [Tar-sha]*   أطرش

death *moht*   موت

December *di-**sim**-bir*   ديسمبر

decide *yi-**qar**-rar*   يقرر

delicious *la-**zeez**   لذيذ

deliver *yi-**sal**-lim*   يسلم

demonstration *mu-**Zah**-ra*   مظاهرة

dentist *Ta-**beeb** 'as-**nehn***
طبيب أسنان

depart, leave *yim-shee/yi-seh-fir*
يغادر، يسافر

department *qism (pl.) aq-**sehm***
قسم، أقسام

depend (on) *yic-**ti**-mid*
(^ca-la)   (يعتمد (على

deposit (noun) *ta'-meen*,
^car-boon   عربون، تأمين

descend *yin-zil*   ينزل

desert *SaH-ra*   صحراء

desserts *Ha-la-wee-yeht*   حلويات

destroy *yi-**dam**-mar*   يدمر

detour *taH-**wee**-la*   تحويلة

develop (film) *yi-**Ham**-maD*
يحمض

development *ta-**Taw**-wur*   تطور

dialect *lah-ga (pl.) lah-geht*
لهجة، لهجات

diamond *'al-**maaz***   الماس

diarrhea *'is-hehl*   إسهال

dictionary *qa-**moos***   قاموس

die *yi-**moot***   يموت

diesel (gas) *dee-zil*   ديزل

diet *ri-**jeem***   نظام غذائي

different *mukh-ta-lif*
[mukh-ta-li-fa]   مختلف

difficult *Sa^cb*   صعب

difficulty *Su-^coo-ba*   صعوبة

dig *yuH-fur*   يحفر

dine *yit-^cash-sha*   يتعشى

dining room (in hotel) *maT-^cam*
مطعم

dinner *^ca-sha*   عشاء

direct (adj.) *mu-**beh**-shir*   مباشر

director *mu-**deer***   مدير

directory *da-**leel***   دليل

dirty *wi-sikh [wis-kha]*   قذر، وسخ

disaster *mu-**See**-ba*   مصيبة

disc *disk*
*(pl.) dis-**keht***   قرص، أقراص

discount *takh-**feeD***   تخفيض

disease (illness) *ma-raD*
*(pl.) 'am-**raaD***   مرض، أمراض

dish *Ta-ba"*
*(pl.) 'aT-**baa"***   طبق، أطباق

dishwasher *ghas-seh-lit Su-Hoon* غسالة صحون

distance *ma-seh-fa* مسافة

distribution *taw-zee^c* توزيع

district *man-Ti-qa* منطقة

do *yi^c-mil* يعمل

doctor *Ta-beeb, duk-toor* طبيب، دكتور

documents *'aw-reh"* أوراق

dog *kalb* (pl.) *ki-lehb* كلب، كلاب

dollar *do-laar* (pl.) *do-la-raat* دولار، دولارات

donkey *Hu-maar* حمار

door *behb* باب

doorman (doorkeeper) *baw-wehb* (pl.) *baw-weh-been* بواب

down (stairs) *taHt* تحت

downtown *fi wiST il-ba-lad* في وسط المدينة

dress (noun) *fus-tehn* فستان

dressed *leh-bis* [*lab-sa*] لابس

get dressed *yil-bis* يلبس

drink (verb) *yish-rab* يشرب

drinks *mash-roo-beht* مشروبات

drive (verb) *yi-soo"* يسوق

drugs *mu-khad-da-raat* مخدرات

drugstore *'ag-za-kheh-na, Say-da-lee-ya* أجزخانة، صيدلية

drunk *sak-raan* [*sak-raa-na*] سكران

dry *neh-shif* [*nash-fa*] جاف، ناشف

dry cleaning *it-tan-Deef in-neh-shif* التنظيف الجاف

Dutch *ho-lan-dee* [*ho-lan-dee-ya*] هولندي

E

each *kull* كل

ear *widn* أذن

early *bad-ree* مبكر، باكر

earn *yik-sab* يكسب

earrings *Ha-la"* حلق

East (Orient) *shar"* شرق

Middle East *ish-sharq il-'aw-Sat* الشرق الأوسط

Eastern *shar-"ee* [*shar-"ee-ya*] شرقي

easy *sahl* سهل

eat *yeh-kuhl* يأكل

economics *'iq-ti-Saad* اقتصاد

education *ta^c-leem* تعليم

eggs *beyD* بيض

eggplant *bi-din-gehn* باذنجان

Egypt *maSr* مصر

Egyptian *maS-ree* [*maS-ree-ya*] (pl.) *maS-ree-yeen* مصري

eight *ta-man-ya* ثمانية

electricity *kah-ra-ba* كهرباء

elevator *'a-san-Seer* مصعد

embarrassed *mak-soof* [*mak-soo-fa*] مكسوف

embassy *sa-faa-ra* سفارة

emergency *Ta-waa-ri'* طوارئ

employee *mu-waZ-Zaf* موظف

empty *faa-Dee, feh-righ* فارغ

energetic *na-sheeT* نشيط

engine *mo-toor, ᶜid-da* موتور، محرك

engineer *mu-han-dis* مهندس

engineering *han-da-sa* هندسة

England *in-gil-ti-ra* إنجلترا

English *in-gi-lee-zee* [*in-gi-lee-zee-ya*] إنجليزي

enjoy *yit-mat-taᶜ (bi—)* يتمتع (بـ)

enough *ki-feh-ya* كفاية

enter *yud-khul, yi-khushsh* يدخل

entertainment *ma-leh-hee* ملاهي

entrance *du-khool* دخول

no entry *mam-nooᶜ id-du-khool* ممنوع الدخول

envelope *Zarf (pl.) Zu-roof* ظرف، ظروف

especially *khu-Soo-San* خصيصا

Europe *u-rub-ba* أوروبا

European *u-rub-bee* أوروبي

even *Hat-ta* حتى

evening *mi-seh', magh-rib* مساء، مغرب

every *kull* كل

everything *kul-li Ha-ga* كل شيء

exact *maZ-booT* مضبوط

exactly *biZ-ZabT* تماما، بالضبط

exam *im-ti-Hehn (pl.) im-ti-Heh-neht* امتحان

(for) example *ma-sa-lan* مثلا

excellent *mum-tehz* ممتاز

except *'il-la* إلا

exchange (money) *yi-Haw-wil* يحول

exchange rate *siᶜr it-taH-weel* سعر التحويل

excuse (noun) *ᶜuzr* عذر

Excuse me. *is-maH-lee* اسمح لي

exhibition *maᶜ-raD* معرض

exit *khu-roog* خروج

no exit *mam-nooᶜ il-khu-roog* ممنوع الخروج

expensive *gheh-lee* [*ghal-ya*] غالي

experience *khib-ra* خبرة

explain *yish-raH, yi-fah-him* يشرح

eye *^ceyn* [pl.] *^ci-yoon*   عين، عيون

eyeglasses *naD-Daa-ra*   نظارة

F

face *wishsh*   وجه

facial massage *tad-leek*   تدليك

factory *maS-na^c*   مصنع، مصانع
   (pl.) *ma-Saa-ni^c*

fall (verb) *yu-"a^c*   يقع

family *^cey-la/us-ra*   أسرة، عائلة

famous *mash-hoor*   مشهور
   [*mash-hoo-ra*]

fan *mar-wa-Ha*   مروحة

far *bi-^ceed*   بعيد

fare *'ug-ra*   أجرة

fast (adj.) *sa-ree^c*   سريع

fast (adv.) *bi sur^c-a*   بسرعة

fast (verb) *yi-Soom*   يصوم

fat *ti-kheen*   سمين

father *'abb*   أب

   my father *'a-boo-ya*   أبي

faucet *Ha-na-fee-ya*   حنفية

fear (verb) *yi-khehf*   يخاف

feast *^ceed*   عيد

February *fib-reh-yir*   فبراير

fence *soor*   سور

ferry *mi-^cad-dee-ya*   معدية

festival *^ceed*   عيد

fever *su-khu-nee-ya*   حمى

field *Ha"l*   حقل، حقول
   (pl.) *Hu-"ool*

fight (with) *yit-kheh-ni"*   يتخانق (مع)
   (*ma-^ca*)

fill *yim-la*   يملأ

filling (tooth) *Hashw*   حشو

film *film* (pl.) *'af-lehm*   فلم، أفلام

find *yi-leh-"ee*   يلقي

fine (noun) *mu-khal-fa*   غرامة

fine (adj.) *mum-tehz*   ممتاز

finger *Su-baa^c*   أصبع، أصابع
   (pl.) *Sa-waa-bi^c*

finish *yi-khal-laS*   يكمل

finish (intrans.) *yikh-laS*   يخلص

finished! (it's over!) *kha-laas!*   إنتهى

fire (verb) *yir-fid*   يطرد

fire (noun) *naar*   نار

first *'aw-wil* [*'oo-la*]   أول [أولى]

first class *da-ra-ga 'oo-la*   درجة أولى

first time *'aw-wil mar-ra*   المرة الأولى

fish *sa-mak*   سمك

five *kham-sa*   خمسة

fix *yi-Sal-laH*   يصلح

flashlight *kash-shehf* مصباح كهربائي

flat (apartment) *sha*"-"*a* شقة ، شقق
(pl.) *shu*-"a"

flies *dib-behn* ذباب

floor *dohr* (pl.) *'ad-waar* دور ، طابق

floor show *ᶜarD, ka-ba-rey* عرض ، كاباریة

florist *ma-Hall zu-hoor* محل زهور

flour *di-"ee"* دقيق

flowers *zu-hoor, ward* زهور ، ورد

folk dancing *ra"S shaᶜ-bee* رقص شعبي

food *'akl* طعام ، أكل

foot *rigl, "a-dam* قدم

football *koh-ra* كرة قدم

for *li, ᶜa-shehn* لـ

for example *ma-sa-lan* مثلا

forbidden *mam-nooᶜ* ممنوع

foreign(er) *'ag-na-bee* أجنبي
['*ag-na-bee-ya*]

forgive *yi-seh-miH* يسامح

fork *shoh-ka* شوكة

forward "*ud-dehm* إلى الأمام/قدام

four *ar-ba-ᶜa* أربعة

France *fa-ran-sa* فرنسا

free (unoccupied) *faa-Dee* خالي

(for nothing) *bi-ba-lehsh, mag-geh-nan* مجانا

freedom *Hur-ree-ya* حرية

freezer *free-zar* فريزر

French *fa-ran-seh-wee* فرنسي
[*fa-ran-sa-wee-ya*]

fresh *Taa-za* طازج

Friday (yohm) *ig-gum-ᶜa* يوم الجمعة

fried *ma"-lee* مقلي

friend *Saa-Hib* صاحب ، صديق
(pl.) '*aS-Haab*

friendship *Sa-daa-qa* صداقة

frighten *yi-khaw-wif* يخوف

from *min* من

in front of "*ud-dehm* أمام ، قدام

fruit *fak-ha* فاكهة

fry *yi*"-*lee* يقلي

full *mal-yehn* [*mal-yeh-na*]، ملئ

fundamentalist '*u-Soo-lee* أصولي ، أصوليو
(pl.) '*u-Soo-lee-yeen*

furniture *farsh* فرش

G

galabiyya *gal-la-bee-ya* جلابية

garbage *zi-beh-la* زبالة

garbage collector *zab-behl* زبال

garden *gi-ney-na* حديقة، جنينة
(pl.) *ga-neh-yin*

garlic *tohm* ثوم

gasoline *ban-zeen* بنزين

gas station *ma-HaT-Tit* محطة بنزين
ban-zeen

gate *ba-weh-ba* بوابة

gears *na"-leht, tu-roos* تروس

generous *ka-reem* كريم، كرماء
[*ka-ree-ma*] (pl.) *ku-ra-ma*

German *al-meh-nee* ألماني
[*al-ma-nee-ya*]

Germany *al-man-ya* ألمانيا

get *yi-geeb* يحضر

get in, on (vehicle) *yir-kab* يركب

ghee *sam-na* سمن

gift *ha-dee-ya* هدية، هدايا
(pl.) *ha-deh-ya*

girl *bint* (pl.) *ba-neht* بنت، بنات

glass *"i-zehr* زجاج

glass (drinking) *kub-beh-ya* كأس

go *yi-rooH* يذهب

Let's go! *yal-la!* هيا بنا

go away *yim-shee* يرحل، يغادر

go home *yi-raw-waH* يرجع للبيت

go in *yud-khul* يدخل

God *'al-laah* الله

gold *da-hab* ذهب

golf *golf* جولف

good (things) *kway-yis* جيد، كويس
[*kway-yi-sa*]

good (people) *Tay-yib* طيب
[*Tay-yi-ba*]

Good afternoon. *mi-seh'* مساء الخير
il-kheyr

Good-bye. *ma-ᶜa s-sa-leh-ma* مع السلامة

Good evening. *mi-seh' il-kheyr* مساء الخير

Good morning. *Sa-baH il-kheyr* صباح الخير

Good night. *tiS-baH ᶜa-la kheyr* تصبح على خير

government *Hu-koo-ma* حكومة

grandfather *gidd* جد

gradmother *gid-da* جدة

grapes *ᶜi-nab* عنب

grateful *mam-noon* ممنون

grave *ma"-ba-ra* مقبرة، مقابر
(pl.) *ma-"eh-bir*

gray *ra-maa-Dee* رمادي

great *ᶜa-Zeem* عظيم

Greece *il-yu-nehn* اليونان

greedy *Tam-maaᶜ* طماع
[*Tam-maa-ᶜa*]

Greek *yu-neh-nee* يوناني
[*yu-neh-nee-ya*]

green *'akh-Dar* [*khaD-ra*] أخضر

grilled **mash**-wee مشوي

grocery store ba"-**ehl** محل بقالة، بقال

ground 'arD أرض

guard **Heh**-ris حارس، حراس
(pl.) Hur-**raas**

guest Deyf ضيف، ضيوف
(pl.) Du-**yoof**

guide, guidebook da-**leel** دليل

guilty **muz**-nib مذنب

gulf kha-**leeg** خليج

H

hair sha^cr شعر

hairdresser ˈHal-leh", حلاق
kwa-**feer**

hairdryer sesh-**waar** مجفف شعر

half nuSS نصف

hand ˈeed (pl.) 'a-**yeh**-dee يد، أيدي

hanger sham-**meh**-^ca شماعة

happen **yiH**-Sal يحصل

happy mab-**SooT** مبسوط
[mab-**Soo**-Ta,
far-**Haan** [far-**Haa**-na] فرحان

harbor **mee**-na ميناء

hashish Ha-**sheesh** حشيش

hat bur-**ney**-Ta قبعة، برنيطة

have ^cand — عند ــ، مع ــ
or ma-^ca — + pronoun

I have ^can-dee, عندي، معي
ma-ceh-ya

hay fever zu-**kehm** زكام ربيعي
ra-**bee**-^cee

he **huw**-wa هو

head raas رأس

headache Su-**daa**^c صداع

headlight kash-**shehf** النور الأمامي

health **SiH**-Ha صحة

hear **yis**-ma^c يسمع

heart "alb قلب

heart attack 'az-ma qal-**bee**-ya
أزمة/نوبة قلبية

heat (verb) yi-**sakh**-khan يسخن

heavy ti-"**eel** ثقيل

heel ka^cb كعب

Hello. (on the phone) a-**loh** آلو

help (verb) yi-**seh**-^cid يساعد

Help! il-Ha-"**oo**-nee! النجدة!

here **hi**-na هنا

hide (verb) yi-**khab**-bee يخبئ

high ^c**eh**-lee عالي

highway Ta-**ree**" طريق رئيسي
ra-'**ee**-see

hire yi-'**ag**-gar يؤجر، يستأجر

historical ta-**ree**-khee تاريخي

history ta-**reekh** تاريخ

hit **yiD**-rab يضرب

hobby *hi-weh-ya* هواية

hold *yim-sik* يمسك

holiday *'a-geh-za* عطلة/إجازة

Holland *ho-lan-da* هولندا

home *beyt* بيت، منزل

    at home *fil-beyt* في البيت

honest *sha-reef*, شريف، أمين
    'a-meen

honey *ᶜa-sal* عسل

(I/we) hope so *'in shaa' al-laah* إن شاء الله

horse *Hu-Saan* حصان

hospital *mus-tash-fa* مستشفى

hostage *ra-hee-na* رهينة، رهائن
    (pl.) *ra-haa-yin*

hot (weather) *Harr* حار

    (people) *Har-raan* حران

    (food, etc.) *sukhn* ساخن

hot (spicy) *Heh-mee* متبل، حامي

hotel *'u-teel, fun-du''* اوتيل، فندق

hour *seh-ᶜa* ساعة، ساعات
    (pl.) *sa-ᶜeht*

    per hour *fis-seh-ᶜa* في الساعة

house *beyt* بيت، منزل
    (pl.) *bu-yoot*

housewife *sit-ti beyt* ربة بيت

how? *iz-zayy/keyf?* ازي، كيف؟

How do you do? *iz-zay-yak?* ازيك؟
    [*iz-zay-yik?*]

How are you? *keyf il-Hehl?* كيف حالك؟

How much/many? *kam? bi kam?* كم، بكم؟

hubble bubble *shee-sha* شيشة
    (water) pipe

humidity *ru-Too-ba* رطوبة

hundred *mee-ya* مئة، مئات
    (pl.) *mee-yeht*

hungry *ga-ᶜehn* جائع، جوعان
    [*ga-ᶜeh-na*]

(in a) hurry *mis-taᶜ-gil* مستعجل
    [*mis-taᶜ-gi-la*]

hurt *yiw-gaᶜ* يؤلم، يوجع

husband *gooz/zohj* زوج

I

I *a-na* أنا

ice *talg* ثلج

ice cream *ays kreem* أيس كريم

idea *fik-ra (pl.) 'af-kaar* فكرة، أفكار

if *law* لو

ill *ᶜay-yehn [ᶜay-yeh-na]*, مريض
    ma-reeD [ma-ree-Da]

immediately *Heh-lan* فورا

import *is-ti-raad* إستيراد

important *mu-himm* مهم

impossible *mish mum-kin* غير ممكن

improve *yi-Has-sin* يحسن

in *fi* في،ب

incense *bu-khoor* بخور

indeed *fi^c-lan* حقا

independence *is-tiq-lehl* استقلال

India *il-hind* الهند

Indian *hin-dee [hin-dee-ya]* هندي

indigestion *Hu-moo-Da* حموضة
سوء الهضم

industry *Si-naa-^ca* صناعة

inexpensive *ri-kheeS* رخيص

infection *'il-ti-hehb* التهاب

influenza *il-floo-in-za* انفلونزا

information *is-ti^c-la-meht* معلومات، استعلامات

injection *Hu"-na* حقنة

insect *Ha-sha-ra* حشرة، حشرات
(pl.) Ha-sha-raat

inside *gow-wa* في الداخل

insomnia *^ca-dam in-nohm* أرق

instead of *ba-dal* بدلا من

insult (verb) *yish-tim* يشتم

insurance *ta'-meen* تأمين

intelligent *za-kee [za-kee-ya]* ذكي

interested (in —)
muh-tamm (bi —) (ب) مهتم

interesting *mu-himm* مهم

international *daw-lee* دولي

interview, encounter (noun)
mu-"ab-la مقابلة

introduce X to Y *yi-"ad-dim*
X li Y يقدم X لـ Y

invitation *^cu-zoo-ma* عزومة

invite *yi^c-zim* يعزم

Ireland *ayr-lan-da* إيرلندا

Irish (man) *ayr-lan-dee* إيرلندي
[ayr-lan-dee-ya]

iron *mak-wa* مكواة

ironer *mak-wa-gee* محل كي، مكوجي

ironing *kayy* كي

Islam *'is-lehm* إسلام

Islamic *'is-leh-mee* إسلامي

island *gi-zee-ra* جزيرة، جزر
(pl.) gu-zur

Israel *is-ra-'eel* إسرائيل

Israeli *is-ra-'ee-lee* إسرائيلي
[is-ra-'ee-lee-ya]

Italian *i-Taa-lee* إيطالي
[i-Taa-lee-ya]

Italy *i-Taal-ya* إيطاليا

ivory *sinn il-feel* سن الفيل

J

jack (car) *ku-reek*, *jehk*
جك، مرفاع سيارة

jacket *ja-kit-ta*   جاكتة

jail *sign*   سجن

jam *mu-rab-ba*   مربي

January *ya-neh-yir*   يناير

Japan *il-ya-behn*   اليابان

Japanese *ya-beh-nee*   ياباني
[ya-beh-nee-ya]

jasmine *yas-meen*   ياسمين

Jerusalem *il-quds*   القدس

jewelry *ga-weh-hir,*   مجوهرات
mu-gaw-ha-raat

jewelry store *ga-wa-hir-gee*   جواهرجي

Jewish *yu-hoo-dee*   يهودي
[yu-hoo-dee-ya]

job, post *wa-Zee-fa*   وظيفة

joke *nuk-ta*   نكتة

Jordan *il-'ur-dun*   الأردن

Jordanian *'ur-du-nee*   أردني

journalist *Sa-Ha-fee*   صحفي

juice *ᶜa-Seer*   عصير

July *yul-yoo*   يوليو

June *yun-yoo*   يونيو

K

key *mif-tehH*   مفتاح، مفاتيح
(pl.) ma-fa-teeH

kidnap *yikh-Taf*   يخطف

kill *yi-maw-wit, yiʰ-til*   يقتل

kilo *kee-loo*   كيلو

kind (noun) *Sanf (pl.)*   صنف، نوع
'aS-naaf, nohᶜ (pl.) 'an-wehᶜ

kind (adj.) *la-Teef*   لطيف
[la-Tee-fa] (pl.) lu-Taaf

king *ma-lik (pl.) mu-look*   ملك

kiosk *kushk*   كشك، كشكات
(pl.) kush-keht

kiss (verb) *yi-boos*   يبوس

kiss (noun) *boh-sa*   بوسة

knife *sik-kee-na*   سكينة، سكاكين
(pl.) sa-ka-keen

knock *yi-khab-baT, yi-duʰʰ*   يدق

know *yic-raf*   يعرف

Koran *'il-qur-'ehn*   القرآن

Kuweit *'ik-ku-weyt*   الكويت

Kuweiti *ku-wey-tee*   كويتي

L

laboratory *maᶜ-mal*   معمل

ladder *sil-lim*   سلم

lady *sitt (pl.) sit-teht*   سيدة، سيدات

lake *bu-Hey-ra*   بحيرة

lamb *Daa-nee*   لحم خروف، ضاني

lamp *lam-ba*   لمبة

table lamp *'a-ba-joo-ra*   مصباح كهربائي

land, earth *'arD*   أرض

language *lu-gha*   لغة

large *ki-beer [ki-bee-ra]*   كبير

larger, largest *'ak-bar*   أكبر

last (adj.) *'a-kheer*   أخير

    (at) last! *'a-khee-ran!*   أخيرا

late *wakh-ree,*   متأخر
mut-'akh-khir

later *ba^c-deyn*   بعد ذلك

laugh *yiD-Hak*   يضحك

laundry *gha-seel*   غسيل
(washing place) *magh-sa-la*   مغسلة

lavatory *twa-litt,*   تواليت، دورة مياه
doh-rit il-may-ya

law *qa-noon*   قانون

lawyer *mu-Heh-mee*   محامي

laxative *mu-lay-yin*   ملين

lazy *kas-lehn*   كسول

learn *yit-^cal-lim*   يتعلم

leather *gild*   جلد

leave (tr.) *yi-seeb*   يترك

leave (intr.) *yim-shee*   يغادر

Lebanon *lib-nehn*   لبنان

Lebanese *lib-neh-nee*   لبناني

left *shi-mehl, yi-saar*   يسار

leg *rigl*   رجل

legal *qa-noo-nee*   قانوني

lemon *la-moon*   ليمون

lend *yi-sal-lif*   يسلف

lens *^ca-da-sa*   عدسة، عدسات
    (pl.) *^ca-da-seht*

lentils *^cads*   عدس

lesson *dars* (pl.) *du-roos*   درس، دروس

letter *ga-wehb*   خطاب
    (pl.) *ga-weh-beht*

liar *kad-dehb*   كذاب

library *mak-ta-ba*   مكتبة

Libya *lib-ya*   ليبيا

Libyan *lee-bee*   ليبي

license, permit *rukh-Sa*   رخصة

lie (noun) *kid-ba*   كذبة

lie (verb) *yik-dib*   يكذب

light (noun) *noor*   نور

light (verb) *yi-wal-la^c*   يشعل

light (in color) *feh-tiH*   فاتح
[fat-Ha]

light (in weight) *kha-feef*   خفيف
[kha-fee-fa]

lighter (noun) *wal-leh-^ca*   ولاعة

like (verb) *yi-Hibb*   يحب

like (prep.) *zayy/keyf*   زاي/مثل

limit (verb) *yi-Had-did*   يحدد

line *khaTT*   خط، خطوط
    (pl.) *khu-TooT*

lip **shif**-fa شفة، شفائف
(pl.) sha-**feh**-yif

liquor **kham**-ra خمرة

list "**ay**-ma قائمة

listen **yis**-ma^c يستمع

little Su-**ghay**-yar صغير

(a) little **shway**-ya قليل

live (verb) **yus**-kun, يسكن، يعيش
yi-^c**eesh**

loaf ri-**gheef** رغيف، أرغفة
(pl.) 'ar-**ghi**-fa

local ma-**Hal**-le محلي

long Ta-**weel** طويل

look, appearance shakl مظهر، شكل
he (she) looks — **shak**-loo
[shak-**la**-ha] مظهره —، شكله —

look (at) yit-**far**-rag (^c**a**-la)
(إلى) ينظر

look (for) yi-**daw**-war (^c**a**-la)
(عن) يبحث

loose (clothes) **weh**-si^c واسع

lose yi-**Dee**^c يفقد

(get) lost yi-**tuuh** يتيه، يضلل الطريق

a lot ki-**teer** كثير

love (noun) Hubb حب

love (verb) yi-**Hibb** يحب

low **waa**-Tee منخفض، واطئ

luck bakht, haZZ حظ

luggage **shu**-naT/^cafsh أمتعة

lunch (noun) **gha**-da غذاء

(verb) yit-**ghad**-da يتغذى

M

machine **ma**-ka-na, 'eh-la آلة

magazine ma-**gal**-la مجلة، مجلات
(pl.) ma-**gal**-leht

magnificent ^ca-**Zeem** عظيم

maid khad-**deh**-ma خادمة

mail ba-**reed** بريد

make **yi**^c-mil يعمل

man **raa**-gil رجل، رجال
(pl.) rig-**geh**-la

manager mu-**deer** مدير

mangoes **man**-ga منجو

manicure ma-ni-**keer** مانيكير

many ki-**teer** كثير

map kha-**ree**-Ta خريطة

March **meh**-ris مارس

market soo" سوق

married mit-**gaw**-wiz متزوج
[mit-gaw-**wi**-za]

marry yit-**gaw**-wiz يتزوج

massage tad-**leek** تدليك

(football) match matsh (**koh**-ra)
مباراة (كرة)

matches kab-**reet** كبريت

(it doesn't) matter *may-him-mish*   غير مهم

mattress *mar-ta-ba*   فرشة

May *may-yoo*   مايو

maybe *yim-kin*   يمكن، ربما

meal *'akl*   طعام، أكل

measure *yi-"ees*   يقيس

meat *laHm*   لحم

medicine *da-wa*   دواء
   (pl.) *'ad-wee-ya*

Mediterranean *il-baHr il-'ab-yaD*   البحر الأبيض

meet *yi-"eh-bil*   يقابل

meeting *ig-ti-meh^c*   اجتماع

melon *sham-mehm*   شمام

member *^cuDw*   عضو، أعضاء
   (pl.) *'a^c-Daa'*

mend *yi-Sal-laH*   يصلح

menu *min-yoo/"ay-ma*   منيو، قائمة

message *ri-seh-la*   رسالة

meter (taxi) *^cad-dehd*   عداد

meter (measurement) *mitr*   متر

Middle East *ish-sharq il-'aw-saT*   الشرق الأوسط

military *^cas-ka-ree*   عسكري

milk *la-ban/Ha-leeb*   لبن، حليب

million *mil-yohn*   مليون، ملايين
   (pl.) *ma-la-yeen*

(never) mind! *ma-^ca-lish!*   معلهش !لا بأس!

mind *^ca"l*   عقل

mine *bi-teh-^cee*   لي

minister *wa-zeer*   وزير

ministry *wi-zaa-ra*   وزارة

mint *ni^c-neh^c*   نعناع

minute (time) *da-"ee-"a*   دقيقة، دقائق
   (pl.) *da-"eh-yi"*

mirror *mi-reh-ya*   مرايا

Miss — *il-eh-ni-sa* —   الآنسة —

mistake *ghal-Ta*   غلطة

mistaken *ghal-Taan*   غلطان

modern *^caS-ree/Ha-dees*   عصري، حديث

moment *laH-Za*   لحظة

monastery *deyr*   دير

Monday *(yohm) lit-neyn*   يوم الأثنين

money *fi-loos*   فلوس

money exchange *mak-tab Sarf*   مكتب الصرف

month *shahr*   شهر، أشهر
   (pl.) *shu-hoor*

monument *'a-sar*   أثر، آثار
   (pl.) *'a-saar*

more *'ak-tar*   أكثر

morning *SubH/Sa-baaH*   صبح، صباح

in the morning *iS-SubH*
صباحا

mosque *geh-mi^c* جامع، جوامع
(pl.) *ga-weh-mi^c*

mosquitoes *na-moos* ناموس

mother *'umm* أم

mountain *ga-bal* جبل، جبال
(pl.) *gi-behl*

mouse *faar* (pl.) فار، فئران
fi-rehn

mouth *bu""/fumm* فم

Mr. — *is-say-yid* — ـ السيد ـ

Mrs. — *is-say-yi-da, ma-dehm* السيدة، مدام ـ
—

museum *mat-Haf* متحف

music *mu-see-qa* موسيقى

Muslim *mus-lim [mus-li-ma]* مسلم
(pl.) *mus-li-meen*

(I, you, etc.) must — *leh-zim* — يجب أن ـ

mustache *sha-nab* شنب، شارب

N

name *'ism* اسم، أسماء
(pl.) *'a-seh-mee*

napkin *foo-Ta* فوطة، منشفة
(pl.) *fo-waT*

sanitary napkin *foo-Ta* فوطة صحية
siH-Hee-ya

narrow *day-ya"* ضيق

national, nationalist *qaw-mee* قومي

nationality *gin-see-ya* جنسية

natural *Ta-bee-^cee* طبيعي

naughty *sha-"ee* شقي، شرير

near (to) *"u-ray-yib (min)* قريب
(من)

nearby *"u-ray-yib* قريبا

nearly *ta"-ree-ban* تقريبا

(it is) necessary *leh-zim* يلزم

(I) need *^ca-wiz* أريد، أحتاج
[^caw-za]

neighbor *gaar* جار، جيران
(pl.) *gi-rehn*

never *'a-ba-dan* أبدا

new *gi-deed* جديد

news *'akh-baar* أخبار

newspaper *ga-ree-da* جريدة، جرائد
(pl.) *ga-raa-yid*

next *gayy* قادم

night *ley-la* ليلة

at night *bil-leyl* ليلا

Nile *in-neel* النيل

nine *tis-^ca* تسعة

no *la'* لا

nobody *ma-Had-dish* لا أحد

noise *daw-sha* دوشة، صخب

noon *Duhr* ظهر

north *sha-mehl* شمال

nose *ma-na-kheer* أنف

not *mish* ليس، ما، لا

notebook **noh**-ta دفتر جيب

nothing *wa-la Ha-ga* لا شيء،

novel (noun) *ri-weh-ya* رواية

November *nu-vim-bir* نوفمبر

now *dil-wa"-tee* الآن

Nubia *in-noo-ba* النوبة

Nubian *noo-bee* نوبي

number **nim**-ra/ra-qam رقم

number (quantity) *ᶜa-dad* عدد

nurse *mu-mar-ri-Da* ممرضة

O

oasis *weh-Ha* واحة، واحات
(pl.) *wa-Heht*

(I've/we've no) objection.
*ma feesh meh-ni*ᶜ ليس عندي مانع

obvious *waa-DiH* واضح

October *ok-too-bar* أكتوبر

of course **Tab**-ᶜan طبعا

offer *yi-"ad-dim* يقدم

office **mak**-tab مكتب

office worker *mu-waZ-Zaf* موظف
[*mu-waZ-Za-fa*]

officer **Zaa**-biT ضابط، ضباط
(pl.) *Zub-baaT*

often *ki-teer* كثيرا

oil *zeyt* زيت

olive oil *zeyt zey-toon*
زيت زيتون

oil (petroleum) *bit-rohl, nafT*
بترول، نفط

okay! **meh-shee!** لا مانع

old (people) *ki-beer* كبير، كبار
[*ki-bee-ra*] (pl.) *ku-baar*

old (things) "*a-deem* قديم
["*a-dee-ma*]

I'm — years old.
ᶜ*an-dee* — *sa-na* عمري — سنة

How old are you? ᶜ*an-dak*
[ᶜ*an-dik*] *kam sa-na?*
عمرك كم سنة؟

olives *zey-toon* زيتون

on ᶜ*a-la* على

on foot ᶜ*a-la rig-ley-na*
ماشيا، على الأقدام

on time *fil-ma-ᶜehd* في الميعاد

once *mar-ra waH-da* مرة واحدة

one *weh-Hid* واحد، واحدة
[*waH-da*]

one another *baᶜD* بعض

onions *ba-Sal* بصل

only (just) *bass* فقط

only (sole) *wa-Heed* وحيد

open *yid-taH* يفتح

open (adj.) *feh-tiH*, *maf-tooH*
مفتوح

opportunity *fur-Sa* فرصة ، فرص
(pl.) *fu-raS*

optician *naD-Da-raa-tee*
محل نظارات

or *'aw*; *wal-la* (in questions)
أو ؛ أم

orange *bur-tu-'aan* برتقال

order (verb) *yuT-lub* يطلب

ordinary *ceh-dee* عادي

organize *yi-naZ-Zam* ينظم

organization *mu-naZ-Za-ma*
منظمة

origin *'aSl* أصل

other *teh-nee* [*tan-ya*], آخر
'eh-khir [*'ukh-ra*]

out of order *caT-laan* معطل

outing, break *fus-Ha* فسحة

outside *bar-ra* في الخارج

oven *furn* فرن

over *foh"* فوق

It's over; that's it! *kha-laaS!*
خلاص!

overcoat *bal-Too* بالطو ، معطف

(on my) own *li waH-dee*
وحدي

(on your) own *li waH-dak*
[*li waH-dak*] وحدك

P

package *Tard* طرد ، طرود
(pl.) *Tu-rood*

packet *cil-ba* (pl.) *ci-lab*,
beh-koo (pl.) beh-ku-*weht*
علبة ، علب

pail *gar-dal* دلو

pain *wa-gac/'a-lam* وجع ، ألم

palace "*aSr* قصر

Palestine *fi-lis-Teen* فلسطين

Palestinian *fi-lis-Tee-nee* فلسطيني

palm trees *nakhl* نخل

panties *kee-lott*
سروال داخلي نسائي

pants, trousers *ban-Ta-lohn*
بنطلون

paper *wa-ra"* ورق ، أوراق
(pl.) *'aw-reh*"

parcel *Tard* طرد ، طرود
(pl.) *Tu-rood*

Pardon me, but — *is-maH-lee* —,
law sa-maHt —
اسمح لي

park *gi-ney-na* حديقة
(pl.) *ga-neh-yin*

park (verb) *yu-"af* يقف

parking *'in-ti-Zaar* انتظار

party *Haf-la* حفل

passenger *reh-kib* راكب ، ركاب
(pl.) *ruk-kehb*

passport *bas-boor/* جواز السفر
ga-wehz is-sa-far

past (noun) *maa-Dee* ماضي

pasta *ma-ka-roh-na* مكرونة

pastries *Ha-la-wee-yeht* حلويات

pastry shop *Ha-la-weh-nee* حلواني

patience *Sabr* صبر

pay (verb) *yid-fa^c* يدفع

peach *khokhh* خوخ

peanuts *fool su-deh-nee* فول سوداني

peasant *fal-lehH* فلاح
(pl.) *fal-la-Heen*

pen, pencil "*a-lam* قلم

pension *ma-^cehsh* راتب تقاعدي

people *nehs* ناس

pepper *fil-fil* فلفل

percentage *nis-ba mi-'a-wee-ya* نسبة مئوية

perhaps *yim-kin* يمكن، ربما

person *na-far* نفر، أنفار
(pl.) *'an-faar, shakhS*
(pl.) *'ash-khaaS* شخص، اشخاص

personal *shakh-See* شخصي

personally *shakh-See-yan* شخصيا

petrol *ban-zeen* بنزين

Pharaonic *far-^coo-nee* فرعوني

pharmacy *'ag-za-kheh-na,* اجزاخانة، صيدلية
Say-da-lee-ya

photograph, picture *Soo-ra* صورة، صور
(pl.) *So-war*

photograph (verb) *yi-Saw-war* يصور

pickles *Tur-shee/* طرشي، مخلل
mi-khal-lil

pigeon *Ha-mehm* حمام

pillow *mi-khad-da* مخدة

pills *Hu-boob* حبوب

sleeping pills حبوب منومة
Hu-boob mi-naw-wi-ma

(what a) pity! *ya kh-Saa-ra!* يا خسارة

place *ma-kehn* مكان، أماكن
(pl.) *'a-meh-kin*

plain *seh-da* سادة

plants *na-ba-teht* نباتات

plate *Ta-ba"* طبق، أطباق
(pl.) *'aT-baa"*

platform *ra-Seef* رصيف

play (verb) *yil-^cab* يلعب

play (theater) *mas-ra-Hee-ya* مسرحية

pleasant (things) *Za-reef* ظريف
(people) *la-Teef* لطيف
[*la-Tee-fa*] (pl.) *lu-Taaf*

please — *min faD-lak* — من فضلك ـ
[*min faD-lik*]

pleased, happy mab-**SooT**, far-**Haan**　سعيد، فرحان، مبسوط

Pleased to meet you.
it-shar-**raf**-na, **fur**-Sa sa-**ʿee**-da　فرصة سعيدة، تشرفنا

plumber sab-**behk**　سباك

police bu-**leeS**/**shur**-Ta　بوليس، شرطة

policeman ʿas-ka-**ree**　شرطي
(pl.) ʿa-**seh**-kir

politics si-**yeh**-sa　سياسة

poor fa-"**eer**　فقير، فقراء
(pl.) **fu**-"a-ra

popcorn fi-**shaar**　فشار

popular (of the people) sha**ʿ**-bee　شعبي

porter shay-**yehl**　شيال، حمال

possible **mum**-kin　ممكن

post ba-**reed**　بريد

postcard kart bus-**tehl**　كارت بوستال، بطاقة بريدية

post office **mak**-tab il-ba-**reed**　مكتب البريد

potatoes ba-**Taa**-Tis　بطاطس

sweet potatoes ba-**Taa**-Ta　بطاطا

pottery fukh-**khaar**　فخار

pound (currency) gi-**ney**　جنيه

pound (weight) raTl　رطل

pour yi-**Subb**　يصب

pray yi-**Sal**-lee　يصلي

prefer yi-**faD**-Dal　يفضل

pregnant **Heh**-mil　حامل

prepare yi-**gah**-hiz,　يحضر
yi-**HaD**-Dar

prescription ru-**shit**-ta　روشتة

present (gift) ha-**dee**-ya　هدية
(pl.) ha-**deh**-ya

present (adj.) maw-**good**　موجود

president ra-**'ees**　رئيس

press (noun) Sa-**Haa**-fa　صحافة

pretty Hilw　حلو

prevent **yim**-naʿ　يمنع

price **ta**-man, siʿr　ثمن، سعر

print (photo) nus-kha　نسخة

private khaaS　خاص

problem mush-**ki**-la، مشكلة، مشاكل
(pl.) ma-**sheh**-kil

profession **mih**-na　مهنة

professor 'us-**tehz**　أستاذ

promise (verb) **yiw**-ʿid　يعد

prophet **na**-bee　نبي

public ʿamm　عام

pull yi-**shidd**　يشد

pupil til-**meez**　تلميذ، تلامذة
(pl.) ta-**lam**-za

purse, wallet maH-**fa**-Za　محفظة

purse, bag **shan**-Ta
(pl.) **shu**-naT   شنطة، حقيبة

push yi-**zu**''''   يدفع

put yi-**HuTT**   يضع

pyramids il-**ha**-ram   أهرام

Q

quantity ᶜa-dad, qee-ma   عدد، قيمة

quarrel (verb) yi-**kheh**-ni"   يخانق

question (query) su-'ehl
(pl.) 'as-'i-la   سؤال، أسئلة

queue Ta-**boor**   طابور

quick sa-**reeᶜ**   سريع

quickly bi-**sur**-ᶜa   بسرعة

quiet **heh**-dee   هادئ

R

rabbit 'ar-nab
(pl.) 'a-**reh**-nib   أرنب، أرانب

race (competition) si-**beh**"   سباق

radio **rad**-yoo   راديو

railroad is-**sik**-ka il-Ha-**deed**   السكة الحديدية

railroad station ma-**HaT**-Tit
il-"aTr   محطة القطار

by rail bil-"aTr   بالقطار

rain (noun) **ma**-Tar   مطر

rain (verb) ti-**maT**-Tar   تمطر

rare (unusual) **neh**-dir   نادر

rate of exchange siᶜr it-taH-**weel**   سعر التحويل

rather (somewhat) **shway**-ya   إلى حد ما، قليلا

raw nayy   خام، نيء

razor blades 'am-wehs Hi-**leh**-"a   أمواس حلاقة

read **yi**"-ra   يقرأ

ready **geh**-hiz [**gah**-za]   جاهز

really? Sa-**HeeH**?   صحيح؟

to the rear **wa**-ra   إلى الوراء

reason **sa**-bab
(pl.) 'as-**behb**   سبب، أسباب

receipt waSl   إيصال

reception is-ti"-**behl**   استقبال

recipe **waS**-fa   وصفة

record (music) is-Ti-**waa**-na   اسطوانة

record (verb) yi-**sag**-gil   يسجل

recover (health) yi-**khiff**,
yish-fee   يشفي

red 'aH-mar [**Ham**-ra]   أحمر

reduction takh-**feeD**   تخفيض

reef **shiᶜ**-ba   شعبة

refrigerator tal-**leh**-ga   ثلاجة

region man-**Ti**-qa   منطقة

relation *"a-reeb* قريب، أقرباء
(pl.) *"a-raa-yib*

remember *yif-ti-kir* يفتكر، يتذكر

remind *yi-fak-kar* يفكر

rent (verb) *yi-'ag-gar* يؤجر، يستأجر

repair (verb) *yi-Sal-laH* يصلح

(noun) *taS-leeH* تصليح

repeat *yi-kar-rar* يكرر

reply (verb) *yi-rudd* يرد

republic *gum-hoo-ree-ya* جمهورية

reservation *Hagz* حجز

reserve *yiH-giz* يحجز

respect (noun) *iH-ti-raam* احترام

responsible *mas-'ool* مسؤول

rest (verb) *yis-ta-ray-yaH* يستريح

restaurant *maT-ᶜam* مطعم، مطاعم
(pl.) *ma-Taa-ᶜim*

restroom *twa-litt* تواليت، دورة للمياه

return (verb) *yir-gaᶜ* يعود، يرجع

rice *ruzz* أرز

rich *gha-nee* [*gha-nee-ya*] غني
(pl.) *'agh-nee-ya*

ride (verb) *yir-kab* يركب

right (correct) *maZ-booT* صحيح، مضبوط

right (direction) *yi-meen* يمين

ring (jewelry) *kheh-tim* خاتم

rise *yi-"oom* يقوم

river *nahr* نهر

road *Ta-ree"* (pl.) *Tu-ru"* طريق، طرق

sik-ka (pl.) *si-kak* سكة، سكك

roast *mash-wee* مشوي

robe, dressing gown *rohb* ثوب، روب

rock *Sakhr* صخر

roof *SatH* سقف، سطح

room *'oh-Da* (pl.) *'o-waD*/ غرفة، غرف
ghur-fa (pl.) *ghu-raf*

roses *ward* ورد

rug *sig-geh-da* (pl.) *sa-ga-geed*, سجادة، سجاجيد، كليم، أكلمة
ki-leem (pl.) *'ak-li-ma*

run *yig-ree* يركض

Russia *roos-ya* روسيا

Russian *roo-see* روسي

S

sad *Ha-zeen* حزين

safe *khaz-na* خزنة

sailboat *yakht, fa-loo-ka* يخت، قارب

sailor *baH-Haar* بحار

salad **sa**-la-Ta سلطة

salary ma-**hee**-ya, مرتب
mu-**rat**-tab

sale bee^c بيع

salt malH ملح

(the same) — nafs il —ﺍﻟـ نفس

sand raml رمل

sandstorm zaw-**ba**-^ca عاصفة رملية

sandals **san**-dal صندل
(pl.) sa-na-**deel**

sandwich **sand**-witsh
(pl.) sand-wit-**sheht**
سندويتش، سندويتشات

sanitary napkins **fo**-waT فوطة صحية
SiH-**Hee**-ya

sardines sar-**deen** سردين

Saturday (yohm) is-**sabt** يوم السبت

sauce **Sal**-Sa صلصة

sausages su-**gu**" " سجق

save (time, money) يوفر
yi-**waf**-far

say yi-"**ool** يقول

scarf 'i-**sharb**, ku-**fee**-ya
منديل الرأس

scene, view **man**-Zar
(pl.) ma-**naa**-Zir منظر، مناظر

schedule **gad**-wal il-ma-wa-^c**eed**
جدول المواعيد

school mad-**ra**-sa
(pl.) ma-**deh**-ris مدرسة، مدارس

science ^c**ilm** (pl.) ^c**u**-loom
علم، علوم

scientific ^c**il**-mee علمي

scissors ma-"**aSS** مقص

scotch (whiskey) **wis**-kee ويسكي

screen **sheh**-sha شاشة

screwdriver mu-**fakk** مفك مسامير
ma-sa-**meer**

sea baHr بحر

search for yi-**daw**-war ^c**a**-la
يبحث عن

seashore shaTT (البحر) شاطئ

season faSl فصل

second teh-nee [**tan**-ya] ثاني

secretary si-kir-**teer**
[si-kir-**tee**-ra]
سكرتير، [سكرتيرة]

security 'amn أمن

see yi-**shoof** يرى

sell yi-bee^c يبيع

send **yib**-^cat يرسل، يبعث

September sib-**tim**-bir سبتمبر

serious gadd جاد

seriously bi-**gadd** بجد

service **khid**-ma خدمة

seven **sab**-^ca سبعة

sew *yi-khay-yaT* يخيط

shampoo *sham-poo* شامبو

shark "*irsh* (pl.) "*u-roosh*
سمك القرش

shave *yiH-la*" يحلق

she *hee-ya* هي

sheep (and goats) *gha-nam* غنم

shells *Sa-daf* صدف

ship *mar-kib/sa-fee-na*
مركب، سفينة

shirt "*a-meeS* قميص، قمصان
(pl.) "*um-Saan*

shoemaker *gaz-ma-gee* جزمجي

shoes *gaz-ma* حذاء، جزمة

shop *duk-kehn* (pl.) *da-ka-keen*
دكان، دكاكين،

ma-Hall (pl.) *ma-Hal-leht*
محل، محلات

short "*u-Say-yar* قصير

shoulder *kitf* كتف

show (stage, floor) *^carD* عرض

show (verb) *yi-war-ree* يري

shower *dush* دش

shrimp *gam-ba-ree* جمبري

shy *mak-soof* [*mak-soo-fa*]
مكسوف

sick *^ay-yehn* [*^ay-yeh-na*],
ma-reeD [*ma-ree-Da*] مريض

sight *man-Zar* (pl.) *ma-naa-Zir*
منظر، مناظر

sign (verb) *yim-Dee* يمضي

silent (of people) *seh-kit* ساكت
[*sak-ta*]

silk *Ha-reer* حرير

silver *faD-Da* فضة

Sinai *see-na* سيناء

sing *yi-ghan-nee* يغني

singer *mu-ghan-nee* [مغنية] مغني
[*mu-ghan-nee-ya*]

sister '*ukht* أخت

sit *yu*"-*^ud* يقعد

six *sit-ta* ستة

size *ma-"ehs* مقاس

skin *gild/bash-ra* جلد، بشرة

skirt *gu-nil-la* جيبة، جونلة

sky *sa-ma* سماء

slaughter *yid-baH* يذبح

sleep (verb) *yi-nehm* ينام
(noun) *nohm* نوم

sleeping pills *Hu-boob*
mi-naw-wi-ma حبوب منومة

slippers *shib-shib* شبشب

slow *ba-Tee'* بطيء

slowly *bir-raa-Ha* ببطء

Slow down! *^a-la mah-lak!*
قلل السرعة، على مهلك!

small *Su-ghay-yar*   صغير
[*Su-ghay-ya-ra*]

smell (noun) *ree-Ha*   رائحة

smoke (verb) *yi-dakh-khan* يدخن

smoking *tad-kheen*   تدخين

snake *ti^c-behn*   حية

snow *talg*   ثلج

so, thus *ki-da*   هكذا

soap *Sa-boon*   صابون

soap opera *mu-sal-sal*
(pl) *mu-sal-sa-leht*
مسلسل، مسلسلات

soccer *koh-ra*   كرة القدم

soccer match *matsh koh-ra*
مباراة في كرة القدم

socialist *ish-ti-raa-kee* اشتراكي

socks *sha-raab*   شرابات، جوارب

soldier *^cas-ka-ree*   عسكري
(pl.) *^ca-seh-kir*

some — *ba^cD* —   ـ بعض ـ

somebody *Hadd*, *weh-Hid* واحد

something *Ha-ga*   شيء

sometimes *sa-^ceht*,   أحيانا
'aH-yeh-nan

son *'ibn*   ابن

soon *"u-ray-yib*   قريبا

Sorry! *'eh-sif!* [*'as-fa!*]   آسف!

sort, kind *noh^c* (pl.) *'an-weh^c*
نوع، أنواع

sound, voice *Soht*   صوت

soup *shur-ba*   شربة

south *ga-noob*   جنوب

Spain *as-ban-ya*   إسبانيا

Spanish *as-beh-nee*   إسباني
[*as-ba-nee-ya*]

spark plugs *boo-jey-heht*
بوجيهات، شمعة الشرارة

speak *yit-kal-lim*   يتكلم

speak to *yi-kal-lim*   يكلم

special *makh-SooS*   مخصوص

spend *yiS-rif*   يصرف

in spite of *bir-raghm min*
بالرغم من

sponge *si-fing*   إسفنج

spoon *ma^c-la-"a*   ملعقة

sports *ri-yaa-Da*   رياضة

spring (season) *ra-bee^c*   ربيع

square (place) *mi-dehn*   ميدان

stairs *sil-lim*   سلم

stamps *Ta-waa-bi^c*   طوابع

stand (up) *yi-"oom*   يقوم

standing *weh-"if*   واقف [واقفة]
[*wa"-fa*]

star *nig-ma*   نجمة، نجوم
(pl.) *nu-goom*

start *yib-ti-dee*   يبدأ

state (noun) *daw-la*   دولة، دول
(pl.) *du-wal*

station *ma-HaT-Ta*   محطة

stay (in, at) *yin-zil (fi)*, *yu"-ᶜud*   ينزل، يبقي

steal *yis-ra"*   يسرق

still (adverb) *lis-sa*   لا يزل

stockings *sha-raab*   شربات، جوارب

stomach *miᶜ-da*, *baTn*   معدة، بطن

stone *Ha-gar*   حجر

stop (noun) *maw-"af* (pl.) *ma-weh-"if*   موقف

stop (verb) *yu-"af*   يقف

store *duk-kehn* (pl.) *da-ka-keen*   دكان، دكاكين،

   ma-Hall (pl.) *ma-Hal-leht*   محل، محلات

story *Hi-keh-ya*   قصة، حكاية

straight (on) *dugh-ree*   إلى الأمام، دغري

strange *gha-reeb*   غريب

strawberries *fa-raw-la*   فراولة

street *sheh-riᶜ* (pl.) *sha-weh-riᶜ*   شارع، شوارع

strong *qa-wee* [*qa-wee-ya*]   قوي

student *Taa-lib* [*Taa-li-ba*] (pl.) *Ta-la-ba*   طالب، طلبة

study *yid-ris*   يدرس

stupid *gha-bee* [*gha-bee-ya*]   غبي

style *'us-loob*   أسلوب

subway *mit-roo*   مترو

suddenly *biS-Sud-fa*   بالصدفة

sugar *suk-kar*   سكر

sugarcane *"a-Sab*   قصب

suit *bad-la*, *kis-wa*   كسوة، بدلة

suitable *mu-neh-sib*   مناسب

summer *Seyf*   صيف

sun *shams*   شمس

Sunday (*yohm*) *il-Hadd*   يوم الأحد

sunglasses *naD-Daa-rit ish-shams*   نظارة الشمس

suntan lotion *kreym li Hi-meh-yit il-bash-ra*   كريم الحماية للبشرة

sweater *bu-loh-var*   بلوفر

sweet *Hilw*   حلو

swim *yis-ta-Ham-ma*, *yi-ᶜoom*   يستحم، يسبح

swimming pool *Ham-mehm si-beh-Ha*   حمام سباحة

system *ni-Zaam*   نظام

T

table *Ta-ra-bey-za*   طاولة، طربيزة

tailor *tar-zee*, *khay-yaaT*   ترزي، خياط

take *yeh-khud*   يأخذ

take off (plane) *yiT-laᶜ*   يقوم،

take off (clothes) *yi"-laᶜ*, *yikh-laᶜ*   يقلع، يخلع

take a picture yi-**Saw**-war   يصور

talk (noun) ka-**lehm**   كلام

tapes sha-**raa**-yiT   شرائط

taste (noun) Ta^cm   طعم

tax Da-**ree**-ba   ضريبة، ضرائب
   (pl.) Da-**raa**-yib

taxi **tak**-see   تاكسي

taxi stand **maw**-"af tak-see
   موقف تاكسي

tea shayy   شاي

teach yi-**dar**-ris   يدرس

teacher mu-**dar**-ris   مدرس، معلم
   (mu-dar-**ri**-sa]

team fa-**ree**"   فريق

T-shirt fa-**nil**-la
   فانلة، قميص نصف كم

telegram til-li-**ghrehf**
   برقية، تلغراف

telephone ti-li-**fohn**   تليفون

telephone call mu-**kal**-ma   مكالمة

telephone number **nim**-rit/
   ra-qam ti-li-**fohn**   رقم تليفون

television ti-li-viz-**yohn**   تليفزيون

tell yi"-**ool**   يقول

tell me... "**ul**-lee...   ...قل لي

temperature Ha-**raa**-ra   حرارة

temple **ma**^c-bad   معبد، معابد
   (pl.) ma-^c**eh**-bid

ten ^ca-**sha**-ra   عشرة

tent **khey**-ma   خيمة

terrible ra-**heeb**   رهيب

terrorism 'ir-**hehb**   إرهاب

terrorist 'ir-**heh**-bee   إرهابي

thank you **shuk**-ran   شكرا

the — il —   الـ

theater **mas**-raH   مسرح

there hi-**nehk**   هناك

there is/are — fee –   يوجد/توجد
   is/are there? fee?
   هل يوجد/توجد ؟

there isn't/aren't ma **feesh**   لا يوجد

thief Ha-**raa**-mee   حرامي

thin ru-**fay**-ya^c   رفيع

thing **Ha**-ga   شيء، أشياء
   (pl.) Ha-**geht**

think yi-**Zunn**   يظن

thirsty ^caT-**shaan**   عطشان

thousand 'alf   ألف، آلاف
   (pl.) 'a-**lehf**

three ta-**leh**-ta   ثلاثة

throat zohr   حنجرة

Thursday yohm il-kha-**mees**
   يوم الخميس

thus **ki**-da   هكذا

ticket taz-**ka**-ra   تذكرة، تذاكر
   (pl.) ta-**zeh**-kir

tidy (adj.) mu-rat-**tab**   مرتب

tight **day**-ya" ضيق

time wa"t, **za**-man وقت، زمن

What time is it? is-**seh**-ᶜa kam? كم الساعة؟

tip (gratuity) ba"-**sheesh** بقشيش

tired taᶜ-**behn** متعب

tiring **mut**-ᶜib متعب

to li إلى

today in-na-**haar**-da/ اليوم
il-**yohm**

together **sa**-wa سويا

tomb ma"-**ba**-ra, مقبرة، مقابر
(pl.) ma-"**eh**-bir

tomorrow **buk**-ra غدا

too, also ka-**mehn** أيضا

(on) top foh" فوق

tooth sinn سن، أسنان
(pl.) 'as-**nehn**

tourist saw-**wehH** سائح، سواح
[saw-**weh**-Ha]
(pl.) suw-**wehH**

towel **foo**-Ta (pl.) **fo**-waT منشفة، مناشف، فوطة، فوط

traditions ta-qa-**leed** تقاليد

traffic mu-**roor** مرور

train (noun) "aTr قطار
(pl.) "u-Tu-**raat**

translate yi-**tar**-gim يترجم

travel (verb) yi-**seh**-fir يسافر

tree **sha**-ga-ra شجرة، شجر
(pl.) **sha**-gar

trip **riH**-la رحلة

true Sa-**HeeH** صحيح

Tuesday (yohm) it-ta-**leht** يوم الثلاثاء

two it-**neyn** اثنان

typewriter 'eh-la **kat**-ba آلة كاتبة

U

ugly **wi**-Hish [**wiH**-sha] قبيح

uncle (paternal) ᶜamm عم

(maternal) khehl خال

under taHt تحت

undershirt fa-**nil**-la فانلة، قميص تحتاني

understand **yif**-ham يفهم

undo yi-**fukk** يفك

unemployed ᶜaa-Til عاطل

unfortunately ma-ᶜal-'a-saf مع الأسف

United States il-wi-la-**yeht** الولايات المتحدة
il-muH-**ta**-Hi-da

university **gam**-ᶜa جامعة

unlikely mish min بعيد الاحتمال
il-muH-**ta**-mal

until li **gheh**-yit إلى

up foh" إلى فوق

get up yi-"**oom** يقوم

Upper Egypt *iS-Si-*c*eed*   الصعيد

use (verb) *yis-*ta*c*-mil*   يستعمل

useful *mu-feed*   مفيد

usually *c*a-*da*-tan*   عادة

V

vacation *'a-*geh*-za*   عطلة، إجازة

valley *weh-dee*   وادي

vegetables *khu-*Daar*   خضر

vegetarian *na-beh-tee*   نباتي

veil *Hi-gehb*   حجاب

very "*a*-wee, *gid*-dan*   جدا

video *vid-yo*   فيديو

view *man-*Zar*   منظر، مناظر
   (pl.) ma-*naa*-Zir*

village *qar-ya*   قرية، قرى
   (pl.) *qu*-ra*

villager *fal-lehH*   فلاح، فلاحون
   (pl.) fal-la-*Heen*

visa *vee-za*   تأشيرة

visit (verb) *yi-*Zoor*   يزور

voice, vote *Soht*   صوت، أصوات
   (pl.) 'aS-*waat*

voltage *volt*   فولت

W

wages *ma-*hee*-ya*   ماهية

wait *yis-*tan*-na/yin-ti-*Zir*   ينتظر

wake up (trans.) *yi-*SaH*-Hee*   يصحي

walk *yim-shee, yit-*mash*-sha*   يمشي، يتمشى

wallet *maH-*fa*-Za*   محفظة

want *c*a-wiz [*c*aw-za]*   عريز

war *Harb*   حرب

warm *deh-fee*   دافئ

wash (verb) *yigh-sil*   يغسل

   (noun) *gha-seel*   غسيل

waste *yi-*Day*-ya*c*   يضيع

watch (verb) *yit-*far*-rag (*c*a-la)*   ينظر إلى

watch (noun) *seh-*c*a*   ساعة

water *may-ya*   ماء، مياه

  hot water *may-ya *sukh*-na*   مياه ساخنة

watermelon *baT-*Teekh*   بطيخ

waves (water, air) *'am-*wehg*   أمواج

way *Ta-ree"*   طريق

we *iH-na*   نحن

weak *Da-*c*eef*   ضعيف

wear *yil-bis*   يلبس

weather *gaww, Ta"S*   جو، طقس

wedding *fa-raH*   عرس

Wednesday (yohm) *lar-ba*c*   يوم الأربعاء

week *'is-boo^c* أسبوع، أسابيع
(pl.) *'a-sa-bee^c*

welcome! *mar-Ha-ba!* مرحبا!
You're welcome, don't
mention it. *^caf-wan* عفوا

well *kway-yis* كويس، بخير

well done (meat) *mis-ti-wee*
تام النضج

West (Occident) *gharb* غرب

Western *ghar-bee* غربي
[*ghar-bee-ya*]

wet *mab-lool* مبلول

What? *'eyh?* ما؟

What!! (surprise) *ya sa-lehm!!* يا سلام!

What time? *is-seh-^ca kam?*
كم الساعة؟

wheel *^ca-ga-la* عجلة

When? *'im-ta?* متى؟

when *lam-ma* لما

Where? *feyn?* أين؟

Where from? *mi-neyn?* من أين؟

Which? *'an-hee?* أي؟

which (relative) *il-lee* الذي

whiskey *wis-kee* ويسكي

white *'ab-yaD* أبيض

Who? *meen?* من؟

Why? *leyh?* لماذا؟

wide *weh-si^c* [*was-^ca*] واسع

wife *ma-ra*, زوجة
sitt/zoh-ga

win *yik-sab* يكسب

window *shib-behk* شباك، شبابيك
(pl.) *sha-ba-beek*

wine *ni-beet* نبيذ

winter *shi-ta* شتاء

wish (verb) *yit-man-na* يتمنى

with *ma-^ca, bi* مع، بـ

without *min-gheyr. bi-doon* بدون

woman *ma-ra* (pl.) *ni-seh'*, امرأة، سيدة
sitt (pl.) *sit-teht*

wonderful *mum-tehz*, ممتاز، عظيم
^ca-Zeem

wood *kha-shab* خشب

wool *Soof* صوف

word *kil-ma* كلمة

work (verb) *yish-ta-ghal*
يعمل، يشتغل

work (noun) *shughl* عمل، شغل

world *'il-^ceh-lam, dun-ya* عالم، دنيا

worried *"al-"ehn* قلق، قلقان

worse *'aw-Hash* أوحش

wrap *yi-liff* يلف

write *yik-tib* يكتب

writer *keh-tib, mu-'al-lif*
كاتب، مؤلف

writing pad *blok noht*

دفتر، كراسة للكتابة

wrong ***gha**-laT*

خطأ، غلط

X

X rays *'a-**shi**c-ca*

أشعة

Y

year ***sa**-na*

سنة، سنوات

(pl.) *si-**neen***

this year *is-sa-**neh** dee*

هذه السنة

last year *is-**sa**-na*

*il-lee-**feh**-tit*

السنة التي فاتت

yellow *'aS-far [Saf-ra]*

أصفر

yes *'**ay**-wa, na-cam*

نعم

yesterday *im-**beh**-riH/'ams*

أمس

(not) yet ***lis**-sa*

حتى الآن

you (sing.) ***in**-ta [in-tee]*

أنت

you (pl.) *in-**tum**-ma*

أنتم

You're welcome, don't mention it.
caf-wan

عفوا

young *Su-**ghay**-yar*

صغير

[Su-ghay-**ya**-ra]

younger, youngest *'aS-ghar*

أصغر

young man *shabb*

شاب، شباب

(pl.) *sha-**behb***

yours *bi-**teh**-cak*

لك

Z

zipper ***sus**-ta*

سوسته

zone *man-**Ti**-qa*

منطقة

zoo *gi-**ney**-nit il-Ha-ya-wa-**neht***

حديقة الحيوان

ARABIC-ENGLISH DICTIONARY

The verbs are given in the third person singular present form ("he goes," etc.), beginning with *yi-*. For other forms of the verb see the Notes on Grammar on page 212.

As in the text, feminine forms are given in square brackets.

The following alphabetical order is used:

″ or ′, a, b, d, D, e, f, g, h, H, i, j, k, kh, 1, m, n, p, q, r, s, S, sh, t, T, u, v, w, y, z, Z, ᶜ

″ or ′

′a-ba-dan never

′abb father

″abl before (prep.)

″ab-li ki-da before (now)

′a-boo ga-lam-boo crab

′a-boo-ya my father

′ab-yaD [bey-Da] white

″a-deem [″a-dee-ma] old

′a-gaa-za holiday, vacation

′ag-na-bee [′ag-na-bee-ya] foreign

′ag-za-kheh-na pharmacy (chemist's)

′ah-lan! Hi!

′ah-raam pyramids

″ah-wa coffee, café

′aH-mar [Ham-ra] red

′aH-san better

′ak-bar bigger

′akl food

′akh-baar news

′akh-Dar [khaD-ra] green

′a-kheer last

′a-khee-ran! at last!

′al-maaz diamonds

′a-lam pain

″al-′ehn worried

″a-lam pen, pencil

″a-lam gaff ballpoint pen

″alb heart

′alf (pl.) ′a-lehf thousand

″a-meeS (pl.) ″um-Saan shirt

′amn security

′am-wehg waves

*'am-**wehs** Hi-**leh**-"a* razor blades

'an-hee? which?

'arD land, earth

'ar-khaS cheaper

*'ar-nab (pl.) 'a-**reh**-nib* rabbit

*'a-san-**Seer*** elevator, lift

*'a-sar (pl.) 'a-**saar*** monument, ruin

*'as-mar [**sam**-ra]* brown-skinned

*'a-**shi^c-^c**a* X rays

"a-Sab sugar cane

*'aS-far [**Saf**-ra]* yellow

'aS-ghar smaller, younger

'aSl origin

"aSr palace

*'aS-**waan*** Aswan

"aTr train

*'aT-rash [**Tar**-sha]* deaf

'aw or

'aw-Hash worse

*'aw-**reh*** papers, documents, bills

'aw-reh" na"d paper money

*'aw-wil ['**oo**-la]* first

"ay-ma list, menu

'ay-wa yes

'ayy any

'az-ma crisis

*'az-ma qal-**bee**-ya* heart attack

*'az-ra" [**zar**-"a]* blue

'a^c-ma [^cam-ya] blind

*'eed (pl.) 'a-**yeh**-dee* hand

"eh-dir ['ad-ra] able

*'eh-khir ['**ukh**-ra]* other

'eh-la machine

*'eh-la **kat**-ba* typewriter

'eh-sif! ['as-fa!] sorry!

'eyh? What?

"ib-Tee Coptic

'ibn son

*'i-**daa**-ra* administration

'il-la except

*'il-ti-**hehb*** infection, inflammation

*'im-**sehk*** constipation

'im-ta? when?

'in shaa' al-laah God willing (I hope so).

*'in-ti-**Zaar*** waiting, parking

*'iq-ti-**Saad*** economics

*"irsh (pl.) "u-**roosh*** piastre

*"irsh (pl.) "u-**roosh*** shark

*'is-**boo^c** (pl.) 'a-sa-**bee^c*** week

*'is-**hehl*** diarrhea

'is-kin-di-**ree**-ya
  Alexandria

'is-**lehm**   Islam

'ism (pl.) 'a-**seh**-mee   name

'is-wid [**soh**-da]   black

'is-^c**ehf**   ambulance service

'i-**sharb**   scarf

"**ish**-Ta   cream

"i-**zehz**   glass

"i-**zeh**-za (pl.) "a-**zeh**-yiz
  bottle

'i^c-**lehn**   advertisement

'oh-Da (pl.) 'o-**waD**   room

"ud-**dehm**   in front (of)

"uf-**Taan** (pl.) "a-fa-**Teen**
  caftan

'**ug**-ra   fee, rent

"**ul**-lee ["u-**lee**-lee]   tell
  me . . .

"u-**mehsh**   cloth, material

'umm   mother

"u-**ray**-yib   soon

"u-**ray**-yib (min)   near (to)

'**ur**-du-nee   Jordanian

'us-**loob**   style

'us-**tehz**   professor

"u-**Say**-yar   short

'u-**teel**   hotel

'u-tu-**bees** (pl.) 'u-tu-bee-
  seht   bus

"**uTn**   cotton

a

a-**loh**   hello

a-na   I

af-**reeq**-ya   Africa

a-**ghuS**-Tus   August

ak-tar   more

al-**man**-ya   Germany

al-**meh**-nee [al-ma-**nee**-ya]
  German

am-**ree**-ka   America

am-ree-**keh**-nee [am-ree-ka-
  nee-ya]   American

ar-**ba**-^ca   four

as-**ban**-ya   Spain

as-bee-**reen**   aspirin

as-**beh**-nee [as-ba-**nee**-ya]
  Spanish

ayr-**lan**-da   Ireland

ayr-**lan**-dee [ayr-lan-**dee**-ya]
  Irish

ays **kreem**   ice cream

b

ba"-"**ehl**   grocery store

ba-"ar   cows

ba"-**sheesh**   tip, gratuity

baar   bar

ba-dal   instead of

bad-la   suit

bad-ree   early, sooner

baH-**Haar**   sailor

baHr   sea

ba-**laH**   dates

ba-lad   town, country

bal-Too   overcoat

ban-Ta-**lohn**   pants, trousers

ban-yoo   bathtub

ban-**zeen**   gasoline

bank (pl.) bu-**nook**   bank

ba-ra-**zeel**   Brazil

ba-ra-zee-lee [ba-ra-zee-**lee**-ya]   Brazilian

bard   cold (noun)

bar-**dehn** [bar-**deh**-na]   cold

bar-**Doo**   also

ba-**reed**   post, mail

bar-ra   outside

bas-**boor**   passport

bas-ka-**weet**   biscuits, cookies

bass   only, just

bash-ra   skin

ba-Sal   onions

ba-**Taa**-Ta   sweet potatoes

ba-**Taa**-Tis   potatoes

ba-**Tee'**   slow

baT-Ta-**nee**-ya   blanket

baT-Ta-**ree**-ya   battery

baT-**Teekh**   watermelon

ba-**weh**-ba   gate

ba^{c}d   after

ba^c-**deyn**   afterwards, later

ba^c-di **buk**-ra   the day after tomorrow

ba^{c}d iD-**Duhr**   in the afternoon

ba^{c}D   one another

ba^{c}D —   some of —

bee-ra   beer

bee^c   sale

beh-"ee   remainder, change

behb   door

beh-rid [**bar**-da]   cold

beyD   eggs

beyn   between

beyt (pl.) bu-**yoot**   house

bi ba-**lehsh**   free, for nothing

bi-din-**gehn**   eggplant (aubergine)

bi-**doon**   without

bil-"aTr   by train

bil-ba-**reed** ig-**gaw**-wee   by airmail

bi-lehj, plehj   beach

bi-nas   hairpins

bing   anesthetic

bint (pl.) *ba-neht* girl, daughter

bi-sur-^ca fast

bi-teh^c — belonging to —

biS-Sud-fa suddenly

bi-Taa-qa (pl.) *bi-Taa-qaat* card

bi-^ceed far

boh-*sa* kiss

bloo-*za* blouse

boo-jey-heht spark plugs

bri-Taa-nee [bri-Taa-nee-ya] British

bri-Tan-ya Britain

bu" " mouth

bu-feyh dining car

bu-Hey-ra lake

bu-khoor incense

bu-leeS police

bu-loh-var sweater

bunn (ground) coffee

bun-*nee* brown

bur-ney-Ta hat

bur-tu-"aan oranges

d

da"n chin, beard

dafn burial

da-*hab* gold

da-*jehj* chicken

da-leel guide, guidebook

da-leel 'al-wehn color chart

damm blood

da-*ra-ga* class

dars (pl.) *du-roos* lesson

da-*wa* (pl.) *'ad-wee-ya* medicine

daw-*la* (pl.) **du**-*wal* state

daw-*lee* international

daw-*sha* noise

day-*man* always

day-*ya"* tight, narrow

dee-*zil* diesel fuel

deh-*fee* warm

deyr monastery

di-"ee" flour

dib-behn flies

dil-wa"-tee now

di-reh^c arm

di-sim-bir December

dohr (pl.) *'ad-waar* floor

do-laar (pl.) *do-la-raat* dollar

dugh-*ree* straight on

duk-kehn (pl.) *da-ka-keen* shop, store

duk-toor [duk-too-ra] doctor

du-khool entry

dun-*ya* world

dush shower

D

Daa-*nee* mutton, lamb

Dahr back

DakhT id-**damm** blood pressure

*Da-**ree**-ba (pl.) Da-**raa**-yib* tax

*Deyf (pl.) Du-**yoof*** guest

Didd against

Duhr noon

f

*fa-"**eer** (pl.) **fu**-"a-ra* poor

faa-*Dee [**faD**-ya]* free, unoccupied

*faar (pl.) fi-**rehn*** mouse, rat

faD-*Da* silver

fak-*ha* fruit

fak-*ka* small change

*fal'-**lehH** (pl.) fal-la-**Heen*** villager, farmer

*fukh-**khaar*** pottery, ceramics

*fal-**lehH** (pl.) fal-la-**Heen*** peasant farmer

*fa-**loo**-ka* sailboat

*fa-**nil**-la* T-shirt, undershirt

*fann (pl.) fu-**noon*** art

*fan-**nehn*** artist

*fa-**raa**-mil* brakes

fa-raH wedding

*fa-**ran**-sa* France

*fa-ran-**seh**-wee [fa-ran-sa-**wee**-ya]* French

*fa-**raw**-la* strawberries

far" difference

*fa-**ree"*** team

farsh furniture

far^c branch

far-^coo-nee Pharaonic

*fa-**sehd*** corruption

faSl season, class, classroom

*fa-**Sul**-ya* beans

*fa-**Zee**^c* dreadful

fee there is/are

feh-*righ [**far**-gha]* empty

feh-*tiH [**fat**-Ha]* light (colored)

feyn? where?

fi in, at

*fib-**reh**-yir* February

fik-*ra (pl.) 'af-**kaar*** idea

fil-*fil* pepper

*fi-lis-**Teen*** Palestine

*fi-liS-**Tee**-nee* Palestinian

*fil-ma-^c**ehd** on time, punctually

*film (pl.) 'af-**lehm*** film

fi-loos   money

fi-rehkh   chicken

fis-seh-^c^a   per hour

fi-saal   bargaining

fi-shaar   popcorn

fi-Taar   breakfast

fi^c^-lan   indeed

foh"   above, on top

foo-Ta (pl.) fo-waT   towel

foo-Ta SiH-Hee-ya
sanitary napkin

fool   pureed beans

fool su-deh-nee   peanuts

fumm   mouth

fun-du"   hotel

furn   oven, bakery

fur-Sa   chance,
opportunity

fur-sha   brush

fus-Ha   outing, break

fus-tehn   dress

g

gaar (pl.) gi-rehn   neighbor

ga-bal (pl.) gi-behl
mountain

gad-wal il-ma-wa-^c^eed
timetable

gadd   serious

   bi gadd   seriously

gal-la-bee-ya   galabiyya

ga-mal   camel

gam-ba-ree   shrimps,
prawns

gam-^c^a   university

ga-noob   south

gar-dal   pail, bucket

ga-ree-da (pl.) ga-reh-yid
newspaper

ga-toh (pl.) ga-to-heht
cake

ga-wa-hir-gee   jeweler's

ga-weh-hir   jewelry

ga-wehb [ga-weh-beht]
letter

ga-wehz is-sa-far   passport

gaww   weather, atmosphere

gayy   coming, next

gaz-zaar   butcher's

gaz-ma   shoes

gaz-ma-gee   shoemaker

ga-^c^ehn   hungry

geh-hiz [gah-za]   ready

*geh-mi^c^ (pl.) ga-weh-mi^c^*
mosque

gib-na   cheese

gidd   grandfather

gid-da   grandmother

gi-deed   new

gi-hehz ka-sitt   cassette
player

gild   leather

*gi-**ney*** pound (currency)

*gi-**ney**-na (pl.) ga-**neh**-yin*
garden, park

*gi-**neyn**-t il-Ha-ya-wa-**neht***
zoo

*gin-**see**-ya* nationality

gism body

*gi-**zee**-ra (pl.) **gu**-zur*
island

gohz husband

***gow**-wa* inside

*gum-hoo-**ree**-ya* republic

***gum**-ruk* customs

*gu-**nil**-la* skirt

gh

***gha**-bee [gha-**bee**-ya]*
stupid

***gha**-da* lunch

***gha**-laT* wrong

***ghal**-Ta* mistake

*ghal-**Taan*** mistaken

***gha**-nam* sheep (and
goats)

gharb west

***ghar**-bee [ghar-**bee**-ya]*
Western

*gha-**seel*** laundry

***gheh**-lee [**ghal**-ya]*
expensive

***gheh**-yib [ghay-ba]* absent

*ghi-**wey**-sha* bracelet

***ghur**-fa (pl.) **ghu**-raf*
room

h

*ha-**dee**-ya (pl.) ha-**deh**-ya*
gift

*han-**da**-sa* engineering

***hee**-ya* she

***heh**-dee [**had**-ya]* quiet,
calm

***hi**-na* here

***hin**-dee [hin-**dee**-ya]*
Indian

*hi-**nehk*** there

*hi-**weh**-ya* hobby

*ho-**lan**-da* Holland

*ho-**lan**-dee* Dutch

*hu-**doom*** clothes

***huw**-wa* he

H

***Ha"l** (pl.) Hu-"ool* field

***Haa**-Dir* certainly

***Ha**-beeb* beloved

***Heh**-lan* immediately

Hadd someone

Had-sa   accident

Haf-la   party, concert

Haf-la mu-si-**qee**-ya
concert

Ha-ga   thing, something

Ha-gar   stone

Hagz   reservation

Ha-la-wee-**yeht**   desserts

Ha-la-**weh**-nee
confectioner's

Ha-**leeb**   milk

Hal-**leh**″   barber's

Ha-**mehm**   pigeons

Ham-**mehm**   bathroom

Ham-**mehm** si-**beh**-Ha
swimming pool

Ha-na-**fee**-ya   faucet, tap

Han-**Toor**   horsedrawn
carriage

Ha-**raa**-mee (pl.) Ha-ra-
mee-ya   thief

Ha-**raa**-ra   temperature

Ha-**reer**   silk

Har-**raan**   hot (people)

Harr   hot

Ha-sa-**see**-ya   allergy

Ha-sha-**raat**   insects

Ha-**sheesh**   hashish

Hashw   filling

Ha-**weh**-lee   about

Hat-ta   even

Ha-ya-**wehn**   animal

Ha-**zeen**   sad

Heh-mee   hot, spicy

Heh-mil   pregnant

Heh-ris   guard

Hi-**gehb**   veil

Hi-**keh**-ya   story

Hilw   sweet, lovely

Hi-**sehb**   bill, check

Hi-seh-**beht**   accounts

Hi-**zehm**   belt

Hu″-na   injection

Hubb   love

Hu-**boob**   pills

Hu-**boob** mi-naw-**wi**-ma
sleeping pills

Hu-**koo**-ma   government

Hu-**maar**   donkey

Hum-mus   chickpeas

Hu-**moo**-Da   acidity,
indigestion

Hur-**ree**-ya   freedom

i

ig-ti-**meh**c   meeting

iH-na   we

ik-ku-**weyt**   Kuwait

il —   the —

il-'eh-**ni**-sa —   Miss —

il-'Ur-dun   Jordan

il-hind   India

il-lee   who, which

il-qaa-hi-ra   Cairo

il-quds   Jerusalem

il-qur-'aan   the Koran

il-wi-la-yeht il-mut-ta-Hi-da   the United States

il-ya-behn   Japan

il-yohm   today

il-yu-nehn   Greece

im-beh-riH   yesterday

im-ti-Hehn (pl.) im-ti-Heh-neht   exam

in-floo-in-za   influenza

in-gi-lee-zee [in-gi-lee-zee-ya]   English

in-gil-ti-ra   England

in-na-haar-da   today

in-noo-ba   Nubia

in-ta [in-tee]   you (sing.)

in-tum-ma   you (pl.)

ir-ri-yaa-Da   sport

is-maH-lee   pardon me

is-ra-'eel   Israel

is-ra-'ee-lee [is-ra-'ee-lee-ya]   Israeli

is-say-yid —   Mr. —

is-say-yi-da —   Mrs. —

is-ti''-behl   reception

is-ti-raad   import

is-tiq-lehl   independence

is-ti^c-la-meht   information

is-Ti-waa-na   disc, record

iS-Seen   China

iS-SubH   (in the) morning

ish-sharq il-'aw-saT   the Middle East

ish-ti-raa-kee   socialist

it-neyn   two, both

it-shar-raf-na   Pleased to meet you.

i-Taa-lee [i-Taa-lee-ya]   Italian

i-Taal-ya   Italy

iz-zayy?   how?

is-zay-yak? [iz-zay-yik?]   How are you?

j

ja-kit-ta   jacket

jehk   jack (mechanical)

k

ka-ba-rey   floor show

kab-reet   matches

kad-dehb   liar

kah-ra-ba   electricity

kalb (pl.) ki-lehb   dog

ka-lehm talk

kam?, bi kam? How much/many?

ka-mehn also

ka-me-ra camera

ka-na-da Canada

ka-na-dee [ka-na-dee-ya] Canadian

kart (pl.) ku-root card

kart bus-tehl postcard

ka-sitt (pl.) ka-sit-teht cassette

kash-shehf headlight, flashlight

ka^{c}b heel, ankle

kee-loo kilo

kee-lott briefs, panties

keh-mil complete

keh-tib clerk

keyf how, like

keyf il-Hehl? How are you?

ki-beer [ki-bee-ra] (pl.) ku-baar big, old

ki-da thus, so

kid-ba lie (noun)

ki-feh-ya enough

ki-leem (pl.) 'ak-li-ma woven rug

ki-nee-sa church

kis-wa suit

ki-teer much, many, often

ki-tehb (pl.) ku-tub book

kitf shoulder

koh-ra ball, football

ko-lon-ya cologne

kom-byoo-tar computer

kreym (cosmetic) cream

kreym li 'i-zeh-lit il-mak-yaj cold cream

kreym li Hi-meh-yit il-bash-ra suntan cream

kri-dit kard credit card

kub-beh-ya glass

kub-ree (pl.) ka-beh-ree bridge

ku-fee-ya headscarf

kuH-Ha cough

kull each, every

kul-lee-ya college

kul-li Ha-ga everything

ku-reek jack (mechanical)

ku-rumb cabbage

kushk (pl.) 'ik-shehk kiosk

kwa-feer hairdresser

kway-yis [kway-yi-sa] good, well

kh

khaa-lis (not) at all

khaaS private

khadd (pl.) khu-dood cheek

khad-**deh**-ma servant (fem.)

kha-**feef** [kha-**fee**-fa] light (in weight)

kha-**laaS**! That's enough! I've finished.

khal-**laaT** blender

kham-ra liquor

kham-sa five

kha-**reef** autumn

kha-**ree**-Ta map

khass lettuce

kha-shab wood

kha-Tar danger

kha-**Teer** dangerous

khaTT (pl.) khu-**TooT** line

khay-**yaaT** [khay-**yaa**-Ta] tailor, dressmaker

khaz-na safe (noun)

khehl (maternal) uncle

kheh-la (maternal) aunt

kheh-tim ring

kheh-yif [**khay**-fa] afraid

khey-ma tent

khib-ra experience

khid-ma service

khi-**yaar** cucumber

khohkh peaches

khubz bread

khu-**Daar** vegetables

khu-**roog** exit

khu-**Saa**-ra pity

khu-**Soo**-san especially

1

la' no

la-ban milk

lag-na committee

laHm, **laH**-ma meat

laH-ma ba-"a-ree beef

laH-Za moment

lam-ba lamp, lightbulb

lam-ma when

la-**moon** lemon

la-**Teef** [la-**Tee**-fa] (pl.) lu-**Taaf** kind, nice

law sa-**maHt**... Excuse me...

la-**zeez** delicious

lee-bee Libyan

leh-zim — it is necessary, must —

leyh? why?

ley-la night

li to, for

lib-**nehn** Lebanon

lib-**neh**-nee Lebanese

lib-ya Libya

lit-**neyn** both

lis-sa still, (not) yet

*li **waH**-dee* on my own

*lohn (pl.) 'al-**wehn*** color

lohz almonds

*los-**yohn*** lotion

m

maa-Dee past (noun)

ma-"aSS scissors

ma-"ehs size, mesurement

*ma"-**ba**-ra (pl.) ma-"**eh**-bir* tomb, grave

*ma"-**fool*** closed

ma"-lee fried

*mab-**lool*** wet

*mab-**rook**!* Congratulations!

*ma-**dee**-na* city, town

ma-dehm — Mrs. —, madame

mad-fan cemetery

*mad-**ra**-sa (pl.) ma-**deh**-ris* school

ma feesh there isn't/aren't (any)

*maf-**tooH*** open

*ma-**gal**-la (pl.) ma-gal-**leht*** magazine

*mag-**geh**-nan* free, for nothing

mag-lis council

*mag-**noon*** crazy

*magh-**sa**-la* laundry, launderette

*ma-**hee**-ya* salary

*ma-**HaT**-Ta* station, stop

*ma-**HaT**-Tit 'u-tu-**bees*** bus stop

*ma-**HaT**-Tit ban-**zeen*** gas station

*ma-**Hat**-Tit il-"**aTr*** railway station

*ma-**Hall** (pl.) ma-Hal-**leht*** shop

*ma-**Hall** zu-**hoor*** flower shop

*maH-**fa**-Za* wallet, pocketbook

*maH-**roo"*** burned

*ma-**ka**-na* machine

*ma-ka-**roh**-na* pasta

*ma-**kehn*** place

*mak-**soor** [mak-**soo**-ra]* broken

mak-tab office, desk

*mak-tab il-ba-**reed*** post office

mak-tab Sarf money exchange

*mak-**ta**-ba* bookshop, library

mak-wa iron

*mak-**wa**-gee* ironer

*mak-**yaj*** makeup

*ma-**khad**-da* cushion

***makh**-baz* bakery

*makh-**SooS*** special

*ma-**leh**-hee* entertainment

malH salt

ma**-lik (pl.) mu-**look king

*mal-**yehn** [mal-**yeh**-na]* full

*mam-**noon*** grateful

*mam-**noo**ᶜ* forbidden

*ma-na-**kheer*** nose

***man**-ga* mangoes

*ma-ni-**keer*** manicure, nail polish

*man-**Ti**-qa* area

***man**-Zar (pl.) ma-**naa**-Zir* view

*ma-ra (pl.) ni-**seh'*** woman

*ma-**raD** (pl.) 'am-**raaD*** disease, illness

*ma-**reeD** (pl.) [ma-**ree**-Da]* ill

*mar-**Ha**-ba!* welcome

***mar**-ka* brand

***mar**-kaz* center (institution)

***mar**-kib (pl.) ma-**reh**-kib* boat

***mar**-ra **waH**-da* once

*mar-**ta**-ba* mattress

*mar-**wa**-Ha* fan

***ma**-sa-lan* for example

*mas-'**ool*** responsible

*mas-**dood*** blocked

*ma-**see**-Hee* Christian

*ma-**seh**-fa* distance

*mas-**loo"*** boiled

***mas**-raH* theater

*mas-ra-**Hee**-ya* play

***maS**-naᶜ (pl.) ma-**Saa**-niᶜ* factory

maSr Egypt, Cairo

***maS**-ree [maS-**ree**-ya]* Egyptian

*mash-**ghool*** busy

*mash-**hoor** [mash-**hoo**-ra]* famous

*mash-roo-**beht*** drinks

***mash**-wee* grilled

***mat**-Haf* museum

*matsh (**koh**-ra)* (football) match

*ma-**Taar*** airport

***ma**-Tar* rain

***maT**-ᶜam (pl.) ma-**Taa**-ᶜim* restaurant

***maw**-"af (pl.) ma-**weh**-"if* stop

***maw**-"af tak-see* taxi stand

*maw-**good*** present (adj.)

***may**-ya* water

***maz**-za* "mezza," appetizers

ma*Z-booT*   exact, precise

ma-*ᶜa*   with

ma-*ᶜa 'inn*   although

ma-*ᶜa l-'a-saf*
   unfortunately

ma-ᶜa-lish!   Never mind!

ma-*ᶜa s-sa-leh-ma*   Good-
bye.

ma*ᶜ-bad (pl.) ma ᶜeh-bid*
   temple

ma-*ᶜehd*   appointment

ma-*ᶜehsh*   pension

ma*ᶜ-mal*   laboratory

ma*ᶜ-raD*   exhibition

meen?   who?

mee-*na*   port, harbor

mee-*ya (pl.) mee-yeht*
   hundred

meh-*ris*   March

meh-*shee!*   okay

meh-*yit [may-ta]*   dead

mi-*dehn*   square (place)

mi-*fal-lis*   bankrupt, broke

mif-tehH (pl.) ma-fa-teeH
   key

mih-*na*   profession

mi-*khad-da*   pillow,
   cushion

mi-*khal-lil*   pickles

min   from

min faD-lak [min faD-lik]
   please

mi-*nab-bih*   alarm clock

mi-*neyn?*   Where from?

min-*yoo*   menu

mi-*reh-ya*   mirror

mi-*seh'*   evening

mi-*seh' il-kheyr*   Good
   evening.

mis-taᶜ-gil [mis-taᶜ-gi-la]
   in a hurry

mis-ti-wee   ripe, cooked

mish   not

mish baT-Taal   not bad

mish-*mish*   apricot

mishT   comb

mit-'ak-kid   certain, sure

*mit-gaw-wiz [mit-gaw-wi-
za]*   married

mitr   headwaiter

mitr   meter

mi-ᶜad-dee-ya   ferry

mi*ᶜ-da*   stomach

moht   death

mohz   bananas

*mo-***toor**   engine

mu-"ab-la   interview,
   encounter

mu-'al-lif   writer, composer

mu-beh-shir   direct

mu-dar-ris [mu-dar-ri-sa]
   teacher

*mu-***deer**   manager, director

mud-min *(bi)*   addicted to

mu-**fakk** ma-sa-**meer** screwdriver

mu-**feed**   useful

mu-**ghan**-nee [mu-ghan-**nee**-ya]   singer

mu-**han**-dis   engineer

mu-**himm**   important, interesting

mu-**Haw**-wil   adapter plug

mu-**Heh**-mee   lawyer

mu-**Heh**-sib   accountant

muH-tamm *(bi —)* interested (in —)

mu-**kal**-ma   phone call

mu-**khad**-da-**raat**   drugs

mu-**khal**-fa   fine

mu-**khay**-yam si-**yeh**-Hee campsite

mukhkh   brain

mukh-**ta**-lif [mukh-ta-li-fa] different

mu-**lay**-yin   laxative

mu-mar-**ri**-Da   nurse

mu-**mas** sil   actor

mu-**mill**   boring

mum-**tehz**   excellent

mi-**nab**-bih   alarm clock

mu-na**Z**-Zam   organized

mu-naZ-**Za**-ma organization

mu-**neh**-sib   suitable

mu-**rab**-ba   jam

mu-**rat**-tab   tidy

mur-**gehn**   coral

mu-**sal**-sal *(pl.)* mu-sal-sa-**leht**   soap opera

mu-**saq**-qaf   cultured

mu-**see**-qa   music

mus-lim [mus-**li**-ma] *(pl.)* mus-li-**meen**   Muslim

mus-**tash**-fa   hospital

mu-**See**-ba   disaster

mush-**ki**-la *(pl.)* ma-**sheh**-kil problem

mu-ta-**was**-siT   average

mu-**Tah**-hir   antiseptic

mu-waS-**laat** communications

mu-**waZ**-Zaf [mu-waZ-**Za**-fa]   employee, official

mu-**weh**-fi″   agreed

muz-nib   guilty

mu-**Zah**-ra   demonstration

n

na″d   cash

na″-**leht**   gears

naar   fire

na-ba-**teht**   plants

na-bee   prophet

naD-**Daa**-ra   eyeglasses

*naD-Da-**raa**-tee*   optician

*naD-**Daa**-rit shams*
  sunglasses

na-*far (pl.) 'an-**faar***
  person, individual

nafs il —   the same —

*nag-**gaar***   carpenter

nahr   river

*na-**Hehs***   copper

nakhl   palm trees

*na-**moos***   mosquitoes

*na-**See**-Ha*   advice

naS-*ya*   (street) corner

na-sheeT   energetic

nayy   raw

na-*^cam*   yes

neh-*dir*   rare

neh-*yim*   asleep

neh-*shif [**nash**-fa]*   dry

*ni-**beet***   wine

*ni-**Deef** [ni-**Dee**-fa]*   clean

nig-*ma (pl.) nu-**goom***   star

nim-*ra*   number

nim-*rit ti-li-**fohn***
  telephone number

*nis-ba mi-'a-**wee**-ya*
  percentage

*ni-**Zaam***   system

*ni^c-**neh**^c*   mint

nohm   sleep

noh-*ta*   notebook

noo-*bee*   Nubian

noor   light

nuk-*ta*   joke

nus-*kha*   copy

nuSS   half

*nu-**vim**-bir*   November

o

*ok-**too**-bar*   October

*os-**tral**-ya*   Australia

q

*qa-**moos***   dictionary

*qa-**naah***   canal, channel

*qa-**noon***   law

*qa-**noo**-nee*   legal

qar-*ya*   village

*qa-wee [qa-**wee**-ya]*   strong

qaw-*mee*   national,
  nationalist

*qum-**bi**-la (pl.) qa-**neh**-bil*
  bomb

*qun-Su-**lee**-ya*   consulate

r

*ra-'**ees***   president

ra's mehl   capital (finance)

ra"S   dance, dancing

*ra"S **ba**-la-dee*   belly dancing

raa-*gil (pl.) rig*-**geh**-*la* man

raa-*gil 'a^c-**mehl*** businessman

raas   head

*ra-**bee**^c*   spring

radd   reply (noun)

rad-*yoo*   radio

*ra-**hee**-na (pl.) ra-**haa**-yin* hostage

*ra-**maa**-Dee*   gray

ra-*qam*   number

*ra-**Seef***   pavement, platform

rash-*wa*   bribe

raTl   pound (weight)

ray-*yis*   boss

*reef (pl.) 'ar-**yehf*** countryside

ree-*Ha*   smell

reh-*kib (pl.) ruk-**kehb*** passenger

rigl   leg

*ri-**gheef** (pl.) 'ar-**ghi**-fa* loaf

riH-*la*   trip

*ri-**jeem***   diet

*ri-**kheeS** [ri-**khee**-Sa]* cheap

*ri-**seh**-la*   message

*ri-**weh**-ya*   novel

rohb   robe, dressing gown

roo-*see*   Russian

roos-*ya*   Russia

*ru-**baaT***   bandages

*ru-**fay**-ya^c*   thin, slim

rukh-*Sa*   license, permit

*ru-**shit**-ta*   prescription

*ru-**Too**-ba*   humidity

ruzz   rice

S

sa-*bab (pl.) 'as-**behb*** reason, cause

sa-*bat*   basket

*sab-**behk***   plumber

sab-^c*a*   seven

sadd   dam

*sa-**faa**-ra*   embassy

*sa-**feer***   ambassador

*sa-**fee**-na*   ship

sahl   easy

*sak-**raan** [sak-**raa**-na]* drunk

sa-la-Ta   salad

sa-*mak*   fish

sam-*na*   ghee

sa-*na*   year

sa-na-**wee**   annual

san-dal *(pl.)* sa-na-**deel**
   sandals

san-**doo"**   box, chest

sand-*witsh* (pl.) sand-*wit-*
   sheht   sandwich

sar-**deen**   sardines

sa-**ree^c**   quick

sa-wa   together

saw-**weh"**   driver

say-**yaa**-ra   car

see-na   Sinai

seh-da   plain

seh-Hil   coast

seh-kit [**sak**-ta]   silent (of
   people)

seh-^ca *(pl.)* sa-^c**eht**   hour,
   time

sesh-**waar**   hairdryer

si-**beh"**   race, competition

sib-**tim**-bir   September

siDr   chest

si-**fing**   sponges

si-**gaa**-ra *(pl.)* sa-**geh**-yir
   cigarette

sig-**geh**-da *(pl.)* sa-ga-**geed**
   carpet

sign   jail

si-kir-**teer** [si-kir-**tee**-ra]
   secretary

sik-ka *(pl.)* **si**-kak   road,
   way

sik-ka **Ha**-deed   railway

sik-**kee**-na   knife

sil-lim   ladder, stairs

sil-**si**-la   chain

si-ni-ma   cinema

sinn il-**feel**   ivory

si-**reer** *(pl.)* sa-**reh**-yir   bed

sitt *(pl.)* sit-**teht**   lady

sit-ta   six

sit-ti beyt   housewife

si-**yeh**-sa   politics

si^cr   price

soo"   market, bazaar

soor   fence

soo-**tyehn**   bra

su-'**ehl** *(pl.)* 'as-'**i**-la
   question

su-**gu"** "   sausage

suk-kar   sugar

sukhn   hot

su-khu-**nee**-ya   fever

sur-^ca   speed

sus-ta   zip fastener

S

Saa-Hee   awake

Saa-Hib *(pl.)* 'aS-**Haab**
   friend

Sa"f ceiling

Sa-baaH morning

Sa-baH il-kheyr Good morning.

Sa-boon soap

Sabr patience

Sa-daa-qa friendship

Sa-daf shells

Sa-Haa-fa press (noun)

Sa-Ha-fee journalist

sa-HeeH? Really?

SaH-ra desert

Sakhr rock

Sa-lohn tag-meel beauty parlor

Sal-sa sauce

Sanf (pl.) 'aS-naaf kind, sort

Sar-raaf cashier

SatH surface, roof

Say-da-lee-ya pharmacy

Sa^cb difficult

See-nee [See-nee-ya] Chinese

Seyf summer

SiH-Ha health

Si-naa-^ca industry

Si-^cee-dee from upper Egypt

Soof wool

Soo-ra (pl.) So-war picture, photo

Soht (pl.) 'aS-waat voice, sound

Su-baa^c (pl.) Sa-waa-bi^c finger

SubH morning

Su-daa^c headache

Sud-fa accidentally

Su-ghay-yar [Su-ghay-ya-ra] small, young

Su-^coo-ba difficulty

sh

sha"-"a (pl.) shu-"a" apartment

sha-"ee naughty

shaa-Tir [shaT-ra] clever

shabb (pl.) sha-behb young man

sha-ga-ra (pl.) sha-gar tree

shagh-ghehl [shagh-geh-la] worker, servant

shahr (pl.) shu-hoor month

shakl appearance, look

shak-loo [shak-la-ha] — he (she) looks —

shakhS (pl.) 'ash-khaaS person

shakh-See personal

sha-mehl north

sham-meh-^ca hanger

sham^c   candles

*sham-**poo***   shampoo

shams   sun

*sham-**see**-ya*   sunshade, umbrella

***sha**-nab*   mustache

***shan**-Ta (pl.) **shu**-naT*   bag, suitcase

*sha-**raab***   socks, stockings

*sha-**raa**-yiT*   tapes

shar″   east

shar-″ee   Eastern, Oriental

*sha-Ta-**rang***   chess

shaTT   beach, shore

shayy   tea

*shay-**yehl***   porter

***sha**^c-bee*   popular

sha^c r   hair

*sheek [shee-**keht**]*   check

*shee-**keht** si-ya-**Hee**-ya*   traveler's checks

***shee**-sha*   nargile, hubble bubble (water pipe)

***sheh**-ri^c (pl.) sha-**weh**-ri^c*   street

*shib-**behk** (pl.) sha-ba-**beek***   window

***shib**-shib*   slippers

***shif**-fa (pl.) sha-**feh**-yif*   lip

*shi-**mehl***   left

shir**-ka (pl.) sha-ri-**keht   company

shir**-kit Tay-ya-**raan   airline

***shi**-ta*   winter

***shi**^c-ba*   reef

*sho-ko-**laa**-ta*   chocolate

***shoh**-ka*   fork

***shuk**-ran*   thank you

***shu**-naT*   bags, luggage

***shur**-ba*   soup

***shur**-Ta*   police

***shway**-ya*   a little, rather

***shway**-yit —*   a bit of —

t

*ta'-**meen***   insurance

*ta-″**ree**-ban*   nearly, roughly

*tad-**kheen***   smoking

*tad-**leek***   massage

*taH-**leel***   analysis

taHt   under, below

*taH-**weel***   exchange (finance)

*taH-**wee**-la*   detour

***tak**-see*   taxi

*tak-**yeef ha**-wa*   air conditioning

*takh-**feeD***   reduction

*ta-**leh**-ta*   three

talg   ice, snow

*ta-**mal**-lee*   always

ta-man   price

ta-man-ya   eight

tan-Deef   cleaning

ta-qa-leed   traditions

ta-reekh   date, history

ta-ree-khee   historical

tar-zee   tailor

taS-leeH   repair, mending

ta-Taw-wur   development

taw-zee^c   distribution

taz-ka-ra (pl.) ta-zeh-hir   ticket

ta-^ceh-la! [ta-^ceh-lee!]   Come on!

ta^c-leem   education

teh-gir   merchant, businessman

teh-nee   again

teh-nee [tan-ya]   another, second

ti-"eel   heavy

ti-gaa-ra   commerce, business

ti-kheen   fat

ti-li-fohn   telephone

til-li-ghrehf   telegram

ti-li-viz-yohn   television

til-meez (pl.) ta-lam-za   pupil

tis-^ca   nine

tiS-baH ^ca-la kheyr   Good night.

ti^c-behn   snake

tohm   garlic

tuf-fehH   apples

twa-litt   lavatory

T

Ta"s   weather

Ta"-Too-"a   ashtray

Taa-lib [Taa-li-ba] (pl.) Ta-la-ba   student

Taa-za   fresh

Ta-ba" (pl.) 'aT-baa"   dish, plate

Tab-baakh   cook

Ta-beeb [Ta-bee-ba]   doctor

Ta-beeb 'as-nehn   dentist

Ta-bee-^cee   natural

Ta-boor   queue

Tab-^can   of course

Ta-ra-bey-za   table

Tard (pl.) Tu-rood   parcel

Ta-ree" (pl.) Tu-ru"   way, road

Ta-ree" ra-'ee-see   highway

Ta-waa-bi^c   stamps

Ta-waa-ri'   emergency

Ta-weel   long, tall

Tay-yaa-ra   airplane

Tay-yib [Tay-yi-ba]   good

Ta^cm taste

Tifl (pl.) 'aT-faal child

Tur-*shee* pickles

u

u-rub-ba Europe

u-rub-bee European

v

vee-*za* visa

vid-*yo* video

volt volt

w

waa-*DiH* obvious

waa-*Tee [waT-ya]* low

wa-ga^c pain

*wa-**Heed*** sole, only

*wa-**keel*** agent

wakh-*ree* late

*wa-la **Ha**-ga* nothing

wa-lad (pl.) 'aw-lehd boy

wal-la (in question) or?

*wa-**leh**-kin* but

*wal-**leh**-^ca* lighter

wa-ra behind

wa-ra″ *(pl.) 'aw-reh″* leaf, paper

ward roses, flowers

war-raa-*nee* back (adj.)

war-*sha* repair shop

waS-*fa* recipe

waSl receipt

wa-zeer minister

*wa-**Zee**-fa* job, post

weh-″if [wa″ fa] standing

weh-Ha *(pl.)* wa-**Heht** oasis

weh-Hid [**waH**-da] one

weh-si^c [**was**-^ca] wide, loose

wi and

widn ear

wi-Hish [**wiH**-sha] bad, ugly

wi-sikh [**wis**-kha] dirty

wis-kee whiskey

wiST, wuST center

wishsh face

*wi-**zaa**-ra* ministry

*wu-**Sool*** arrival

y

*ya-**beh**-nee [ya-ba-**nee**-ya]* Japanese

yakht yacht

yal-la! Let's go!

ya-**neh**-yir January

yas-**meen** jasmine

yee-gee to come

yeh-kul to eat

yeh-khud to take

yi-"**ad**-dim X li Y to introduce, offer X to Y

yi-'**ag**-gar to hire, rent

yi-'**ak**-kid to confirm

yi"-dar to be able

yi-"**ees** to measure

yi-"**eh**-bil to meet

yi"-fil to close

yi"-lee to fry

yi-"**ool** to say, tell

yi-"**oom** to get up

yi"-ra to read

yi-"**til** to kill

yib-"a to become

yi-**bee**^c to sell

yi-**boos** to kiss

yib-**ti**-dee to begin

yib-^cat to send

yi-**dakh**-khan to smoke

yi-**dam**-mar to destroy

yi-**dar**-dish to chat

yi-**dar**-ris to teach

yi-**daw**-war ^ca-la to look for

yid-baH to slaughter, sacrifice

yid-fa^c to pay

yid-ris to study

yi-**Day**-ya^c to waste

yi-**Dee**^c to be lost (objects)

yiD-rab to hit

yi-**faa**-Sil to bargain

yi-**faD**-Dal to prefer

yi-**fah**-him to explain

yi-**fak**-kar to remind

yif-Dal to remain

yif-ham to understand

yif-taH to open

yi-**ti**-kir to think, remember

yif-Tar to have breakfast

yi-**fukk** to undo

yi-**gah**-hiz to prepare

yig-ree to run

yi-**ghan**-nee to sing

yi-**ghay**-yar to change (trans.)

yigh-sil to wash

yi-**Had**-did to limit

yi-**HaD**-Dar to prepare

yi-**Hal**-lil to analyze

yi-**Ham**-maD to develop

yi-**Has**-sin to improve

yi-**Haw**-wil to exchange (money)

yiH-giz to book

*yi-**Hibb*** to like, love

yiH-la" to shave

yiH-ra" to burn

yiH-Sal to happen

*yi-**kal**-lif* to cost

*yi-**kal**-lim* to speak to

*yi-**kam**-mil* to continue

*yi-**kar**-rar* to repeat

yik-dib to lie

yik-sar to break

yik-sab to earn, win

yik-tib to write

*yi-**kuHH*** to cough

*yi-**khab**-bee* to hide (trans.)

*yi-**khal**-laS* to finish

*yi-**khaw**-wif* to frighten

*yi-**khay**-yaT* to sew

*yi-**khehf*** to be afraid

*yi-**kheh**-ni"* to quarrel with

*yi-**khiff*** to get better, recover

yikh-laS to finish (intrans.)

yikh-la^c to undress

yikh-taar to choose

yikh-Taf to kidnap

yil-bis to dress

*yi-**leh**-"ee* to find

yil-ghee to cancel

*yi-**liff*** to wrap

*yil-^c**ab*** to play

*yi-**maw**-wit* to kill

yim-Dee to sign

yim-meen right (direction)

yim-kin perhaps

yim-la to fill

yim-na^c to forbid, prevent

yim-shee to walk, go away

yim-sik to hold, grasp

*yi-**naD**-Daf* to clean

*yi-**naZ**-Zam* to organize

*yi-**nehm*** to sleep

yin-saH to advise

yin-ti-Zir to wait

yin-zil (fi) to get off, stay (at)

*yi-**qar**-rar* to decide

*yi-**raa**-hin* to bet

yir-fid to fire, sack

yir-ga^c to return

yir-kab to get on, ride

*yi-**rooH*** to go

*yi-**rudd*** to reply

yis-'al to ask

*yi-**sag**-gil* to record, check

*yi-**sakh**-khan* to heat

*yi-**sal**-lif* to lend

*yi-**sal**-lim* to greet

*yi-**seeb*** to leave (tr.)

*yi-**seh**-fir* to travel, leave

*yi-**seh**-miH*   forgive

*yi-**seh**-ᶜid*   to help

***yis**-maᶜ*   to hear, listen to

*yi-**soo**"*   to drive

***yis**-ra"*   to steal

*yis-ta-**Ham**-ma*   to bathe

*yis-**tan**-na*   to wait

*yis-ta-**ray**-yaH*   to rest

*yis-**taᶜ**-mil*   to use

*yis-**ti**-lif*   to borrow

*yi-**Sal**-laH*   to repair

*yi-**Sal**-lee*   to pray

*yi-**Saw**-war*   to photograph

***yiS**-raf*   to spend, change (money)

*yi-**Subb***   to pour

*yi-**shag**-gaᶜ*   to support, encourage

***yish**-fee*   to get better

*yi-**shidd***   to pull

*yi-**shoof***   to see

***yish**-rab*   to drink

***yish**-raH*   to explain

***yish**-tim*   to insult

*yish-**ti**-ree*   to buy

*yit-**far**-rag (ᶜa-la)*   to watch, look (at)

*yit-**gaw**-wiz*   to get married

*yit-**ghad**-da*   to have lunch

*yit-**ghay**-yar*   to change (intrans.)

*yit-**kal**-lim*   to speak, talk

*yit-**kheh**-ni" (ma-ᶜa)*   to quarrel, fight (with)

*yit-**man**-na*   to hope

*yit-**mash**-sha*   to take a walk

*yit-**mat**-taᶜ (bi —)*   to enjoy

*yit-**naf**-fis*   to breathe

*yit-**tar**-gim*   to translate

*yit-ᶜ**ash**-sha*   to have dinner

*yiT-**Ti**-Sil (bi —)*   to contact

*yi-**waf**-far*   to save

*yi-**war**-ree*   to show

*yi-**waS**-Sal*   to accompany

***yiw**-gaᶜ*   to hurt

***yiw**-Sal*   to arrive

***yiw**-ᶜid*   to promise

*yi-**zu**""*   to push

*yi-**Zoor***   to visit

*yi-**Zunn***   to think

*yi-ᶜ**eesh***   to live

***yiᶜ**-mil*   to do, make

***yiᶜ**-oom*   to swim

*yiᶜ-**ti**-mid (ᶜa-la)*   to depend (on)

***yiᶜ**-zim*   to invite

*yohm (pl.) 'ay-**yehm***   day

*yoh-**meyn***   two days

*(yohm) ig-**gum**-ᶜa*   Friday

*(yohm) il-**Hadd***   Sunday

*(yohm) il-kha-**mees***
Thursday

*(yohm) is-**sabt*** Saturday

*(yohm) it-ta-**leht*** Tuesday

*(yohm) **lar**-ba^c* Wednesday

*(yohm) lit-**neyn*** Monday

yu-"af to stop

yu-"a^c to fall

yu"-^cud to sit down

yud-khul to enter

yuH-fur to dig

yul-yoo July

*yu-neh-nee [yu-neh-**nee**-ya]*
Greek

yun-yoo June

yur-"uS to dance

yus-kun to live

yuT-bukh to cook

yuT-lub to ask for, order

Z

*za-kee [za-**kee**-ya]*
intelligent

*zab-**behl*** garbage collector

*zaw-**ba**-^ca* sandstorm

*za^c-**lehn*** angry

zeyt oil

*zeyt zay-**toon*** olive oil

*zi-**beh**-la* garbage

zib-da butter

*zi-**meel** (pl.) **zu**-ma-la*
colleague

zohg husband

zoh-ga wife

zohr throat

*zu-**hoor*** flowers

*zu-**kehm*** cold (noun)

Z

Zaa-biT (pl.) Zub-**baaT**
(army) officer

*Za-**reef*** pleasant

*Zarf (pl.) Zu-**roof*** envelope

*Zu-**raar** (pl.) Za-**raa**-yir*
button

c

*^c**a**"l* mind

*^caa-**Si**-ma* capital (city)

*^c**aa**-Til* unemployed

*^c**a**-dad* number, quantity

*^ca-dam in-**nohm*** insomnia

*^ca-da-sa (pl.) ^ca-da-**seht***
lens

*^cad-**dehd*** meter

^cads lentils

^caDm bone

^cafsh luggage, furniture

*c**af**-wan* Not at all, don't mention it.

*c**a**-ga-la* wheel, bicycle

*c**a**-la* on

*c**a**-la **fik**-ra . . .* by the way . . .

*c**a**-la **mah**-lak!* slow down!

*c**amm* (paternal) uncle

*c**am**-ma* (paternal) aunt

*c**an* about (concerning)

*c**and* with (= have)

*c**a**-ra-bee [*c**a**-ra-**bee**-ya]* Arab, Arabic

*c**a**-ra-**bee**-ya* car

*c**arD* show (noun)

*c**a**-**rees*** bridegroom

*c**a**-**roo**-sa* bride

*c**as**-**ka**-ree (pl.) *c**a**-**seh**-kir* soldier

*c**a**-**Seer*** juice

*c**aS**-**foor** (pl.) *c**a**-Sa-**feer*** bird

*c**aS**-ree* modern

*c**a**-sha* dinner

*c**a**-shehn, li-ann* because

*c**aT**-**laan** [*c**aT**-**laa**-na]* broken down, out of order

*c**aT**-**shaan*** thirsty

*c**a**-wiz [*c**aw**-za] (pl.) *c**aw**-**zeen*** want

*c**ay**-**yehn** [*c**ay**-**yeh**-na]* ill

*c**a**-**Zeem*** marvelous, magnificent

*c**eed* feast, festival

*c**eed il-mi**-lehd*** Christmas

*c**eed mi**-lehd*** birthday

*c**eh**-dee* ordinary

*c**eh**-lam* world

*c**eh**-lee* high

*c**ey**-la* family

*c**eyn* eye

*c**il**-ba (pl.) *c**i**-lab* packet, can

*c**ilm (pl.) *c**u**-**loom*** science

*c**il**-mee* scientific

*c**i**-**maa**-ra (pl.) *c**i**-**maa**-**raat*** building, block

*c**i**-**nab*** grapes

*c**in**-**wehn*** address

*c**uDw (pl.) 'a*c**-**Daa'*** member, organ

*c**um**-la* currency

*c**um**-la Sa*c**-ba* hard currency

*c**u**-**zoo**-ma* invitation

*c**uzr* excuse (noun)

INDEX